THE AGE OF INTOXICATION

THE AGE OF INTOXICATION

ORIGINS OF THE GLOBAL DRUG TRADE

Benjamin Breen

PENN

University of Pennsylvania Press

Philadelphia

The Early Modern Americas
Peter C. Mancall, Series Editor
Volumes in the series explore neglected aspects of early modern history in the western
hemisphere. Interdisciplinary in character, and with a special emphasis on the At-
lantic World from 1450 to 1850, the series is published in partnership with the USC-
Huntington Early Modern Studies Institute.

Published by
University of Pennsylvania Press
Philadelphia, Pennsylvania 19104-4112
www.upenn.edu/pennpress

Printed in the United States of America on acid-free paper
10 9 8 7 6 5 4 3 2 1

Library of Congress Cataloging-in-Publication Data
Names: Breen, Benjamin, author.
Title: The age of intoxication : origins of the global drug trade / Benjamin Breen.
Other titles: Early modern Americas.
Description: 1st edition. | Philadelphia : University of Pennsylvania Press, [2019] | Se-
    ries: The early modern Americas | Includes bibliographical references and index.
Identifiers: LCCN 2019032803 | ISBN 978-0-8122-5178-4 (hardcover)
Subjects: LCSH: Drug traffic—History—16th century. | Drug traffic—History—17th
    century. | Drug traffic—History—18th century. | Drugs—History. | Pharmacy—
    History. | International trade—History. | Drugs—Social aspects—History. | Drug
    control—History.
Classification: LCC HV5801 .B674 2019 | DDC 382/.4561510903—dc23
LC record available at https://lccn.loc.gov/2019032803

Frontispiece: Hand-drawn depiction of a Turkish coffee drinker, a Chinese tea drinker,
and an indigenous American chocolate drinker from a manuscript copy of Philippe
Sylvestre Dufour (pseudonym), *Tractatus Novi de Potu Caphé, et de Chinesium The*,
circa 1685. Courtesy of University of California, Santa Cruz Special Collections.

Lovingly dedicated to my parents and my brother—

And to Roya, who gives meaning to Rumi's words:

پر ذوق تر از تو من ندیدم شکری

Contents

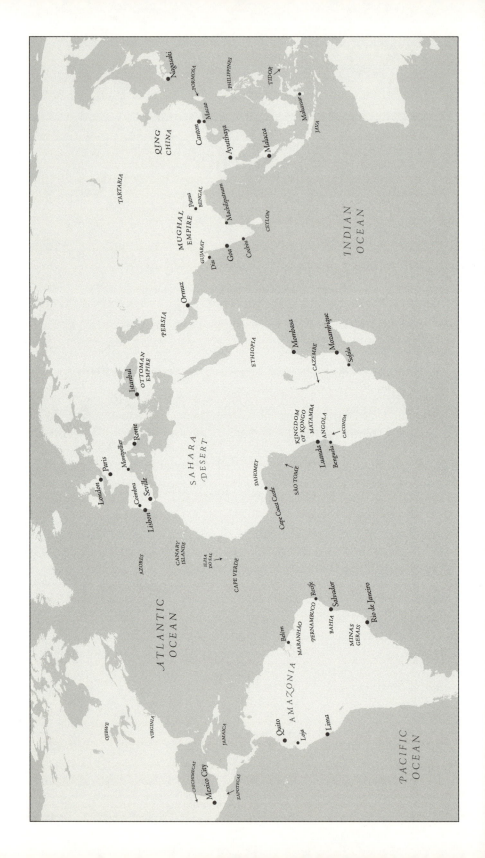

At the Statue of Adamastor

O reckless people . . . you have breached what is forbidden!
—ADAMASTOR TO VASCO DA GAMA, *OS LUSÍADAS*, 1572

I n a city known for its spectacular vistas, one place in Lisbon stands out: a small patch of grass and stone called the Miradouro do Adamastor. It is sleepy during the day, frequented mostly by tourists (and the occasional stray cat) eager to take in its panoramic views. But as the sun sets over the Tejo River, revelers from the city's nightlife districts crowd the south end of this tiny plaza. Dealers in MDMA, hashish, and cocaine begin to ply their wares. By nightfall on a typical Friday, the Miradouro do Adamastor has become one of the busiest drug markets in Portugal.[1]

The north end of the plaza is very different. This side is dominated by an elegant building that happens to house Lisbon's Museum of Pharmacy. One spring evening several years ago, I watched an intoxicated man climb on top of the stone statue that stands at the center of the plaza, his back to the museum. "Lisbon doesn't care about me!" he shouted in Angolan-accented Portuguese. The people behind the statue pretended not to notice. With time, however, the tall iron fence that divides the museum from the plaza began to seem to me like a statement in its own right. The fence proclaims the museum's symbolic and physical distance from the drug dealers and drug users beyond: the scientific realm of the medical, standing apart from the messy world of intoxication.

And as for the statue at the center of it all? The sculpted figure, rising out of rough-hewn rock, is an imperial Portuguese imagining of an African demigod. In The Lusiads, the sixteenth-century poetic epic of the Portuguese Empire, Adamastor is the name given to a giant who battles the navi-

Figure 1. Adamastor's statue in Lisbon, with the Museu da Farmácia in the background. Photograph by the author, July 2018.

gator Vasco da Gama. As da Gama and his men round Africa's Cape of Good Hope, a "deformed and enormous" figure rises in the night air "like a second Colossus of Rhodes, most strange to see . . . its hair curly and filled with earth . . . its mouth black."[2] Adamastor, the "Spirit of the Cape," tries and fails to repel the Portuguese from reaching the "strong and potent drugs" of the Indies.[3] Today, Lisbon's Adamastor stands frozen in an expression of futile rage, staring out to sea. A tiny figure of Vasco da Gama perches on the edge of his beard.

It would be hard to find a better starting point for the stories told in this book. The African god and his Portuguese enemy, united in their silent contemplation of a gateway to the Atlantic Ocean. The drug sellers below, often recent immigrants from Brazil, Angola, or Mozambique, whose personal journeys map onto the older pathways of Portugal's vanished empire. And, looming behind them, the silent wall dividing the street drugs of the miradouro from the medical drugs of the museum.

The Age of Intoxication argues against this division. It is a window into a time when there was no barrier between the museum and the marketplace—

or between the drug dealer and the pharmacist. Here the reader will encounter merchants, slaves, shamans, prophets, *feiticeiros*, inquisitors, witches, alchemists, and natural philosophers. I don't claim that these figures all saw themselves as participating in the same profession, trade, or worldview. On the contrary, the global drug trade emerged out of conflict and difference. It was, and is, rooted in a spectrum of beliefs that are difficult to draw together. A random selection of opinions held by individuals in this book would include the following: Eating the powdered flesh of an Egyptian mummy may cure the plague. Distilled poppies reduce melancholy. A Turkish drink called coffee increases alertness. The arterial blood of a murderer is the best thing for an epileptic, especially when collected and drunk immediately after the murderer's public beheading. Tobacco cures cancer. Possessing an enemy's toenail clippings may allow you to kill them.

The global drug trade was an emergent property, born of a ferment of different beliefs, practices, and conflicts, following a course that was neither planned nor expected. But I believe that it is important to try to see the drug trade as a unified whole. In the early modern era (the period spanning roughly 1500 to 1800 CE) the drug trade became truly global in scope—and the world changed in ways both familiar and forgotten. This book's title, *The Age of Intoxication*, is a deliberate provocation in this regard. It has fallen out of fashion for historians to refer to an "Age of Reason" in the late seventeenth and eighteenth centuries, but the term continues to resonate in the popular imagination.[4] I argue that the globalization of drugs during the same period was an event with impacts on global health, material culture, and intellectual life that were arguably even more transformative than the unevenly distributed intellectual currents of the Enlightenment.[5] Rather than limiting this book to the study of *only* medicinal drugs or *only* recreational ones, I have thus chosen to study psychoactive and medicinal drugs in tandem so as to better capture the full scope of their impacts.

The substances we will learn about fall into different categories today. There are pharmaceuticals like quinine, so-called "traditional remedies" like St.-John's-wort or rhinoceros horn, New Age and homeopathic cures, food-like drugs or drug-like foods such as sugar, and illegal narcotics like heroin. In chronicling how these substances circulated during the first era of globalization, it became clear that the permanence of such divisions—between illicit and licit, recreational and medicinal, modern and traditional—is illusory. These boundaries were radically different in the past, and they are shifting beneath our feet today. In order for people of the present day to guide drug policy toward a fairer and more informed course, we first need to understand who and what set it on its present trajectory.

The chapters that follow trace the drug trade's emergence on a world stage, the main points of contact and conflict that key early modern drugs initiated, and the accompanying backlashes. For instance, the Atlantic slave trade was not just a trade in human beings but also a commerce in psychoactive drugs. The Scientific Revolution, likewise, was partially inspired by questions about how novel "Indies" drugs acted on mind and body, and what latent "virtues" they concealed. The shape taken by globalization was forever altered by this early modern era of drugs. In understanding the age before the pharmacy museum and the recreational drug market became separated by physical and ideological walls, we will learn more about how the modern world itself came into being—and about the age of intoxication that we still live in.

Why Does Drug History Matter?

The range of substances that early modern Europeans classified as "drugs" was truly vast. The term encompassed everything from herbs and spices (like nutmeg, cinnamon, and chamomile) to deadly poisons (like lead, mercury, and arsenic). Some early modern drugs, such as oil of roses or lavender, appealed to the senses. Others revolted against them, like the 1609 recipe that called for the sick to consume "the corpse of an unblemished twenty-four-year-old red-haired man . . . torn into strips and sprinkled with powdered myrrh and aloe."[6] An early modern apothecary—a vendor and preparer of drugs—might sell Egyptian mummies, Neolithic artifacts, narwhal tusks, bird beaks, powdered pearls, and drinkable gold. Drugs could dispel or enact curses, increase sexual desire or banish it, ease the pains of childbirth or induce abortion, kill in agony or dissipate all sensation in an opiated haze. Amid this enormous diversity, however, there were also common traits. The unifying definition of the substances called "drugs" in this book is that they are *things consumed to alter the mind or body*. I sometimes use terms like "psychoactive" or "intoxicating" to refer to these effects, but it is important to remember that contemporary medical definitions of psychoactivity and the more capacious one that I use here are not identical.

It is also worth noting that most of the drugs surveyed in these pages were not effective by modern medical standards. A few, like opium or cinchona bark, are botanical precursors of contemporary pharmaceuticals. In some cases, studying premodern or non-Western drugs has led to significant breakthroughs, like the Nobel Prize–winning antimalarial drug artemisinin (i.e., *qīnghāosù*, 青蒿素), brought to market on the basis of a traditional Chinese remedy, or ibogaine, a compound found in the root of the African *Tabernanthe iboga* tree, which has shown potential for treating addiction.[7] Nevertheless, most drugs studied in this book likely have no empirical therapeutic value. So, leaving aside our natural curiosity about the weird, wizardly contents of apothecary jars or the remarkable lives of drug merchants, cultivators, and consumers, why do their histories matter?

Because this book is about the early modern era, I don't enter here into debates about the deep human past. However, I do proceed from a broad perspective: I believe that it is impossible to understand human history without accounting for the centrality of drug taking as a fundamental human impulse. The desire to alter mental and physical states by ingesting natural products appears to number among the defining traits of our species.[8] It is a behavior that arguably deserves a position alongside the more celebrated human expressive modes, like dance, music, or language.[9] And if the intentional alteration of conscious or physical states is a fundamental element in human behavior, then so, too, is the desire to find meaning in these states. Humans are the only animal that *prepares*, *trades*, and *explains* drugs.[10] Drugs play a significant role in human societal differentiation, cultural and material exchange, and, in some cases, conflict.

Today, nonmedical drug use is often given the label "recreational," but this is a deeply inadequate phrase. The desire to escape the mind's confines is an ancient and profound one. Sometimes the impulse can be destructive; other times, it offers an outlet for dispelling fear or frustration, making sense of hardship or gaining knowledge. In either account, the impulse runs deep. Some archaeologists have theorized that the introduction of alcohol can be identified in the archaeological record of Bronze Age Europe, when new ceramic forms appear to have been linked to the emergence of rituals of intoxication.[11] For the most part, however, the early chapters of drug history stretch so far back into the human past that they remain unwritten and, perhaps, unwriteable. Indeed, humanity's ancient alliances with caffeine and alcohol have become so deeply embedded in many societies around the world that we rarely reflect on the fact that these everyday substances even *are* drugs. They are part of the fabric of our world—and our shared histories, from Peru to Africa to China.

Almost as ancient as the evidence for alcohol and caffeine use are the archaeological records of the use of drugs sometimes known as *entheogens*, a word deriving from the Greek ἔνθεος (*éntheos*), meaning "god within" or "inspired by a god." In Mesoamerica, archaeological records documenting entheogens like peyote (*Lophophora williamsii*) stretches back at least as far as the Olmec era, circa 1200–400 BCE.[12] We should be wary of drawing a clear line between the use of these drugs in spiritual, recreational, or medical settings. They often serve all three simultaneously. An emerging scientific consensus points to the utility of drugs like mescaline and psilocybin as treatments for disorders such as alcoholism, PTSD (post-traumatic stress disorder), and severe depression. They have been lauded as tools for obtaining "self-knowledge and psychological insight."[13] But as we'll see, substances like peyote and psilocybin have also been attacked as dangerous intoxicants. Today, in the United States, both remain classified as Schedule 1 drugs. In the end, I suspect it is impossible to draw a clear line between recreational and therapeutic use of a drug. But this has not stopped modern societies from attempting to do just that.

The chapters that follow document how the early modern drug trade emerged, grew, and split into *licit* (medicinal, scientific, legal) and *illicit* (recreational, irrational, illegal) branches. This book will also explore how drugs have served as a kind of advance guard for both the allure and the dangers of global trade, and as a catalyst for slave traders, scientists, and agents of empire.[14] Newly globalized psychoactive substances from the tropical and subtropical regions, which Europeans called "the Indies," prompted new racialized and religious fears of foreign drugs, as well as new scientific questions and methods.

Today, legacies of the early modern globalization of drugs shape our world in ways both seen and unseen. In the Philippines, an estimated 7,000 people were executed by police and vigilantes because of supposed links to drug dealing in late 2016 and early 2017 alone.[15] Roughly half of the inmates in U.S. federal prisons as of 2015 were serving time for so-called drug offenses.[16] Meanwhile, the trade in *legal* drugs has emerged as one of the planet's largest and most powerful industries.[17] One in six Americans is thought to regularly consume psychiatric drugs. In 2015, an estimated 38 percent of American adults were prescribed opioids.[18] And substances like tobacco, coffee, and alcoholic spirits (which all fell under the early modern definition of drugs) account for a truly massive portion of global advertising budgets and consumer spending.

By reframing certain drugs as foreign invaders or markers of societal decline rather than acknowledging drug taking's ancient role in nearly all human societies, modern states have committed unspeakable crimes. The assumptions underlying drug criminalization include concerns about bodily and mental purity and the trope of intoxication as an enemy of civilization. This book shows how these associations arose out of early modern conceptions of racial difference, fears of non-Christian spirituality, and the commercial imperatives of merchants, slavers, and medical professionals. Drugs became illegal not because of the arbitrary decisions of government leaders in the nineteenth and twentieth centuries but because of deep-seated epistemological, commercial, and social structures that emerged during an earlier age of globalization on the plantation, on the slave ship, and on the surgeon's table.

Defining Drugs, and How to Study Them

In modern English, French, Spanish, and Portuguese, drug/*drogue*/*droga* has a well-known double meaning. It can signify either "a natural or synthetic substance used in the prevention or treatment of disease" or "a substance with intoxicating, stimulant, or narcotic effects used for cultural, recreational or other non-medical purposes."[19] But the genealogy of the word is more tangled than this distinction might imply. It first entered English and several other European languages in the fourteenth century (seemingly from a Middle Dutch word related to dryness, *droge*). At this early stage, the word referred simply to dry goods, from medicinal herbs and spices to dyes, soaps, incenses, or pigments. As we will see, the meaning of "drug" changed subtly in the sixteenth and seventeenth centuries, gaining associations with exotic spices, medicines, and poisons. Dictionaries state that it was not until the late nineteenth century that the word *drug* gained a formal secondary association with recreational usage. Yet, the links among drugs, intoxication, and the illicit actually begin to emerge in the seventeenth and eighteenth centuries, as goods like cannabis and opium acquired labels like "drogas narcoticos," or "stupefying drugs."

These changes in the meanings of "drug" were directly linked to the global expansion of European empires.[20] When Columbus and da Gama sailed in search of the Indies, for instance, they sought not only gold, silver, and slaves but also especiarias (spices) and drogas (drugs). By the early decades of the sixteenth century, the word droga was increasingly being applied to exotic medicinal imports from the New World and Asia, but in a way

Figure 2. Detail of a list of *drogas* (cloves, nutmeg, mace, and cinnamon are listed in the visible portion) available in Cochin, 1525. ANTT Cartas 876/16 "Carte de Manuel Botelho a D. João III sobre a colheita da pimenta e outras drogas," Cochin, January 21, 1525, fol. 2r. Courtesy of the Arquivo Nacional da Torre do Tombo, Lisbon, Portugal.

that continued to blur the boundaries between drug and spice.[21] In a 1525 letter, for instance, a Portuguese factor in Cochin named Manuel Botelho sent the crown a list of drogas that included cinnamon, mace, nutmeg, and cloves (Figure 2). Simão Botelho, another colonial official, wrote in 1552 that "the trading contract in drugs [contrato das drogas] which we maintain with Ormuz, is the most important remedy for [supplying] the necessities of this land [of Goa]."[22] Botelho was referring to items like nutmeg, cloves, mace, and cinnamon, not to substances commonly classified as drugs today.[23]

Given the protean nature of the category itself, any history of drugs must address several different facets of human experience: economic, social, scientific, and spiritual. Historians of early modern science and medicine have studied medicinal drugs like cinchona, guaiacum, and opium as examples of how post-Columbian botanical networks altered ecological practices and theories of nature.[24] Viewed from another angle, the early modern drug trade is a story of profit and loss, of competing participants in a "medical marketplace," and of oppressed workers whose lives were defined by labor and drawn together by the vast wheels of commerce.[25] Finally, this book is indebted to historians who see economic motives as threads in a larger fabric of social relations, cultural practices, and that deep reservoir of unstated beliefs about how the world functions that informs both the history of science and the realm of the spiritual.[26]

This book focuses on the Portuguese and British Empires because these two colonial regimes had what I consider to be the most significant influence on the early modern globalization of drugs. The Portuguese Empire was central to the globalization of drugs and spices; no other empire or state played such a wide-ranging role in the redistribution of flora and fauna that historians call the Columbian Exchange.[27] In the seventeenth and eighteenth centuries, the British Empire emerged as a would-be inheritor of Portuguese dominance in the drug trade. In this aim, British natural philosophers and colonists largely succeeded. However, the story of early modern drugs was not confined to any one region or power. This book takes a broad view, shifting from a Portuguese to a British imperial focus (and at times moving freely beyond either) because drugs themselves had a stubborn tendency to ignore the boundaries imposed by both humans and geography.

It is also important to remember that terms like "Portuguese Empire" or "British Empire" can conceal as much as they clarify. Studying early modern empires requires a highly skeptical view of claims to geographic power. From the idealized perspective of a cartographer, Portuguese holdings were vast indeed. Through the personal union with Spain under the Hapsburgs, the joint monarchs of the Spanish and Portuguese crowns laid claim not only to the kingdoms of Iberia but also to a selection of territories including Athens, Corsica, "the Eastern and Western Indies," "the Islands and Mainland of the Ocean Sea," Burgundy, Flanders, and Jerusalem. After the restoration of an independent Portuguese monarchy under King João IV of the House of Braganza (1640), the kings of Portugal continued to claim a litany of royal titles that included "the Conquest, Navigation, and Commerce of Ethiopia, Arabia, Persia, and India." In reality, however, Portuguese power in the seventeenth and eighteenth centuries rarely penetrated further than a few dozen miles beyond the empire's key colonial outposts: the coastal cities of Brazil; Luanda in present-day Angola; Goa in present-day India; and Macau in present-day China.

Overlaid onto this secular power structure, like a second empire, lay the missionary enterprises of the holy orders.[28] In parts of South America and Asia, Society of Jesus "provinces" (frequently dominated by Lusophone Jesuits) exerted quasi-governmental control. The Franciscan and Dominican Orders also wielded considerable influence in Goa and Macau, as did the

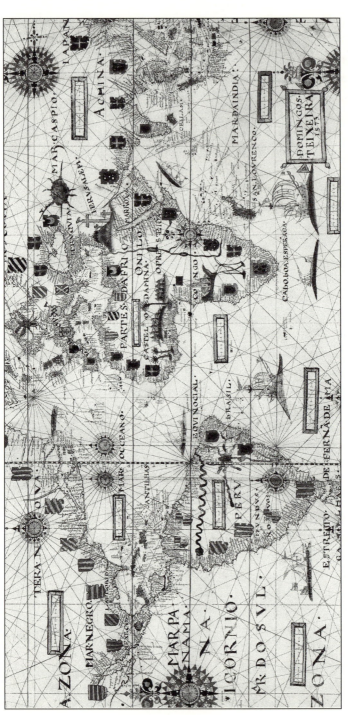

Figure 3. Planisphere of Domingos Teixeira (1573), Bibliothèque Nationale de France. Created seven years before Philip II acceded to the Portuguese throne and initiated the period of Iberian Union (1580–1640), the map paints an exaggerated vision of Portuguese power. Brazil, Angola, Goa, and Macao are labeled with the Portuguese coat of arms, but so too are notional territorial claims in the Cape of Good Hope, the Horn of Africa, and Morocco. Courtesy of the Bibliothèque Nationale de France.

Capuchins in seventeenth-century Angola. Still, the combined population of both missionaries and colonists was surprisingly small. By one estimate, fewer than 10,000 "able-bodied Portuguese" inhabited the colonies claimed by the king of Portugal at the end of the sixteenth century.[29]

Perhaps the defining geographic and demographic feature of the Portuguese and the British Empires was their reliance on the forced labor of captives.[30] Although the largest group of these unwilling immigrants were enslaved Africans transported along the networks of the Atlantic slave trade, they were not the only group to suffer confinement and transportation.[31] In the British context, a substantial proportion of naval crews in the seventeenth and eighteenth centuries consisted of individuals who had been unwillingly conscripted into the Royal Navy—often while they were deeply intoxicated.[32] A significant proportion of Portuguese soldiers, similarly, were *degredados* (exiled convicts) who demonstrated little allegiance to the Portuguese state that had prosecuted them.[33] The "empires" we will encounter in this book were zones of contested control, guided by forces and individuals that often evade the notice of histories focused on a single state.

THIS BOOK'S FIRST part, centered on the Portuguese colonies of Brazil and Angola and on the imperial capital of Lisbon, examines the process by which novel drugs were located, commodified, and consumed in the seventeenth and eighteenth centuries. The British Empire, I argue, owed much of its success in the late seventeenth and eighteenth centuries to cannibalizing these Portuguese drug networks. For this reason, the second part of *The Age of Intoxication* expands into British sources relating to the drug trade. Here, I argue that the global drug trade can offer an alternative history of the Scientific Revolution and its entanglement with the rise of global capitalism.[34] Although cultural understandings of intoxication vary widely, by the eighteenth century a new, more global understanding of intoxication emerged, one guided by both empiricism and orientalism. The division between drugs and pharmaceuticals sprouted in this racialized soil of Enlightenment-era debates about intoxication, science, and empire.

This book's approach, with its emphasis on unusual details and forgotten characters, is an attempt to do justice to a history that has too often been viewed as a simplistic binary between good and bad. As I wrote it, I became convinced that one of the central problems in how societies deal with drugs has been, and remains, a profound lack of empathy and imagination. In this regard, I've found inspiration from the companionable titles of some early modern drug manuals. These books, written in vernacular languages rather than Latin and priced to sell, promised that "the Treasury of Drugs" would be "Unlock'd" for all to see, announced their desire to be "Useful to the Public," or offered entry into the "Watchtower of Life Against the Hostilities of Death."[35] The secrets of drugs were revealed to "the Poor Man" and "Every Woman."[36] The titles of those old drug manuals over-promised: they were often repetitive lists of prescriptions that had been copied and recopied for centuries. But they did manage to cover a surprisingly rich array of topics, from how to make perfume to the proper way to die, from deadly plagues to melancholy, and from tropical poisons to garden herbs. I have tried to evoke something of that eclectic and inquisitive spirit in this book.

Today, deep-seated preconceptions and fears continue to structure how we think about drugs. By understanding the historical origins of these assumptions, we can overcome bias and rethink obsolete policies. What is at stake here is not just our knowledge about a crucial and understudied aspect of world history. My hope is that in some small way, these pages can push contemporary societies toward tolerance and compassion, and away from an obsolete legacy of criminalization and stigma.

PART I

Inventions of Drugs

CHAPTER 1

Searching for Drugs

Inventing Quina in Seventeenth-Century Amazonia

> As for the *china china*, what will be necessary to know it is for the people to see a painting with the colors of the trunk, branches, leaves and fruits, because with samples of the bark alone it will be very difficult to be certain of the tree, not knowing what name the Tapuyas have given it.
>
> —FRANCISCO DE SÁ E MENEZES, 1683

The jungle was large, and Captain Lacerda was small.

Perhaps not in stature. We can't presume to know, although we do know that the average height of a Portuguese soldier in 1720 was a little over five feet and four inches.[1] What was small about Captain Lacerda was his knowledge, and his power. This might have been news to him. After all, Andre Pinheiro de Lacerda was a decorated officer in the Portuguese army, the leader of an imperial vanguard. But it was an empire that was far weaker than it let on. At the moment at which we join him, in the humid tropical winter of 1683, Captain Lacerda was not leading much of anything. In fact, he was lost.

We cannot know the exact physical size of the jungle Lacerda wandered within, either. During the centuries that divide us from him, Amazonia's edges have retreated like a pool of evaporating water. Thousands of species that once thrived within its boundaries are gone now. But the jungle was not large simply because of its physical extent or the number of plants and animals it contained. It was large because this jungle, when viewed from the inside, was a system too complex to be reduced to its constituent parts.

Captain Lacerda, to his repeated frustration, was there to look for parts:

parts of plants and animals, parts to be collected, packaged, sold, and consumed. He called these parts *drogas*.[2] Beyond this, Lacerda didn't know precisely what he was in the jungle to find. He simply knew it was a bark similar to the one that the Portuguese called "quina" or "china china," and which could cure certain types of fever. He had seen dried remains of the plant's bark, pictures of what it might look like when alive, and a list of names that were applied to it in different places.

Yet, he had never laid eyes on a living specimen. And he had no idea what the peoples of this particular corner of the Amazon called the plant. Later, in the early nineteenth century, quina would become one of the planet's most valuable crops, famed as a malaria treatment because of the powerful "febrifuge" (fever-fighting) alkaloids in its bark.[3] For Captain Lacerda, as he stood in 1683 in an indigenous village in the Amazon, miles from any Portuguese settlement, the presence of a thing called "quina" remained little more than a rumor.

Also known as cinchona, Jesuit's bark, or Peruvian bark, the "true" quina of Peru (genus *Cinchona*) had first gained global fame in the middle decades of the seventeenth century. It was said to be a miraculously effective treatment for fevers. Yet, because the most prized type of quina was (wrongly) thought to grow only in Loja, a tropical valley south of Quito, the Portuguese were reliant on their Spanish enemies' goodwill.[4] Lacerda and the man who gave him orders, Governor Francisco de Sá e Menezes, hoped to discover a new variety of quina in the *sertão* (backlands) of the Estado do Maranhão e Grão Pará, an independently administered Portuguese colony straddling the southeastern quarter of the Amazon basin.[5] In so doing, they hoped to make the drug into a tool of Portuguese colonization and a rebuff to Spanish competition.[6]

Lacerda's charge of "making discoveries of drugs . . . among the flora and fauna of the interior" required a deep engagement with Amazonian landscapes, languages, and modes of thought.[7] To find quina in Maranhão, Lacerda first had to develop ties with the people he called the "Tapuya" (a catch-all Portuguese term for non-Tupi speakers in the Amazon, derived from the Tupi word for "enemy").[8] Portuguese hunters for drugs were building on a Spanish and Dutch colonial precedent of commodifying local cures. But they soon found that the act of "discovering" a drug in a new landscape and cultural setting was far from simple. The mental categories Lacerda brought to his task—not just the existence of a specific plant called "quina," recognizable on the basis of its botanical characteristics, but of a specific ailment called "fever" or even a category called "drug"—did not seem to have obvious correlates among the Tapuya.

The Portuguese in Amazonia were discovering that drugs are never a fixed category. A lump of gold might retain its core characteristics, and its value, despite crossing cultural frontiers and undergoing repeated material transformations. But drugs do not. By consuming them, we erase them. By harvesting and preparing them, we obscure their biological origins. In naming them, we sow confusion. And by turning them into tools of sociability, spirituality, or healing, we overlay a constantly changing array of cultural beliefs onto the basic facts of their existence as material objects.

Quina was no exception. As historian Matthew Crawford has pointed out, the drug had a dual identity "as both a natural object and a cultural artifact."[9] The individuals involved in the first phase of quina's existence as a drug—Quechua- and Aymara-speaking indigenous healers—worked within a mental framework of healing that long predated European colonization. But quina turns out *not* to have had a deep history of use as a medicine to treat malarial fever, despite the fact that it was quina's antimalarial activity that made it globally renowned. Instead, the discovery of quina's role as a febrifuge seems to date to the sixteenth century, sparked by the transatlantic transfer of malaria-bearing *Anopheles* mosquitos to the New World by the 1530s, and the resulting search for a cure by Andean healers and colonists.[10]

In a report sent to the Overseas Council in Lisbon, Governor de Sá wrote that he had brought "two small samples" of true quina to Belém, Maranhão's administrative center. De Sá exhibited these samples to "the Indian leaders there who had kin in the *sertão*" and asked them to bring him plants that looked similar. Despite receiving "a great number of medicinal barks," however, de Sá had failed to find what he considered to be an adequate match for his quina samples. Verbal descriptions, names, and physical examples had failed to manifest the governor's imagined Amazonian variant of quina. De Sá now pinned his hopes on a detailed illustration created by artisans in Lisbon, "painted with the colors of the trunk, the branches, the leaves, and the fruit it bears," to communicate the "quina-ness" of quina with the indigenous peoples of the Maranhão interior.[11] This, too, ended in failure.

In the end, it took more than a century for the ambitions of de Sá and Lacerda to be even partially realized: by the end of the eighteenth century, a drug known as "Brazilian quina" (*quina do brasil*) had become a popular fever cure in the Lusophone world. But as we'll see, it *still* remained unclear to Portuguese colonists and healers whether this was "true" quina of genus

Cinchona. Today, half a dozen unrelated plants circulate in Brazilian folk medicine that bear a variant of the name "quina"—but none of them, according to botanists, are actually related to genus *Cinchona*, the "true" quina and precursor of quinine.[12]

I have chosen to begin this book on the ground in the Amazon, in a state of confusion rather than clarity, because these scenes of confusion seem to me more typical of the early modern drug trade than the more famous episodes of success. For every tobacco, chocolate, or coffee—drugs that were, in a fairly short period of time, described and categorized by European savants, transplanted to new continents, and transformed into enormously valuable commodities—there were a host of *failed* drugs whose stories have fallen out of the historical record. In part, this absence is because older histories of drugs tended to begin their story only after a substance made its first appearance in a European medical or botanical text.[13] More recently, historians have looked back to the ecological and epistemic sources of drugs, studying "bioprospectors" as they hunted for new commodities and cures.[14] The stories that have emerged from this work are fascinating: the French botanical spy who smuggled precious cochineal beetles out of colonial Mexico, or the missionary who, strolling in the forests of Quebec, identified a novel species of Canadian ginseng that he recognized from the reports of Jesuits in China.[15]

But what did it really mean to "discover" a drug? The word *bioprospecting*, adopted from mining, summons a mental image of the prospector as a hunter in a natural landscape with a specific and durable quarry, like gold, in mind. In reality, though, searchers for drugs in seventeenth-century tropics had enormous difficulties agreeing on the most basic questions of identification and purpose. After all, quina was not just one species, but several, scattered over a wide growing range and bearing numerous indigenous and European names. Moreover, quina's role as a febrifuge was still quite new, a product of a secretive colonial medical culture rather than ancient and widespread knowledge. In a very real sense, there was no such thing as a single drug called quina, and no clearly-delineated bank of "traditional" knowledge that Europeans could co-opt to discover it.

The multiple reinventions of a drug like quina depended on a complex dance between hyper-localized ecological and linguistic knowledge, ever-changing disease environments, and incommensurate epistemologies of what drugs were and how they worked. More often than not, this was an exchange that ended in confusion. Captain Lacerda, wandering lost in the jungle, carrying the shriveled remains of a drug that no one can recognize, turns out to be more emblematic of the search for drugs in the early modern period than the figure of the triumphant prospector striking gold.

The Deep History of South American Drugs

The idea of the Columbian Exchange—developed by Alfred Crosby, in the 1970s and 1980s, and popularized in the 1990s by Jared Diamond—has been an enormous success. One of the few new historical concepts to filter into popular consciousness over the past decades, it is predicated on a simple argument: The voyages of Columbus and those who came after him didn't just *connect* the biomes of the Old and New Worlds, the argument goes. It unleashed a *differential of power* between them. Afro-Eurasia is thought to have enjoyed certain prior advantages (such as a wider array of domesticated animals, an East-West corridor allowing for lateral transplantation of key crops, and greater exposure to epidemic diseases), which helped enable the Spanish conquest of Mexico and Peru and the colonization that followed.[16]

But there were many dimensions to the Columbian Exchange, not all of them ending in an inevitable conquest of the New World by the Old. It turns out that the Americas, especially tropical Central and South America, were far better equipped than Africa, Europe, and Asia when it came to psycho-active substances and pharmacological knowledge. A kind of reverse colonization took place in the world of drugs, both medicinal and recreational. Within two centuries, American drugs like tobacco, chocolate, guaiacum bark, and Peruvian quina had become the consolations, the cures, and the obsessions of consumers in Africa, Europe, Asia, and beyond.

The Amazon basin is a central hub of global biodiversity that has perhaps yielded more psychoactive substances per acre than any other region in the world.[17] As best contemporary scientists can tell, the tobacco genus (*Nicotiana*) appears to have evolved in the Greater Amazon basin.[18] So, too, did many of the other "breakthrough" drugs of the sixteenth and seventeenth centuries. In addition to those mentioned above, we could add lesser-known substances found in greater Amazonia, such as yopo, ayahuasca, "Occidental" bezoars, ipecacuanha, and copaiba balsam. But there has been more than one Amazon, and more than one Amazonia. The oldest iterations of the river system actually flowed westward, emptying into the Pacific Ocean as they passed through foothills that would eventually become the Andes. They dripped from regions of eternal snow to arid mountainsides, oxbowed through rolling grasslands, and carved channels in the red clay soils of the interior. The waters nourished eagles with twenty-five-foot wingspans, giant sloths, and saber-toothed cats. In the green twilight below the forest canopy, countless creatures waged evolutionary war with chitin claws, prying fingers, hallucinogenic toxins, and parasitic guile. These paths carved by Andean snowmelt became one of the central arteries of life on earth.[19]

When *Homo sapiens* reached the Amazon basin sometime between 30,000 and 15,000 years ago, we set about reshaping this crowded ecosystem. A growing body of archaeological literature points to significant pre-Columbian manipulation of the Amazon River valley as an environmental space, including zones of intensive farming and complex regimes of labor.[20] According to one historian, the peoples of the pre-Columbian Amazon basin "created one of the largest, strangest, and most ecologically rich artificial environments on the planet."[21]

European colonists tended to lump together the diverse cultural and linguistic groups of eastern South America because sixteenth-century Europeans interacted primarily with the Tupi-speaking peoples of the coast. Yet the indigenous societies of Brazil were a patchwork of dozens of often-unrelated linguistic groups. Some (like the Gê people) had resided in the area for millennia, while others, like the Tupi and Guaraní, were relative newcomers, having moved from present-day Paraguay to coastal Brazil around 400 CE and approaching the southern banks of the Amazon shortly thereafter.[22] One feature that bound together all of these linguistic and cultural groupings was a profound knowledge of the biodiversity and pharmacology of rain-forest ecosystems. Whether they were intensive agriculturalists or hunter-gatherers, the Tupi, Gê, and other groups possessed an enormous collective knowledge of the flora and fauna that the Portuguese would come to call *drogas do sertão*—"drugs of the backlands."

Many pre-Columbian societies of the Amazon basin (and beyond) featured a societal category that, for simplicity's sake, we can call the *shaman*.[23] Shamans stood apart from the normal social order, closely guarding hard-won knowledge of a natural landscape that was perceived to be imbued with latent spiritual powers: of gods, ancestors, ambiguous magical forces, or even the spirits of psychoactive plants themselves. In such an arrangement, drug knowledge tended to be socially segregated and highly prized. Although their practices and social positions varied widely, shamans of Greater Amazonia tended to employ at least one mind-altering substance in their rituals: *Nicotiana rustica* was probably the most common, but other documented shamanistic drugs include yopo (*Anadenanthera peregrina*), ayahuasca, and various species of genus *Datura*.[24]

In some cases, shamans who gained power from their perceived ability to commune with psychoactive substances became political leaders. Among Arawakan-speaking groups of the Rio Negro, for instance, "cosmologically adept leaders" consolidated multiethnic groups into larger polities.[25] Arawakan shamans were selected not just on the basis of their mastery of cognitive challenges (such as the memorization of ritual songs and an enormous array of botanicals) but also for their physical and spiritual ability to tolerate the ingestion of psychoactive drugs like yopo or *Nicotiana rusticum*. Another example can be found among the shamans of the Cubeo people (known as *payé*), who utilized ritual intoxication through the use of *chicha*, coca leaves, and tobacco. A period of "fits of visions and dreams" passed into a stage during which the *payé* was believed to gain physical power over nature, such as the ability to "cause small creatures to be born and grow" and "propagate fruits."[26] Profound knowledge of tropical remedies followed from such liminal experiences, and ultimately an appointment to a line of succession, allowing the *payé* to create disciples.[27] It was a role Europeans had no name for, and no prior understanding of. Yet successfully "discovering" a drug in the Amazon often really meant entering, or at least making contact with, this radically unfamiliar epistemology.

Mastering the use of Amazonian drugs required an encyclopedic knowledge not just of where substances could be found but also the proper way of preparing and mixing them. Two examples—manioc and ayahuasca—give a sense of both the complexity of the knowledge system Europeans were trying to adapt to, and of the high stakes. Although manioc root (*Manihot esculenta*) is a common dietary staple throughout South and Central America, it is also potentially deadly. If manioc isn't properly prepared by soaking in water for several days, the tuber can contain a high enough concentration of cyanide as to be neurotoxic and potentially even fatal. In other words, colonists who simply attempted to transplant the manioc without the accompanying technologies of preparation would put their lives at risk.

Similarly, although the Amazonian entheogen known as ayahuasca is often described as if it were a single drug, like tobacco, it is actually a mixture of at least two plants. Typically, though not always, it consists of the bark of *Banisteriopsis caapi* and the leaves of the *Psychotria viridis* vine. Taken separately, neither substance is psychoactive. But when the former, which is a potent monoamine oxidase inhibitor (MAOI), combines with the latter, which contains the potent hallucinogen dimethyltryptamine (DMT), the brew becomes profoundly mind-altering.[28] To hit upon this precise formula through trial and error, out of the hundreds of thousands of potential combinations available, implies an enormous amount of experimentation and carefully acquired knowledge of the effects of the combinations of different drugs.

In short, the drug cultures of Amazonia are the product of an enormous amount of technological know-how—a millennia's worth of careful empiricism, preserved through memorization, stories, songs, and the experimental ingestion of the substances themselves. It took thousands of years for Amazonian peoples to master such a complex pharmacological environment. It is little wonder, then, that the Portuguese spent much of their first decades in the Americas stumbling in the dark, trying and usually failing to make sense of the hallucinogens, poisons, stimulants, and remedies that surrounded them.

In the initial phase of colonization, the emphasis was on only one coastal crop: brazilwood. The tree that the Tupí called *ibirapitanga* ("red tree") became known to the Portuguese as *pau-brasil* ("emberwood") after the Portuguese word for glowing embers, *brasa*. Brazilwood was, after Spanish-traded tobacco and guaiacum, the first New World plant to attract significant attention in Europe. Scenes of Tupinambá harvesting the reddish bark of the tree appeared prominently in a detail from one of the first maps of Brazil, the Vallard Atlas (Figure 4).[29] It is no coincidence that brazilwood had a close correlate in a pre-existing Old World product. When brazilwood began to be shipped back to Europe at scale, it benefited from its close resemblance to an expensive Asian medicine and dye called sapanwood, the substance traditionally used to dye Buddhist monks' robes orange.[30] The success (and, later, the stumbles) of the brazilwood trade pushed the Portuguese into the pharmacological worlds of the Amazon in search of correlates with other potential substitutes for valuable *drogas*—and into direct competition with the Spanish.

Imperial Competition for *Drogas do Sertão*

The hunt for novel drugs by Europeans in the New World dates back to Christopher Columbus's first Atlantic voyage. In his first letter to Ferdinand and Isabella, the Genoese navigator reported that he had found evidence of "rhubarb and other sorts of drugs" on the island that he called Hispaniola

Figure 4. Native Brazilians harvesting brazilwood in a detail from the *Vallard Atlas,* a book of fifteen highly detailed nautical charts created in Dieppe, France, in 1547. Huntington Library, HM 29, fol. 11. Courtesy of the Huntington Library, San Marino, CA.

(present-day Dominican Republic and Haiti).[31] Throughout the sixteenth century, Spanish colonists and missionaries documented cultures of drug use that stood on the brink of transformational change and, in many cases, destruction. The oldest book written by a European in the Americas, the Jeronimite monk Ramón Pané's "Relation of the Antiquities of the Indians" of Hispaniola (c. 1498), is also among the oldest known textual descriptions of psychedelic drug use. Pané described shamanistic use of an entheogen that was commonly used throughout Amazon basin and beyond: yopo snuff, the powdered seeds of the *Anadenanthera peregrina* tree, which contains the psychoactive alkaloid DMT.[32] Healers called *buhuitihu,* Pané wrote, "mimic the diet and the appearance of the sick person." To "purge himself like the sick person," the *buhuitihu* "takes a certain powder called cohoba [yopo], sucking it into his nose, which intoxicates him in such a way that he knows not what he does."[33] Anthropologists have filled in Pané's fragmentary picture, documenting Taíno chiefs (*caciques*) and shamans (*bohitu*) who used hallucinogenic snuffs to commune with both natural and ancestor spirits (*zemís*).[34]

As the Spanish asserted control over an increasingly vast swath of the New World throughout the sixteenth century, they began to draw clear lines between pre-Columbian drugs that they deemed to be demonic and those that could be commodified as medicines in Europe. Entheogens like yopo and peyote typically failed this test; others, however—notably, guaiacum, chocolate, and tobacco—emerged as highly valuable luxury items. When the Flemish engraver Jan van der Strat sat down to depict the "New Inventions" of his modern age in the late 1580s, Spanish-traded guaiacum logs (genus *Guaiacum*, native to the Caribbean) stood in the foreground of his scene, taking their place alongside innovations like gunpowder, eyeglasses, and the printing press (Figure 5).[35]

New World drugs became popular among European consumers in part because of new fears prompted by the post-Columbian globalization of epidemic diseases. Guaiacum, for example, became closely associated with the treatment of the *morbo gallico* (syphilis), a disease that was widely—and, it now seems likely, correctly—thought to have been a disease of the Ameri-

Figure 5. A detail from an engraving in Jan van der Strat's *Nova Reperta* (New Inventions), late 1580s, detail, showing guaiacum at lower right. Courtesy of the John Carter Brown Library, Providence, RI.

cas transmitted to the Old World by Iberian sailors.[36] In one of the earliest detailed accounts of tobacco, the French Brazil colonist Andre Thevet described it as a potential cure for yaws, another New World disease that had no known cure in the existing European pharmacopoeias. Likewise, as noted above, the value of quina as a febrifuge seems not to have been hit upon until malarial mosquitos had spread the illness to South America from Africa, via the Atlantic slave trade.[37]

These drugs faced challenges from Europeans who saw them as potentially dangerous because of both their pharmacological properties and their association with supposedly "heathen" cultures. Writing from Bahia in the 1550s, the Portuguese friar Manuel Nóbrega framed tobacco as an invaluable cure for the ailments endemic to tropical Brazil's wet and humid climate, acknowledging that "I have had need of [tobacco] owing to the humidity and my cough." Yet Nóbrega feared that his use of this "infidel" drug would set a bad precedent: "At present there are none among our Friars who use this [drug]," he wrote, "and so too few of the other Christians use it lest they emulate the infidels who relish it greatly."[38] Within a matter of decades, however, this foreign drug would number among the most prized American medicines, featuring in the daily rituals and sociability of millions throughout the Old World.[39] Part of the value of these "new" drugs derived from their perceived efficacy in treating newly globalized diseases. If a *disease* came from a region unknown to the ancients, the theory went, then perhaps its *cure* could, too.

The hunt for drugs in the early modern tropics was thus part of a larger story of globalization. It was born not just from a profit motive but also from desperation and fear occasioned by the spread of diseases like syphilis, yaws, and malaria that had been unknown to medieval or Greco-Roman medical authorities. In addition, by the beginning of the seventeenth century, the hunt for new drugs was also being driven by the recognition that intensive harvesting of coastal forests was causing ecological devestation. By 1605, the Portuguese crown was already warning against wasteful harvesting practices that might "finish off" the remaining supplies of the brazilwood tree. In 1607, the crown placed a quota of 600 tons a year on exports, which were also deemed royal property.[40] As with brazilwood, which functioned as both dye and medicament, sugar was a food and a drug.[41] In the 1660s, however, Brazilian sugar prices entered a period of decline. The problem was compounded when, in the 1660s, sugar became heavily cultivated in the Dutch, English, and French West Indies, increasing total supply.[42] Meanwhile, the Spanish crown was busy consolidating its control over the vice-royalty of Peru, dispatching missionaries and officials to establish overland routes joining the Andes with the Atlantic. The most famous of these was Pedro Texeira's successful 1637 expedition on the Amazon, moving westward from Belém in Maranhão to Quito in Ecuador.[43] Following the restoration of Portuguese independence in 1640, administrators and colonists grew understandably worried about the prospect of a Spanish Amazon, as well as the arrival of independent Spanish, French, and Dutch colonists and traders lured by the promise of wealth in the *sertão*.

As the Atlantic forest (*mata Atlantica*) that ringed the coastal Portuguese settlements became depleted and as sugar prices fell, colonists looked northward to the Estado do Maranhão and the vast interior rain forests of the Amazon.[44] The decline of brazilwood stocks and sugar prices made the *drogas do sertão* of the Amazonian interior (like copaiba, guaiacum, sarsaparilla, ipecacuanha, wild nutmeg, cinchona, and local subspecies of tobacco) increasingly commercially attractive to colonists. There was a problem, however. The two forests of the *mata Atlantica* and the Amazon had once been joined and had shared many species. But the knowledge required to collect medicines in the *mata Atlantica* didn't necessarily translate to the Amazon. The go-betweens who had made brazilwood extraction possible by locating and prepping trees in the interior were harder to come by outside the coastal Tupí heartlands. Amazonian peoples spoke unfamiliar languages and shamans carefully guarded knowledge of plant species deemed sacred or useful.[45] By the close of the sixteenth century, many colonists had shifted from extraction of brazilwood in forest hinterlands to the cultivation of sugar in coastal plantations—and from Tupi labor to slaves seized in Africa.[46]

The Dutch Republic, newly liberated from Hapsburg control, was quick to realize the commercial potential of Brazilian naturalia. In 1630, the Dutch West India Company launched a successful attack on the Portuguese port of Pernambuco and claimed it as company property. A decade later, under Governor Johan Maurits, the Dutch Brazilian city of Recife hosted the construction of the continent's first botanical garden. The goal was twofold: to highlight the ecological reach of the Dutch state (bananas, newly transplanted from West Africa, were a special focus) and to serve as a site for experimentation with novel drugs, animals, and foods.[47] By 1645, however, the failure of the Dutch to forge effective alliances with sugar planters had combined with political instability in Holland to make Dutch Brazil increasingly untenable. The Dutch formally ceded their remaining possessions in Brazil to Portugal in 1654.

But the Dutch influence, with its emphasis on transplantation and "improvement" of a landscape, remained potent. The frontispiece to *Historia Naturalis Brasiliae*, a treatise written jointly by the German naturalist Georg Marcgrave and by Maurits's personal physician, Willem Piso, turned palm trees into quasi-classical columns and arbors of forest trees into an archway. Inside, riches beckoned.[48] With its "doorway" of trees leading to an Edenic array of natural wonders, the frontispiece framed the Brazilian interior as a potentially knowable—and exploitable—space (Figure 6).[49]

A 1650 letter to the king of Portugal used the language of improvement to laud the benefits of developing Pernambuco's drug trade. The land "yields *drogas*," the author wrote, "not only sugar but also brazilwood, cotton, tobacco, ginger, and also many other products which we have not yet profited from [*aproveitado*]."[50] Even as he enthused about Brazilian nutmeg (*Cryptocarya moschata*) and "abundance of drugs" in the Maranhão, another booster of the drug trade named Domingos Antunes Tomás complained that the Portuguese advantage was "lost because no one knows how to benefit from it." The problem, he wrote, was the inaccessible nature of these *drogas*.[51] Similarly, João de Moura, a Portuguese clerk stationed in Belém in the 1680s, observed that the Maranhão was "the most well-appointed Province in the World," but that the landscape was too dangerous and unknown to be effectively "reduced."[52]

"The Greatest Apothecary . . . Which Has Yet Been Discovered"

In 1611, French traveler François Pyrard called Brazil "a rough and savage land," complaining that it was "almost entirely covered in forests filled with monkeys who are a lot of trouble."[53] Yet when it came to Brazilians themselves, Pyrard's tone changed. The inhabitants of Brazil, he wrote, were "very healthy," being "said to achieve well beyond 100 years." Pyrard described a near total "absence of illnesses, and those who do feel badly can cure themselves with the juice of certain herbs of which they know the properties."[54] Pyrard's statement is shocking given what historians now know: epidemic diseases were devastating populations throughout South America during precisely the decade (1610s) that Pyrard visited Brazil. Although Pyrard acknowledged that the indigenous Brazilians suffered from smallpox, he

Figure 6. Hand-colored frontispiece engraving of the first edition of Willem Piso and Georg Marcgrave, *Historia Naturalis Brasiliae* (Amsterdam: Franciscus Hack, 1648). Courtesy of the John Carter Brown Library.

claimed that "they think little of this ailment" owing to their possession of "the Gayac" with which "they are rapidly cured."[55] Guaiacum bark, as we've seen, was mainly known to Europeans of Pyrard's time as a syphilis cure, but Pyrard seems to have regarded it as a panacea for all serious diseases, part of a larger palette of miraculous tropical cures that Brazilians had mastered.

Other travelers in the Amazon described a dark inverse of these healing abilities. The same knowledge of the "properties" of medicinal drugs that allowed for remarkable cures could also be used for poisons and curses. As he made his way down tributaries of the Amazon in 1639, Cristóbal de Acuña had enthused that "in these uncultivated forests, the natives have, for their sicknesses, the greatest apothecary of medicinal drugs [botica de simples] which has yet been discovered."[56] However, he also feared that these Amazonian drogas were wielded by what he called "sorcerers" (hechizeros) who used them to poison as well as to heal. "All of the people [of the Amazon] hold their sorcerers in great esteem," he wrote, "not so much out of the love they bear them, but out of the dread they forever live under of the damage that they can do."[57] Acuña was convinced that these sorcerers were legitimately powerful. "It is very ordinary for them to speak with the Demon," he wrote. Acuña recorded that the Amazonian hechizeros offered "poisonous herbs [yervas venenosas] with which to take vengeance against enemies." He also described multiday funeral rites involving "great intoxication," in what is possibly another early reference to the use of Amazonian entheogens.[58]

Would-be bioprospectors grappled with the challenges of translating their own conception of drugs and healing into these plant-based and shamanic epistemologies of indigenous Amazonians. What did it mean to be an expert in finding, locating, and transporting New World drugs in the seventeenth century? Were these men performing scientific acts of botanical description, or were they conquistadors searching for "green gold"? Bioprospectors not only were embodying multiple roles simultaneously but also were applying overlapping categories to the natural quarry they sought.

The tendency to equate bioprospecting with botany has led historians to focus on only one facet of drug discovery in the colonial world.[59] Plants, to be sure, were the most important raw material for the drug trade, and the Amazon's natural riches were remarkable.[60] But the learned networks of trained botanists represent a sliver of a larger story. Seventeenth-century individuals—Europeans and indigenous Amazonians alike—categorized plants in a manner foreign to post-Enlightenment botany. Some theorized that minerals grew underground like roots and believed that plants could give birth to animals; others imagined the search for natural knowledge as a hunt (*venatio*) steeped in Hermetic and alchemical lore.[61] Native Brazilians, too, had very different understandings of plant-based drugs, seeing them as potentially sentient natural forces that spiritual initiates could commune with or control. Yet they, too, operated within a mental universe in which Linnaean definitions of plants did not apply.[62] Bioprospecting for *drogas* in the Amazonian hinterlands could just as easily have involved hunting for healing mineral waters, bones, bezoars, pearls, muds, hoofs, claws, and gemstones as it did searching for plants.

Likewise, it was not necessarily the case that Europeans regarded plants and minerals as fundamentally distinct: throughout the colonial Americas and beyond, experts in mining and medicine described metals as "growing," "fermenting," and consuming "food" like living things.[63] A mining official in Peru, for instance, described a mystical correspondence between metals and plants: "The way that metal is created in mountains is similar to how a tree pushes its branches out from its trunk."[64] António Vieira came away from two years of missionary travels in the Maranhão convinced that gems, drugs, and natural philosophical secrets grew in the "bowels" of Brazil.[65] Likewise, in his *Historia natural y moral de las Indias*, Acosta had likened the mineral wealth of Spanish America to "plants hidden in the entrails of the earth" whose underground structures featured *ramos* (branches) and *troncos* (trunks) just like the trees sought by bioprospectors aboveground.[66] These metaphors remind us that the early modern European vision of nature allowed for a much wider range of metamorphoses than modern science does. In the early modern European worldview, even nonbotanical drugs could "grow" or "be created."[67] The lack of clear boundaries among plants, animals, and minerals meant that there were no clear categorical boundaries between individual types of drugs.

Bioprospecting, in short, was emphatically *not* the same thing as a botanical hunt for specimens. For early modern individuals, plants, animals, and minerals had all been created by God, all were organic and in a constant state of metamorphosis, and all could shape mind or body. Bioprospectors might search for gold, animal horns, and rare botanicals in the same conceptual framework, using the same methods, and in the same places. Moreover, unlike naturalists, they *consumed their quarry*. Rather than seeking ideal specimens to display or reproduce in learned works, bioprospectors sought potency and accessibility. And rather than the pristine representations of plants isolated from their surroundings favored in works of botanical description, bioprospectors needed "thick ecological descriptions" of the settings in which drugs might be located—not only information about the drug itself but also about the way it existed within its environment, its colloquial names, its roles in local societies, and its price.

The Lisbon apothecary João Vigier gave a description of quina that reflected a close, firsthand knowledge of the bark yet offered few clues for potential bioprospectors. They needed to know ecological details like the height of the tree, the plants that grew near it, and the altitude at which it thrived. Vigier's description instead offered guidelines for the plant's *consumption*—not its harvesting.[68] This emphasis on the final product was useless from the point of view of bioprospectors, who sought a living organism embedded in a complex ecological context rather than a processed drug in a marketplace.

Yet it did contain a detail that might have given hope to the search for other forms of the drug in regions outside Spanish control. Vigier argued that quina did not take only one form: "There are two species," he wrote, "one wild (*brava*) and one cultivated." This would prove to be an influential belief. As quina globalized, it also became refigured, spreading through hearsay, traveler's tales, and misunderstandings like the branches growing from a central trunk.

Amazonian Quina's Travels from Colony to Court

De Sá and Lacerda's quest for quina hinged on the ecological reasoning that if the cultivated quina thrived in the western reaches of the Amazon, a second variety may well occupy the eastern. Their hunt for this potential plant took place within the context of a vast and haphazard search for gold, gems, dyewoods, "curiosities," and even human beings to take as captives.[69] These efforts culminated during the era of the short-lived Companhia de Comércio do Maranhão (1682–1695), which held both a slave-trading contract and a twenty-year Crown monopoly on Amazonian exports.[70] The convergence of these two privileges thus put a premium on the discovery of new drugs and minerals and their exploitation through the use of enslaved labor.

Maranhão was an almost purely extractive rather than a mixed agricultural colony like Brazil. Its administrators, eager to secure wealth the only way they knew how, were obsessed with making "discoveries" [*descobrimentos*] of new commodities to extract. As historian Rafael Chambouleyron puts it, "One has the impression sometimes that the sertanejos . . .

were sent without even knowing what they were seeking."[71] The push came not only from the colonial administrators themselves but also from wealthy magnates and officials elsewhere in the empire who hoped that their insider knowledge would allow them to corner the market in newly discovered drugs and spices. In January 1684, for instance, Francisco de Sá had asked another lieutenant in the sertão (the Capitão-Mor of a settlement called Tapuitapera) for samples of "drugs and other curiosities to send to Dom Lourenco de Almada," an ambitious young nobleman at the Portuguese court who would go on to become the governor of Brazil (1709). Secular administrators began competing directly with members of the Society of Jesus in the colony, whose finances relied upon monopolizing the labor of mission Indians charged with harvesting drugs and spices. Already by 1681, a Jesuit had lodged an official complaint about a merchant in Belém who had "made a contract with the Indians to take wild cloves [cravo]" from the environs of the Xingu settlement of Taconhape, harming the Jesuit monopoly in the region.[72]

De Sá tended to play up the success of these drug-discovery efforts in his communications with Almada and other elites in Lisbon.[73] The governor claimed that his interest in "bitters" (amargosas) like quina and sarsaparilla had created a local drug trade between the Indian aldeias and the small Portuguese settlement in Belém; "Today," Sá wrote in 1683, "this medicine is sold by a woman for a quarter thousand réis." It was apparently being purchased by the colony's surgeon from the woman, likely an indigenous herbalist.[74] And during Captain Lacerda's continued search for quina, de Sá claimed, he had found two drugs with "medicinal virtues": "a bark much like sarsaparilla" and "a bark like huanó[co]." The latter was likely a reference to a subspecies of quina that became known as Cinchona huanuco in the nineteenth century.[75] Captain Lacerda appears to have been more doubtful. He promised that he "would do more diligence to discover the tree [of the quina-like bark]" but complained that "it was not easy to find, because the sample had been cut from the trunk a long time ago," and he cautioned that the lands where it flourished were "two months' march" into the interior.[76]

Early the next year, in the spring of 1684, the secretary of the Overseas Council wrote to the powerful duke of Cadaval regarding a shipment of twenty pounds of a drug purported to be "chinachina" that an official in Madrid had promised to send to Lisbon. The secretary wanted to know whether de Sá's samples of supposed quina had been "falsified" (falsicava).[77] The Overseas Council, he noted, had "some Chinachina of a more white color"

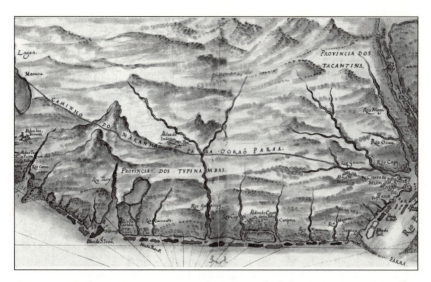

Figure 7. A Portuguese map (c. 1629) showing (at far left) the location of Tapuitapera, a settlement from which Francisco de Sá had requested "drugs and other curiosities." At the far right, another "Aldea de Indios" (village of the Indians) is visible on the Rio Guama, where de Sá had mentioned the presence of a quilombo of runaway African slaves in another letter demanding "discoveries." The road through the *sertão* from Maranhão's capital at Belém to Pará is indicated with a painted line. João Teixeira Albernaz I, "Pequeno atlas do Maranhão e Grão-Pará," c. 1629. Courtesy of the Arquivo Digital da Biblioteca Nacional, Brazil.

than the reddish quina that came from Peru "and it possesses lesser medicinal virtue."[78] The council sought to double-check Governor de Sá's quina against the "true," Spanish-traded quina to be found in Madrid.[79]

Things did not go well from there. The duke of Cadaval was extremely well connected in the medical circles of imperial Lisbon—both the royal surgeon Joseph Ferreira de Moura and the royal apothecary João Vigier dedicated books to him—and he seems to have cast doubt on the Maranhão sample's authenticity.[80] Although the secretary continued to make inquiries about drugs and medical matters among the administrators of colonial Brazil, de Sá's novel *drogas* did not win the commercial success he'd hoped for.[81] De Sá was forced to spend his remaining term as governor quelling Beckman's Revolt (February 1684), an uprising led by a New Christian colonist angered, in part, by the profiteering of leaders like himself.[82]

Half a decade later, in 1689, Artur de Sá e Menezes (Francisco de Sá's kinsman and the new governor of Maranhão) again wrote to the Overseas Council with samples of drogas that included pepper, quina, and a tea-like plant, along with a report on the continuing backlands adventures of Captain Lacerda, who was by now trying and failing to discover cochineal.[83] It was not until decades later, however, with the arrival of fifteen arrobas (roughly four hundred and eighty pounds) of "quina-quina" from Maranhão in Lisbon in 1749 that the trade in "quina" from Portuguese Amazonia seems to have become a commercial reality.[84]

Part of this shift may have been enabled by changes in print culture. By the second half of the eighteenth century, the iconographic strategies of naturalists had made botanical illustrations more functionally useful within the context of bioprospecting. These new depictions lavished attention upon characteristics like color or the shapes of discrete parts of the plant like the stamen or seeds, reflecting the fact that they were increasingly being used as guidelines for the new Linnaean classifications of botanists rather than as illustrations in vernacular medical texts or as advertisements. These images were also disseminated across long distances, both in popular books like Hipólito Ruiz's *Quinologia* and in painted form. In the late 1790s, for instance, Fernando José de Portugal, the governor of Bahia, enlisted a local artist to paint a plant that he believed to be "true" quina. In 1800, he sent the image "drawn on paper with watercolor tints of yellow, beige, black, green and red . . . describing the natural colors of the branches, leaves, flowers and fruits" across the Atlantic to Lisbon.[85]

Even at this later date, though, the ambiguous nature of Brazilian quina persisted. The governor's letter accompanying the painting announced "the discovery of a tree imagined to be quina" in the backlands west of Bahia. Yet the letter concluded with a by-now characteristic note of doubt. "The most experienced apothecaries disagreed" about the identity of the plant, the governor admitted.[86]

From Quina to Quinology

De Sá and other early modern bioprospectors faced a crisis of representation. To invent a drug, and to commodify it, one had to be both certain of its identity and capable of broadcasting that same certainty. But the earliest depictions of quina tended toward ambiguity: they were either allegorical images in generic classical backgrounds or schematics that lacked critical details (Figure 8).

These depictions rarely showed the different parts of the plant. They were in black and white (hence, de Sá's request for a painting showing "the colors

Figure 8. Frontispiece engraving (left) showing an allegorical representation of the Deæ Febri ("God of Fever") decapitated by the powers of quina, which is presented to personifications of Europe and the medical arts by an indigenous child wearing the feathered skirt typical of European depictions of Tupí Indians. From the same text (right), the quina tree ("Arboris Chinæ Chinæ") is depicted with scarce attention to details like the shape of its roots, flowers, or seeds. The tree appears out of context, with no hints as to the ecological niches where it flourishes. Francesco Maria Nigrisoli, *Febris china chinae expugnata* (Ferrara, 1687). Courtesy of the New York Academy of Medicine Library.

of the trunk, branches, leaves, flowers and roots"). And no seventeenth-century depiction of quina showed the plant realistically in its native ecology. The iconographic ambiguity of early images of quina lent itself well to the aesthetics of late seventeenth-century European drug manuals, which emphasized classical references and formal elegance over naturalism.[87] But it made it impossible to locate quina in its actual ecological contexts by relying on European-made images alone.[88]

What is striking, at the remove of centuries, is the profound vagueness, the aimlessness, of the drug-discovery enterprise of de Sá and company. Shall we say that they were seeking a wild, uncultivated twin to the plant we now call *Cinchona officinalis*? Or was it the unrelated yet similarly

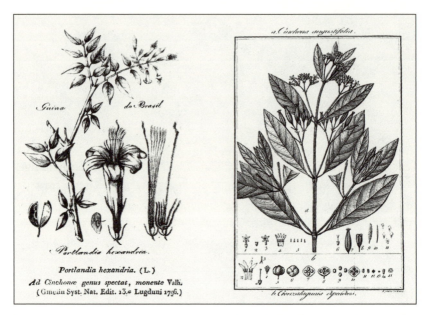

Figure 9. Left, the frontispiece illustration to José Ferreira da Silva, *Observações sobre a propriedade da Quina do Brasil* (Lisbon, 1801), which identifies "Quina do Brasil" as the Linnaean *Portlandia hexandria*. Right, the "true" Quina of Loja, from Hipólito Ruiz, *Quinologia* (Madrid, 1792). Courtesy of the John Carter Brown Library.

fever-reducing plant that, by the 1790s, had come to be known as "Quina do Brasil" (Figure 9)? Or was "wild quina" some other plant entirely, and was its identity *as* quina, its "quinaness," more dependent on perceived fever-fighting properties or on some other cultural or aesthetic characteristic than in any botanical kinship with the quina of Loja? De Sá's attempt to make "discoveries of drugs" in the Amazonian interior leaves us, as it did him, with far more questions than answers.

Early modern naturalists used what art historian Janice Neri calls "specimen logic," turning "nature into object by decontextualizing select creatures and items . . . removing them from their habits, environments, and settings."[89] This practice of decontextualizing nature was a formidable roadblock for bioprospectors. "Pinheiro [de Lacerda] told me that he made efforts to discover [quina] trees," Governor de Sá had told his superiors, but he added that "it will not be easy to find them by showing [the Indians] the trunk cut into pieces, all by itself without branches, or leaves, for the Indians do not recognize them."[90] The properly prepared bark described by drug merchants like João Vigier in Lisbon (carefully sorted, processed, chopped, and packaged) was here blamed for the failure of Europeans to locate new sources of the plant itself. The "specimen logic" of both the printed medical treatise and the apothecary's drawers stymied bioprospecting on the ground.

While most official expeditions to locate drugs in the Amazon (and beyond) met with failure, however, this did not mean that they had no impact. Such false starts and misunderstandings profoundly shaped the formation of the global drug trade. Indeed, figures like de Sá and Lacerda helped invent the very category they sought. In moving between European, indigenous American, and African worlds, these individuals collectively created a hybrid understanding of drugs and tropical nature that attempted to mesh European "authorities" with indigenous experts and creole *sertanejos*. Their false starts and biases would survive long after the samples they found had rotted away, shaping the commodification and consumption of novel drugs in the decades and centuries that followed.[91] To this day, varietals of fever-fighting drugs identified by Portuguese bioprospectors are still called "quina do Brasil" and "quina do Pará" in Brazilian folk medicine, long after their Linnaean classifications had been pinned down, their unrelatedness to "true" quina definitively proven.

The findings presented here accord with other works on botany and empire that stress the misunderstandings and gaps between European and indigenous botanical knowledge.[92] But they also highlight the larger ambiguity of drugs as a category. The theoretical basis behind conceptualizations of where drugs grew and how they might be used tapped into spiritual understandings of the workings of nature. At the same time, it drew on nascent environmental knowledge and the experimental intellectual culture of Iberian colonization.[93] Often, the most lasting legacy of these processes was a state of prolonged confusion and ambiguity around tropical drugs. The epistemological categories that might have allowed de Sá or Lacerda to sort medicinal barks into "quina" and "not quina" were by no means self-evident or translatable. Even the seemingly successful identification of a drug was not enough to render it commercially or scientifically useful.[94] Just as bioprospectors encountered gaps between their own schemas and those of indigenous societies, they, too, were frequently unable to bridge the gap between their colonial "discoveries" and techniques of chemical analysis, specialized medical erudition, and social credibility in Europe.[95]

The result was a confusion of drugs with similar names and effects. Jimson weed (*Datura stramonium*) for instance, is a deliriant drug native to

Mexico, long used in pre-Columbian ritual practices and healing. But by the late seventeenth century, the plant had been transplanted to many sites throughout Africa, Asia, and Europe. And because cannabis, datura, and opium all caused sleepiness and confusion in high doses, physicians and drug merchants found it difficult to distinguish between them despite their different points of origin. The French physician Nicolas Venette claimed that cannabis (*bhanghé*) was the same plant as "the opium of the orient" and datura ("the herb that we call stramonium or bitter apple"). Confusing things even further, he linked the supposed aphrodisiac effects of *bhang* and opium to "the ginseng of the Chinese." Such vagueness might have sold books about exotic drugs, but it did little to establish an effective understanding of the drugs themselves.

The Invention of Drugs

The early modern drug trade depended more on improvisational encounters across cultural frontiers than it did on the careful categorizations of botanists and pharmacists in the centers of empire.[96] Our understanding of early modern drug discovery is thus radically altered when we confront it from the perspective of creole colonists and indigenous peoples, rather than from that of the European scientists who would, in the eighteenth and nineteenth centuries, follow them in search of new products. Exchanges of knowledge about drugs moved along vernacular, colonial pathways long before they reached natural philosophers in Europe. These improvised acts of translating information about early modern drugs, taken in aggregate and over a long timescale, ultimately helped constitute that very knowledge.[97]

If we follow this logic, "to make discoveries of drugs" (*fazer descobrimentos de drogas*), as de Sá had put it, contains an etymological contradiction at its core. "Discovery," or "descobrimento" (from late Latin *discooperire*, to uncover), implies the revelation of an existing thing. Yet the interpretive work that went into "finding" drugs—amassing knowledge of existing remedies, gathering visual depictions, surveying landscapes, interrogating experts—was actually an act of *invention*.

One important result of this state of affairs is that drug names—what we might, with some anachronism, call the branding of drugs—were of prime importance in turning regional drugs into global commodities. The profusion of names for the same (or related) substances as they passed cultural and epistemological boundaries produced lasting misunderstandings.

Antonie van Leeuwenhoek, who examined "the bark called china chinae" under a microscope in 1707, wondered "whether the china chinae be of two sorts of trees."[98] He was far from alone. By the time Charles Alston compiled his two-volume treatise on "the natural history of drugs" in the 1750s, "quina" had amassed more than a dozen ostensibly synonymous names: Cortex, Cortex Peruvianus, China China, Quinaquina office[inalis], Arbor febrifuga Peruviana, China Chinae, Quinquina, Gannana, Hispanis Palos de calenture, cortex arboris, pulvis partum, pulvis Cardinalis de Lugo, the Jesuit's powder, Kina Kina, Cinchona, the Jesuit's bark, the bark, and Peruvian bark.[99] The act of translating South American quina into new languages, functions, and social settings was an act of transformation, leading to widespread confusion between substances that contemporary biologists regard as distinct species, along with arbitrary divisions on the basis of criteria (like age; potency; color; or the age, health, gender, or geographic origin of the user) that contemporary science disregards when making a classification.

These misunderstandings built over time, one upon the other, like layers of sediment. Over decades and centuries, they profoundly shaped the historical trajectories of early modern drugs—and of the rise of drugs as a cross-cultural category. Drugs that could successfully be invented, or reinvented, according to actionable models of their ecological climate, potency, and effect made their way into global pharmacopoeias. Drugs that failed this test stayed in their regional cultures of use—and, in later centuries, became targets of the drive to stigmatize and render illegal some forms of drug use.

During their tenures as colonial officials, Governor Francisco de Sá and Captain Pinheiro de Lacerda blamed their failure to "discover" a new source of quina on a lack of support, a lack of time, and a lack of funds. But in the end, perhaps it was due to something simpler: they had failed to invent it.

CHAPTER 2

Selling Drugs

Early Modern Apothecaries and the Limits of Commodification

I do remember an apothecary,
And hereabouts he dwells, which late I noted
In tatter'd weeds, with overwhelming brows,
Culling of simples; meagre were his looks,
Sharp misery had worn him to the bones.

—WILLIAM SHAKESPEARE, *ROMEO AND JULIET*, 1597

A knave apothecary that administers the physic, and makes the medicine, may do infinite harm, by his old obsolete doses, adulterine drugs, [and] bad mixtures.

—ROBERT BURTON, *THE ANATOMY OF MELANCHOLY*, 1621

Maria Coelho knew how to make mithridate. She knew how to tell good camphor from bad. She knew every alley and road that ran between her shop and the castle gates. She knew the rabbits (her namesakes) that lived in the fields outside the walls, and the ruins of an ancient city that lay a day's walk beyond that. But one thing she didn't know was what would become of her in the jails of the Portuguese Inquisition.

Maria was born into the business of *drogas*, a daughter and sister of apothecaries, as well as a drug professional in her own right.[1] The records of the Inquisition for the city of Coimbra tell us that Maria Coelho was taken into jail on January 8, 1666, where she was interrogated on charges of *judaísmo*. The inquisitors learned that she was the unmarried daughter of Felipe and Maria, who ran an apothecary shop in Montemor-o-Velho, a village

within the orbit of the ancient university city of Coimbra. She had lived for
five years (perhaps as a kind of apprentice apothecary) with a half brother
who also ran a *botica*. The matriarch of the family, Maria Pinto, was a forced
convert from Judaism. According to the Inquisition records, the family continued to "follow the Law of Moses" and maintained "a back room for Jewish
ceremonies."[2] By August 1666, Maria was still being held in jail. It was not
until more than three years after her capture, in April 1669, that she was
convicted of heresy, excommunicated, and sent to Brazil, penniless.[3] As far
as the Inquisition sources are concerned, this "boticaria," or female apothecary, was never heard from again.

During Maria's imprisonment in Coimbra, another apothecary in the
city, also bearing the last name Coelho and perhaps a relative of Maria, was
writing a manuscript that he called the *Pharmaca of Jozeph Coelho*.[4] In it,
we find a drawing of a man and woman facing one another over a stylized
representation of an apothecary's chest (Figure 10). They seem to be pointing
at it. "Botica[ria]" reads the caption above the woman's head, and "Boticario"
above the man's: apothecaress and apothecary. Regardless of whether Jozeph
was kin to Maria, the image stands as a mute testimony to the role played by
women and other oppressed groups in shaping the early modern drug trade.

Figure 10. The *boticária* and *boticário* of the Botica da Rua Larga in Coimbra. BNP,
Cod. 2259. José [Jozeph] Coelho, *Pharmaca, de Jozeph Coelho que fes sendo
boticario no anno de mil e seis sentos e sesenta outo na botica da rua larga* (Coimbra, [1668]), fol. 76r. Courtesy of the Biblioteca Nacional de Portugal.

In Chapter 1, we saw how the work of making a drug global was an act of creative destruction, built upon misinformation, rumor, and the gaps between differing epistemologies of drugs and nature. Here we will see what happened when drugs *did* commodify: namely, how the drug trade relied on self-assertions of purity that sought to separate the "good" drugs (and drug sellers) from the "bad."

An early division between *licit* and *illicit* began to emerge from the posturing and punishment of early modern individuals involved in the marketing and sale of drugs. Some drug professionals reaped enormous profits from the increasing popularity of novel drugs. Others, like Maria Coelho, were excluded, falling prey to claims of corruption, counterfeiting, or membership in groups (Jews, women, non-Europeans) that the trade's networks of sociability and credit refused to accept. To establish the necessary social capital to sell controversial drugs, apothecaries and merchants needed to carefully weed out competitors who were in danger of appearing suspicious or fraudulent to consumers. That process resulted in the increasing commercialization of "Indies drugs" in the seventeenth century. It also led to the erasure of the women, Jews, and other subaltern groups who helped make the trade possible.

Historians of medicine have documented how seventeenth-century European cities witnessed a crisis in medical authority.[5] In the continent's commercial centers, it has been argued, a new "medical marketplace" emerged in the mid- to late seventeenth century that gave ordinary consumers access to a greatly expanded field of treatment options, thus reducing the centrality of traditional medical authorities.[6] Economic historians have, likewise, documented a major increase in the value and diversity of medicinal drugs available to consumers in the second half of the seventeenth century.[7] These changes allowed the ancient profession of the apothecary to move up in the world. Apothecaries increasingly began working as independent healers in their own right, rather than as adjuncts to licensed physicians.

In this regard, apothecaries and drug merchants can be seen as pioneers of global capitalism. In cities like Madrid, Paris, and Lisbon, the most ambitious were soon branching out into auxiliary ventures like publishing medical manuals and seeking lucrative court appointments and sinecures. Some apothecaries, like Jacob de Castro Sarmento in Portugal and William Salmon in England, became successful participants in the realm of print culture, producing vernacular books with eye-catching titles like *A New Mystery in Physick Discovered* (1681) that ran into multiple editions and translations.[8] But their rise was accompanied by a proportionate increase in the suspicion and condemnation directed at the most "foreign" and otherwise vulnerable participants in the trade.

The apothecary Pierre Pomet, who wrote perhaps the most famous early modern drug manual of all (*Histoire Générale des Drogues*), was representative of the professional class that benefited from the commodification of exotic drugs.[9] Pomet boasted that he "kept up a trade in letters with the Indies of the East and West to have true accounts [*relations fidèles*] of Drugs which are not yet known in Europe." In addition to being an author and an apothecary who sold his own wares out of his shop on the Rue des Lombards at "the sign of the Golden Beard," Pomet became the superintendent of the *materia medica* in the gardens of Louis XIV and a correspondent with both the Royal Society of London and the Académie des Sciences in Paris.[10] He died rich, convinced that he had pursued his vocation "with all the good faith and duty that ought to attend a man of honor." As Pomet put it, "The knowledge of Drugs that are used in Medicine" had grown into "a commerce that is not only the greatest in the Kingdom, but also the most useful and important to the life of men."[11]

So it went for the apothecary elite in Paris. By contrast, stories like those of Mario Coelho are, for historians of medicine, something akin to the "missing" dark energy that bedevils contemporary physics. We know that figures like crypto-Jewish, female, and African healers existed in the early modern medical marketplace, and we know they were important. But they tend to elude the reach of our observations. When Maria Coelho left Portugal for Brazil, she disappeared into an archival event horizon.[12] The processes of invention, and then commodification, that brought tropical drugs from Brazil to Europe, or tobacco and sugar cane rum from Brazil to Africa, were a reversal of the pathways of people like Maria Coelho. Exotic drugs flowed into the mainstream of commercial and social success; some of those who sold them moved on an opposite trajectory.

Seventeenth-century texts relating to the drug trade are rich with epithets and slanders directed at the supposed deceitfulness of the members of what we might call this "drug underground": empirics, cunning women, African healers, crypto-Jews. It is in this push and pull over the respectability, trustworthiness, and "purity" of the drug seller that some of the first signs of a division between illicit and licit drugs begins to appear.

Drugs and the Exotic

We cannot know what Maria Coelho's apothecary shop looked like. But from contemporary literary and visual sources, we can imagine it: rows of blue and white ceramic drug jars on wood shelves mounted behind a counter, perhaps interspersed here and there by seashells, corals, or horns.[13] We know that Maria worked alongside family members. She may well have been the primary individual with whom customers interacted, following the division of labor we find in Figure 11, with a male and apprentice boy engaged in prep work and a female apothecary at the front of the shop selling to a female customer base.[14] Apothecary shops of Coelho's generation were distinctively cluttered spaces, piled with the powdered or bottled vestiges of living things. They challenged the senses with stinking unguents, decaying animal parts, aromatic perfumes, and heady vapors of distillation. Many featured dangling tortoises and alligators, which seem to have served as a kind of totem

Figure 11. Wolfgang Helmhard Hohberg, *Georgica curiosa aucta; Das ist: Um-ständlicher Bericht und klarer Unterricht Von dem Adelichen Land- und Feld-Leben* (Nuremberg: Martin Endters, 1697). Courtesy of the Wellcome Library.

of the apothecary's links to long-distance trade and foreign ecologies. These shop spaces were the vanguard of a new form of capitalism—one reliant on differentiation through branding.[15]

The value proposition of the early modern drug trade was not just that drugs created cures. It was also a commerce of *potential* potencies. Drug merchants transported substances that, when paired with appropriate knowledge, unlocked virtues that altered the mind and body. The substances alone were of ambiguous utility; they required someone with the knowledge of how to prepare them. Apothecaries were the intellectual go-betweens in this schema, the artisans who drew the active virtues out of "simples"— the term of art for unmixed, individual drugs bought directly from drug merchants—and transformed them into remedies. But the other side of this arrangement was the implicit threat of apothecaries using their proprietary knowledge to manipulate, to mislead, or even to poison. Apothecaries who belonged to already-persecuted groups were particularly vulnerable to such charges.

In Portugal, some licensed physicians wielded Inquisitorial trials as a professional weapon, punishing individuals who they perceived to be a threat to the elite medical order.[16] There was much to punish, in their view. Proponents of "Indies" drugs in the seventeenth century were a strikingly mobile cohort, crossing emerging national and confessional boundaries and forming new identities: there is the German-Portuguese apothecary/gardener Gabriel Grisley and the unlettered Portuguese teenager turned self-proclaimed Brazilian "physician" (and slave owner) João Cardoso de Miranda. One of the most famous Iberian apothecaries, Cristóvão da Costa, even described himself as "Africano."[17] Throughout the seventeenth century, Portuguese physicians and Inquisitorial agents systematically targeted "New Christian" apothecaries reputed to be secretly Jewish or of otherwise "impure" blood. African and folk healers (*curandeiros*) were similarly prosecuted in a number of inquisition trials.[18] Although no such institutional apparatus existed in Britain outside of the increasingly ineffectual Company of Physicians, English-language print culture abounded with attacks on foreign quacks, "empirics," "fetisheers," and other representatives of the newly globalized medical marketplace.[19]

Garcia da Orta, the crypto-Jewish apothecary and physician who was among the first Europeans to advocate for Indian drugs, stood at the boundary between the privileged world of elite apothecaries and the shadowlands inhabited by persecuted figures like Maria Coelho. In his lifetime, da Orta's

Jewish identity was shielded from Inquisitorial eyes thanks to the patronage of allies like Martim Afonso de Sousa, the viceroy of Portuguese India from 1542 to 1545. In death, however, da Orta was not so lucky. A year after his passing, in 1569, da Orta's sister was burned at the stake on orders of an Inquisitorial court, and da Orta's own body was later exhumed and his bones were burned.[20] Da Orta's *Coloquios* (1563) announced its subject matter as "medicinal simples, and drugs, and other medical things of the Oriental Indies."[21] Written in the form of a dialogue between European and Hindu medical practitioners, the *Coloquios* was the third European book published in Asia, and one of the first European works to devote substantial attention to non-Christian sources of pharmacological knowledge. Da Orta's interlocutor in the *Coloquios* begins the work by announcing his "great desire to learn of the *drogas medicinais* [medicinal drugs]" from the Indies. The commenter, Ruano, explains that he's referring to "those that in Portugal are called *de botica* [i.e., of the apothecary shop]."[22] This emphasis on *drogas de botica* reflected da Orta's own participation in Indies commerce. The doctor also doubled as a merchant, investing in voyages to Ceylon and Bengal and dabbling in the gemstone trade.[23] Da Orta's practical approach to natural knowledge turned the *Coloquios* (largely through the Latin translation and revision of Carolus Clusius) into the leading sixteenth-century guide to non-European medicines and, in the process, helped to shape an emerging conception of drugs as separate from spices.[24]

Da Orta's posthumous burning at the stake was a shot across the bow of a movement to "purify" the drug trade.[25] Spanish and Portuguese physicians, apothecaries and drug merchants who recorded information about Indies drugs fell under increasing scrutiny in the aftermath of this event and of other revelations of crypto-Jewish identities among the medical trades. Likewise, in Britain, many drug merchants and physicians suffered damaged reputations or worse owing to a widespread belief that Jewish and Converso healers engaged in fraud or were tainted by their association with non-Christian or non-European knowledge. For instance, Doctor Rodrigo Lopez, a Portuguese Converso who rose to become a personal physician to Queen Elizabeth, became an object of intense public scorn. The writer Gabriel Harvey noted that Lopez claimed to be Christian, but Harvey believed that "by a kind of Jewish practis," Lopez "hath growen to much wealth."[26] In 1594, Lopez was accused of attempting to poison the queen and was publicly executed, perhaps serving as inspiration for Shakespeare's character of Shylock in *The Merchant of Venice*.[27]

At issue in these fears of "corruption" in the drug trade was not just the identities of the drug sellers but the larger implications of a trade that was predicated on consuming substances with uncertain origins in faraway lands. By the late seventeenth century, the terms drug/*drogue*/*droga* were increasingly becoming defined in direct relation to geographical distance and exotic origin. In *Paradise Lost*, Milton compared Satan (enjoying a "solitary flight" above the Gates of Hell) to a fleet of Indies vessels "close sailing from Bengala, or the isles / of Ternate and Tidor, whence merchants bring / their spicy drugs."[28] In his *Dictionnaire universelle* (originally published in 1690), Antoine Furetière defined *drogue* as "merchandise of various types sold by spicers, above all from faraway lands, which are used in Medicine, by dyers and by Artisans. . . . The apothecaries must stock in their *boutique* all sorts of drugs."[29] Widespread skepticism directed at those who dealt in drugs palpably emanates from early dictionaries like Furetière's. Indeed, the *Dictionnaire universel* offered a secondary definition of *drogue* with a decidedly moralistic slant: "It is said also of things that have little value . . . one says proverbially that a fellow 'knows well how to value his drugs,' which is to say, that he is a charlatan."[30]

Fifty years later, Samuel Johnson offered a second meaning of "to drug" as "to tincture with something offensive."[31] Elsewhere in the *Dictionnaire universel*, the phrase "Qui pro quo" (meaning a mistaken identity, rather than the more common "quid pro quo") is glossed as "a Latin term which refers to an error by an Apothecary, who gives to one person a medicine prepared for another . . . from which we have the proverb, God Guard us from the *qui pro quo* of the Apothecary."[32] Even more damning was the assertion that mumia (supposedly the "balsamic" remains of actual Egyptian mummies) was frequently counterfeited by Jewish apothecaries, who some sources claimed resorted to murder to obtain more raw materials (see the final entry in Table 1). The claim was repeated often enough that it seems to have functioned as a sort of apothecary-specific variant of the blood libel.

As can be seen in Table 1, the lexical and conceptual terrain of drugs in the seventeenth and early eighteenth centuries remained expansive: they could be dyestuffs, spices used in cooking, recreational intoxicants, or artisanally prepared chemical medicines. A significant proportion were minerals and animal products, while others were "chymically" prepared substances. What bound them together was their exotic nature. Whether it was a botanical from the Indies or an iatrochemical formula created by an artisan, the

Table 1. Substances Identified as "Drugs" in Early Dictionaries

P = *plant* • M = *mineral* • A = *animal* • O = *other*

Furetière's *Dictionnaire*, 1690 (French)	Bluteau's *Vocabulario*, 1712 (Portuguese)	Johnson's *Dictionary*, 1755 (English)
Crystal: "a drug which one takes in medicines." [M]	Almegega gum: "suspends the vomit." [P]	Acacia: "a drug brought from Egypt." [P]
Jonc: "There is an odiferous *jonc*, which the apothecaries call *pature de chameau*." [P]	Amianto: "A French Author in his *Apararatus Medico-Pharmaco-Chimico* says this is a drug." [M]	Agaric: "a drug of use in physick, and the dying trade." [O]
"Oeuil lucide": "a drug called *lyceum*." [P]	Camphor: "The ancients knew this drug." [M]	Ambergris: "a fragrant drug . . . . many of the orientals imagine it springs out of the sea." [A]
Orchanette: "a strange drug which is not so good." [P]	Gorviam: "a drug used in medicines for horses." [P]	Ammoniac: "the name of a drug." [M]
Mace: "The Dutch have a great traffic in it, which is a drug highly esteemed." [P]	Mataleste: "a drug which resembles jalap." [P]	Elemi: "brought from Aethiopia . . . it is very rare in Europe." [P]
Mummy: "a medicinal drug, viscous and bituminous, from the mountains and forests of Arabia and other hot places in the Orient." [A]	Mummy: "A dead body which is embalsamed and aromatized . . . the most perfect mummies are the corpses of Princes and great Lords of Egypt and Syria . . . their balsam can be drunk with wine." [A]	Lac: "Authors leave us uncertain whether this drug belongs to the animal or the vegetable kingdom." [P]
Myrrh: "an odorant drug." [P]	Segapenum: an Arabian resin.	Mummy: "What our druggists are supplied with is the flesh of executed criminals, or any other bodies the Jews can get." [A]
Spikenard: "a drug liquid and potable." [P]		Myrrh: "Our myrrh is the very drug known by the ancients under the same name." [P]
		Nepenthe: "a drug that drives away all pains." [P]

seventeenth-century drug was beginning to be defined by its mysterious origins and controversial social role. To sell drugs was to stake a commercial, epistemological, and ethical claim to that role: to announce one's access to knowledges and material pathways that were not always considered savory in Europe, but that held an unmistakable allure for consumers.

In short, the widening scope of what apothecaries could do with drugs created new opportunities for societal power and wealth. Yet this power was undercut by ties to supposedly corrupt or foreign practices, from herbalists who were accused of witchcraft, to "Judaizing" apothecaries, to murderous mummy merchants, to traveling African healers.[33] By obscuring the nature and origin of "simples" and blending them into "compound medicines" with vague names like mithridatum, Venetian treacle, or aqua celestia, apothecaries could (it was feared) cheat their customers.[34] Their close control over such an intimate category—substances designed not just to be *put* in the body but to *change* it—transformed apothecaries into a uniquely suspect group, and figures like Maria Coelho paid the price.

Gender and the Drug Trade

Only a handful of female apothecaries gained public renown in print or at court in the early modern period. These were typically women from elite backgrounds.[35] However, within non-elite pathways of drug knowledge built on word of mouth and manuscript culture, drug recipes written by and for women circulated widely. Recipes gained annotations, corrections, and experimental modifications as they passed from healer to healer and household to household.[36] In England, for instance, the countess of Arundell, Lady Anne Howard (1557-1630), created and distributed drug recipes of her own invention, such as "A drink for the Plague or Pestilent Feaver" and "The Countess of Arundels drink for the Scurvy." These recipes were published in a 1662 compendium called *The Queens Closet Opened*, one copy of which was owned by the women of the Busby family. As the inscriptions on their heavily annotated copy imply, Howard's cures were modified by female heads of household for decades afterward (Figure 12).[37]

Perhaps the most famous female-authored drug manual was that of Madame Fouquet (1590-1681), whose "recipes" went through more than seventy editions in French, Spanish, and Italian in the decades after the first edition appeared in 1675.[38] Fouquet's recipes were part of a new genre of drug manual, one that was aimed directly at "common" folk unable to afford physi-

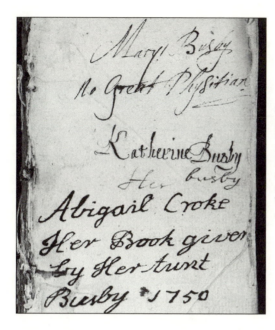

Figure 12. "No great physitian": inscriptions by three different female members of the Busby household on the flyleaf of a copy of *The Queens Closet Opened* (1662) owned by the Wellcome Library. Courtesy of the Wellcome Library.

cians, and which combined avant-garde alchemical medicine and tropical drugs with an older tradition of quasi-magical cures, such as the recipe that bids the reader to "take the dung of a black horse that has been grazing in the month of May."[39] The discussion, at times, grew heady enough that Fouquet insisted, "This is not magic, although the effects can seem miraculous to us."[40] Above all, Fouquet's recipes and their counterparts in manuscript recipe books written by women show a deep sensory and tactile engagement with the technology of drugs, lavishing attention on laborious processes of drug-making at the most practical level. These books abound with grinding, sifting, straining, fermenting, macerating, drying, diluting, pounding, and distilling.

Drug books aimed at women sometimes referred to their contents as the opening up of a "closet," which in the early modern period meant not just a space for clothes but any kind of private, internalized, typically femininized space.[41] The role of female labor in the drug trade was beginning to come into view, not just in the circulation of written works but in the performative aspect of apothecary shops as sites of public display. Visitors to a seventeenth-century apothecary shop would have seen women at work, both at the counter and in the workshop, distilling, grinding, pounding and decocting medicines. Wolfgang Helmhard Hohberg's *Georgica Curiosa Aucta*,

Figure 13. Women performing distillations using retorts and making a medicinal beverage in Hohberg's *Georgica Curiosa Aucta.* Courtesy of the Wellcome Library.

Figure 14. Anonymous (French school), Drug Warehouse, c. 1740. University R. Descartes in the Faculty of Pharmaceutical and Biological Sciences in Paris. Credit: J. L. Charmet/Science Source.

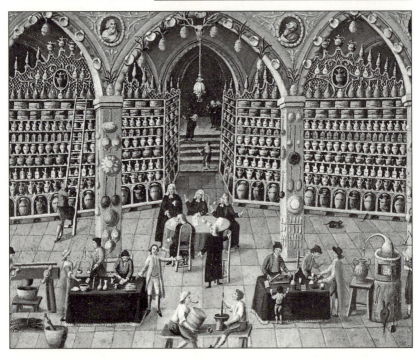

a popular proto-encyclopedia that was reprinted throughout the 1680s and 1690s, offered no less than three distinct images of female apothecaries or apothecary assistants physically preparing drugs. In one, two women attend to a complex distillation apparatus, while in another, a woman pours a recently prepared medicine beside a table covered with chopped roots, a drug vessel and a mortar and pestle (Figure 13).

In an anonymous eighteenth-century French painting (Figure 14), two women, one with a pipe clenched jauntily between her teeth, are doing the actual drug preparation while an African boy waits on a male apothecary. The space demonstrates an almost manic display of exotica, from the ten pineapples adorning the arches to the twenty-two shells and the moose skull chandelier. In the sixteenth and seventeenth centuries, female-authored "receipt books" had typically prescribed local European herbs. But by the time Mary Kittilby created her "Collection of Receipts in Physick and Surgery" in 1714, she assumed that her readers would have access to such exotics as balsam of Peru, crab eyes, "prepared pearls," sassafras, sarsaparilla, Virginia snakeweed, ambergris, balm of Gilead, "smaragd" [Persian emeralds?], "spic'd diatragacanth," tamarinds, and sandalwood.[42]

The commodification of drugs, through "branding" in ornate shop displays and performances of exotic origins, was often oriented toward women. According to historian Patrick Wallis, shops like the one depicted in Hohberg's image allowed exotic drugs to "be appropriated into a socially and sexually exclusive pattern of leisure activity. . . distinct from searching markets for necessities or the disordered, inclusive, and sometimes grotesque pleasures of the fair."[43] The apothecary shop not only *reflected* changing gender roles—it may have helped reshape them.

Drugs, Fraud, and Secrets

We have seen how medicinal drugs became increasingly associated with the exotic in the seventeenth century. The process of commodifying drugs relied on non-European sources of knowledge and material culture, and hence offered a niche for diasporic communities like Jews and African healers. Women also became more publicly involved in the drug trade, both as producers and as consumers. But this globalization of the trade, and widening of its social scope, exposed drug sellers to charges of fraud, heresy, and "impurity"—charges that inordinately fell upon subaltern groups. How did this concept of impurity or corruption begin to be applied to these drug sellers? What motivated it, and what effects did it have on the larger division of the drug trade into illicit and licit sectors?

In 1731, a slave named José Francisco Pereira, originally from the Mina Coast of Africa but at that time a resident in Lisbon, was brought before the Inquisition on charges of being a *feiticeiro* (one who crafts magical objects, a sorcerer or healer).[44] Pereira's crime was to have crafted pouches known as *bolsas de mandinga* that, he claimed, conferred special powers on the wearer, such as protection from disease or from knife wounds.[45] There was nothing inherently distinctive about this claim: indeed, the trope of an amulet or a substance offering magical protections was an ancient one in Europe, appearing everywhere from the writings of Marsilio Ficino to Francis Bacon. It was the practitioner who was the problem, not his claims.

A trade based on secrets only helped those who society believed could be trusted with them. The Lisbon apothecary and drug seller João Curvo Semedo stands as a counterexample to the sad fate of Pereira. Semedo, too, prescribed quasi-magical amulets based on secret knowledge—indeed, he was so associated with occult secrets that books promising to reveal the "secrets of Semedo" circulated in both Spanish and Portuguese long after his death.[46] Semedo also explicitly acknowledged his debt to African and South Asian healers. In the introduction to a pamphlet praising various Indies drugs, Semedo cited the practices of "Gentile" [i.e., Hindu] physicians, and defended a wide range of Indies drugs, including bezoar.[47] Figures like Semedo and João Vigier straddled the boundary between metropolitan European medical practice and the more cosmopolitan world of Jewish, female, and non-European actors who sustained the global drug trade. Indeed, Semedo devoted almost half of a pamphlet, which advertised the exotic drugs available for sale at his shop, to African animal and root medicines. Semedo described the medicinal virtues of the bones of various Angolan creatures and implicitly demonstrated his reliance on indigenous knowledge by citing (in at least two cases) the Bantu names for the *materia medica* he was describing. The apothecary boasted that he had gathered this knowledge from "certain persons who have travelled in the Indies and other regions of the earth" and had also himself "discovered various manuscripts which have informed me of the virtues of the aforesaid stones, powders, roots and fruits [from the Indies]."[48]

Here Semedo was making a rhetorical move that was typical of the seventeenth-century drug trade. He was appealing to his readers' hunger for exotica but was remaining coy as to *who*, precisely, these "certain persons who have travelled in the Indies" actually were. This was, I believe, a conscious strategy adoped by the figures who most benefited from the commodification of drugs—licensed, published apothecaries like Semedo—to highlight their connections to global drug networks while also concealing the precise identity of these figures, such as non-Europeans or non-Christians, who could potentially cast their profession into disrepute. The drug trade's connections to non-Christian spirituality and healing, and its susceptibility to fraud, made it a dangerous trade indeed for individuals who did not benefit from existing social protections such as court patronage or membership in the Inquisition.[49] The drug trade needed scapegoats, and it soon found them.

Legal forces brought to bear on these groups did not depend on an outright prohibition of the drugs they were associated with. Rather, drug sellers became linked with other crimes like counterfeiting and heresy. To be sure, there *were* attempts to ban drugs associated with foreign traders or that corrupted physical and mental health. Bans on the sale and use of tobacco were announced by Sultan Murad IV in Turkey (1633) and in Russia (1633-34).[50] This series of dates is somewhat misleading, however, because these attempts were all failures. Early modern states simply did not have sufficient power to put such a sweeping restriction into effect. The earliest drug laws to enter the books in both Iberia and England, instead, attempted to insulate drug buyers from the risk of purchasing remedies with suspect or dangerous ingredients. A 1555 law issued by the court of Charles V in Spain offered an early insight into the ways that sixteenth-century lawmakers differentiated between the medical professions, mandating that "physicians, surgeons, apothecaries and barbers" be examined by a court physician, or *protomedico*, but also stipulating that "the examination must not include midwives, druggists [*drogueros*] or spicers [*especiaros*]."[51] By the seventeenth century, these "druggists" had fallen under increased scrutiny. The ordinances of the city of Zaragoza feature a 1669 statute attempting to rein in the abuses of "Boticarios y Drogueros," levying fines on their sale of "false and sophisticated medicines, and stale drugs [*drogas añejas*]."[52] In cities from Edinburgh to Seville, official pharmacopoeia enforced legal strictures governing the composition of remedies.

The problem was not just counterfeiting. It was price gouging that resulted from the application of secret knowledge to a given set of "simple" or pure and uncompounded drugs. The licensed physician John Moyle wrote in 1704 that "we must distinguish betwixt Drugs, and the *Medicins* prepared of them." For Moyle—whose comments appeared within the context of a larger argument about the merits of fixing the prices of key medicines—"No certain Price indeed can be put upon Drugs, but then it does not properly belong to the Apothecary to sell these, but to the Druggist."[53] In Moyle's estimation, "drugs" referred to the raw materials of healing, traded as commodities. "Medicins" were what resulted when drugs fell into the hands of apothecaries, who used compounded individual drugs (simples) that had undergone various mechanical (grinding, decocting, pounding, infusing) or "iatrochemical" (distilling, fermenting) processes. This distinction is what Semedo had in mind when he described how Indies drugs were compounded in Europe and sold back to consumers in the Indies at a markup. The true value of a medicament, Moyle argued, resulted from the artifice of the individual who prepared it, not the scarcity or exotic nature of the drugs of which it was composed.[54]

Making Exotic Drugs Illicit

We have seen how a Coimbra apothecary named Joseph Coelho filled a notebook in 1688 with sketches and notes that included an apparent self-portrait of Coelho and a female relative working together in their apothecary shop, the Botica da Rua Larga. Coelho's notebook offers an invaluable glimpse into a vanished world in which centuries-old beliefs about pharmacy were confronting new information from overseas. It shows us, first, the degree to which even drug professionals in cities like Coimbra were influenced by innovations from the tropical world and non-Western drug traditions. And, second, it highlights how debates about "foreign" ways contributed to a backlash against exotic drugs. In these debates, the *foreignness* of a drug—its embeddedness in both non-European cultures and unfamiliar ecologies—became conflated with its potential moral and physical dangers. This was a trope that would play out again and again in the later history of drugs, as questions of psychoactivity and healing became tied to nativism, racism, and fears of poisoning and intoxication.

   Coelho's notebook, which includes entries in multiple different hands, ranges from translated extracts of Latin, Greek, and Persian medical texts to inventories of specific wares for sale, and includes numerous doodles.[55] The excerpts included in the book hew quite closely to the traditional Greco-Roman-Muslim synthesis of Mediterranean pharmacy that apothecaries had been learning for centuries by Coelho's time. But the records of drugs for sale tell a different story.[56] Although the Coelho *Pharmaca* largely consists of extracts from Greco-Roman authorities like Dioscorides or medieval Islamic and Byzantine physicians like Mesue (Yūhannā ibn Māsawayh) and Nicolaus Myrepsus, the presence of Indies drugs in the Coelhos' inventories reveals the interpenetration of materials from Portugal's tropical colonies even in a provincial shop.

Jozeph Coelho's *Pharmaca*—and, perhaps, Maria Coelho's shop as well—stood on the boundary of two different approaches to pharmacy. It looked backward to a medieval legacy, with a strong grounding in what historian Paula de Vos calls the "Mediterranean tradition" of pharmacy: a blend of Persian and Arabic authorities like Mesue with Greco-Roman medical texts, overlaid onto an eclectic assemblage of folk knowledge of the medicinal herbs, roots, and animal products native to the Mediterranean basin.[57] But it also exemplified a new trend toward quietly folding "modern drugs" in with this familiar blend of Greco-Roman, Muslim, and medieval Christian cures. For instance, Coelho described the use of guaiacum, an American drug.[58] In this, however, the provincial apothecary hedged his bets. He listed guaiacum as an analogue to ancient Mediterranean drugs, not as something entirely new.[59]

Although they were delayed for decades or even centuries by hedging of the sort employed by Jozeph Coelho, the globalization of diseases and drugs ultimately forced a reckoning.[60] To what extent would drug professionals, from famous alchemists to the humble Coelhos of Coimbra, adapt themselves to drugs across the seas? To what extent would they break with classical precedent, rather than trying to shoehorn entirely new cures and diseases into obsolete epistemologies?

Portuguese pharmacy was distinctively open to making this shift into the brave new worlds of modern drugs for two reasons. First, because of Portugal's long-standing dominance of tropical trade routes and the resulting cosmopolitanism of Lisbon itself, Lusophone pharmacists and patients were more open than most Europeans to consuming cures that had origins in African, Asian, or American pharmacy. In Coelho's time, around 5 percent of the population of Lisbon was enslaved and perhaps as much as 20 percent of the city's inhabitants were of African descent.[61] A number of Inquisition trials demonstrate the participation of African medical professionals in vernacular communities of healing within Portugal that involved local people accepting African-approved drugs. Although only a handful of working apothecaries' notebooks from Portugal survive, we can compare Coelho's *Pharmaca* with another surviving notebook, this one from a 1730s apothecary.[62] Manuel Ferreira de Castro traded with the Portuguese colonial cities of Bahia and Luanda, as well as selling drugs locally in Lisbon. The wares in a 1738 shipment to Bahia included traditional *materia medica* like dried cherry plums and bushels of poppies, but it also featured novelties like mechoacan root from New Spain, nutmeg oil from the East Indies, and "bezoarticos de Curvo," a newly invented cure incorporating numerous South Asian medicaments created by João Curvo Semedo.[63]

The second distinctive feature of the Portuguese drug trade was its global distribution. The Portuguese Empire may have been in a state of territorial decline, but the world of Portuguese influence was vast. A 1750s handbook of drugs stocked by Jesuit pharmacies in areas of Portuguese control and influence, for instance, ranges across the globe, from Macao to Goa and from Luanda to Brazil.[64] But each entry overlapped with the others: the Jesuits at these outposts were stocking what they would have called "modern" cures, meaning drugs unknown to the Greek, Roman, and medieval Muslim authorities yet widely available in the maritime emporiums in which the Jesuits tended to operate. Semedo himself, creator of the "bezoarticos" stocked in Portuguese Jesuit pharmacies, had explained that his innovations were directly derived from gathering new cures and medical "recipes" from the Indies. "The experience of the Moors and Gentiles [i.e., Hindus] of Asia was the teacher which gave [us] knowledge of the use of such remedies," Semedo wrote.

Semedo also offered some insight into the curious phenomenon of Lisbon-based apothecaries *reselling* tropical drugs to neighboring colonies, such as the case of the Lisbon apothecaries who imported cinchona bark from Peru, only to resell the resulting powdered bark to Amazonia at a huge markup. He admitted that some "doctors, as well as lay folk, take the view that bezoars and remedies which come from India and other foreign lands do not work the same wonders in Portugal that they do in India and in the lands where they originate . . . owing to the difference of the climate when these remedies arrive in Portugal."[65] But for Semedo, the key was that a properly trained apothecary was capable of preparing and reshaping these raw materials to preserve them from "corruption."

Long distances made drugs valuable, but they also made them suspicious. Sixteenth-century medical theory generally upheld the view that human "constitutions" had been ordered by God to benefit from local cures.[66] This view was advanced by figures like the Anglican bishop Godfrey Goodman, who publicly denounced the "farre fetched Indian drugges" that London merchants had begun to import from the tropical world. Along with pearls, rubies, diamonds, incense, and rich textiles, traders with the recently launched English East and West India Companies and the Dutch VOC had begun to import trial amounts of exotic new consumables ranging from guaiacum bark and occidental bezoars to *bhang* (cannabis) and *cha* (tea).[67] Goodman protested that the exotic and colorfully packaged drugs of the apothecaries "doe not agree with our constitution; yet such is our wantonnesse, that sometimes with taking their physicke [medicine], wee overthrow the state of our bodies." Goodman complained, "We make our selves artificiall stomackes, when our English bodies must prove the store-houses of Indian drugges."[68] Conversely, plants that came from a different ecological zone were, as Goodman put it, "separated in nature" and therefore liable to provoke humoral imbalance.[69] The problem was the unfamiliar ecologies and climates in which they were grown. "There is a great distance in the Climat," between Europe and the Indies, Goodman had written, "and therefore we should not rashly undertake such a journey, to joyne together things so farre separated in nature."[70] King James I of England articulated a similar view in his *Counterblaste to Tobacco*. James feared that if the English chose "to imitate the barbarous and beastly manners of the wilde, godlesse, and slavish Indians" by smoking tobacco, they would potentially come to "denie God . . . and adore the Devill, as they doe."[71]

The key issue was the combination of foreignness with unfamiliar effects on mind or body. The most reviled of all were the category of drugs known as narcotics, which were thought to cause harmful "passions" and "hungers." Da Orta claimed that South Asian potentates employed opium and *bhang* (cannabis) to provoke "sweet dreams."[72] For da Orta, the unpleasant psychological effects of *bhang* seem to have contributed to his decision not to include the drug among the substances he advocated for in *Coloquios*, besides mentioning that the drug caused "sadness and nausea."[73] When the coffee bean was introduced to European cities in the 1650s and 1660s, many physicians attacked it as a dangerous new mind-altering drug, but because coffee did not cause "drunkenness," it passed the test.[74] Likewise with substances thought to confer psychological benefits: Giuseppe Donzelli believed that bezoar stones were used in Persia and India not only to cure poisons but also to "root out all sorts of melancholy."[75] Spices, too, often appear in apothecary and medical manuals as substances with psychoactive properties, which dispel melancholy or "enliven the spirit." As late as the 1740s, consumption of ambergris was claimed to make a man "as merry as if he had drunk a great quantity of wine."[76] In short, if an Indies drug was strongly able to alter the subjective experience of those who consumed it, it opened the door to fears of corruption. Thus, both type and degree of psychoactivity became a litmus test for whether a drug could be rendered acceptable—a topic to which we will return in Chapter 5.

Consumerism and Artisanal Purification

Even as some in Europe agonized about the consequences of European bodies ingesting Indies drugs, their contemporaries who smoked Brazilian tobacco, drank Mexican cacao, or took "physicke" with West Indian guaiacum and Persian opium demonstrated that the material worlds of Europe, the Americas, Africa, and Asia were growing together. Robert Pitt complained in 1702 that "Trading Physicians returning from the *Indies*" had "impos'd upon" a gullible public by arguing that bezoar stones were capable of "subduing all sorts of Poysons," when in reality they were little more than "pretty Trifle[s]."[77] Yet by the eighteenth century, such complaints had a backward-looking quality: Indies drugs ranging from chocolate and tobacco to bezoar and quina had triumphed.[78]

In Portugal, vernacular guides to tropical drugs celebrated the abundance of what one drug seller called the "modern drugs from both the Indies." That drug seller, a French-born apothecary in Lisbon, João Vigier, presented his *Pharmacopea Ulyssiponense* (1712) as a practical manual undertaken "for the health of the sick, who each day are continually asking for new *receitas* [medical recipes]."[79] Vigier's book included an appendix titled "Treatise on the virtues and descriptions of diverse plants and animal parts from Brazil and from other parts of America or the Western Indies, along with some from the Eastern discoveries of the past century."[80] Vigier's praise for these "modern drugs" [*drogas modernas*] was part of a larger shift in how drugs were sold (Table 2). Mastering these public presentations of oneself and the drugs one sold helped decide who and what would fall on the *licit* side of the spectrum, avoiding the social condemnation directed at figures like Maria Coelho.

Vigier's list is bracing. It is difficult today to fathom just how much diversity of experience these substances offered, on both sensory and intellectual levels. Francisco Hernández encountered in the *boticas* of Mexico City, "dried fox lungs . . . tapir hooves [and] urine and excrement of animals including the goose, ass, peccary, ox, cow, goat, stork, serpent, horse, chicken,

Table 2. João Vigier's List of "the Virtues of Modern Drugs" from his *Pharmacopea Ulyssiponense* (Lisbon, 1716).

Name	Origin	Virtues
Caju [Cashew]	Brazil	Tree yields a red gum, which is "drying, cooling and condensing."
Ambia [?]	Brazil	"Comforting, sweetening, resolutive;" used to treat "cold wounds."
Ananas [Pineapple]	Brazil	"So corrosive that it eats away the iron in a knife left in it."
Anda [?]	Brazil	"Purgative, somewhat emetic . . . the bark of the fruit in powder is good against curses, and kills fish, as does the coca to the west."
Andira [Brazil wood	Brazil	"A tree of great strength." Its fruits are used to treat worms.
Andiraguacu [Vampire Bat]	Brazil	"The tongue and the heart are poisons."
Anhima [Horned Screamer]	Brazil	Aquatic bird with a "horn" that is "highly esteemed antivenom."
Anil [Indigo]	America	Dye that also treats wounds "when applied in powder."
Anime or Minaea [?]	America	"White resin," "resolves cold humors" and "comforts the brain."
Anisum Chinae [Star anise]	China	Carminative; "comforts the stomach." The Dutch use it in tea.
Armadilho [Armadillo]	America	The tailbone, placed in the ears, "defends against deafness."
Balsam Judaicum [Balm of Gilead]	Arabia	"Comforts the vital parts and excites semen"; however, "the Grand Turk . . . has taken all of these plants . . . they are guarded carefully by his Janisarries."
Balsam Copahu [Copaiba]	Brazil	Good for the stomach, "cures the stone and nephritic colics."
Balsam de São Thomé	São Thomé	"Has the same virtues as Copaiba, but more efficacious for wounds."
Balsam de Tolu	Cartagena	Similar to the above-mentioned balsams, but especially good for asthma.
Balsamum Peruvianum	Peru	"Comforts the heart, the stomach and the nerves." Also from Brazil.
Bangué [Cannabis]	India	"Indians eat the seeds and leaves for appetite, to sleep well, and to free them from disgust and pains. If they wish to have sweet dreams, they mix it with camphor, nutmeg and mace."
Bezoar	E. Indies	"Comforts the heart, cures the plague and most epidemic diseases."
Bezoar Occidental	Peru	"Has the same virtue as Oriental Bezoar, with less efficacy."
Pedro do Porco Espinho	Malacca	"A great preservative against poisons . . . effective against smallpox."
Bezoar Simiae	Makassar	"More sudorific . . . than most other types."
Bezoar serpentinus	Mombasa	"Ground into powder, it is a sovereign remedy for melancholy."
Pedras de cobra	E. Indies	Cures bites from cobras "and other venomous animals and insects."
Pedra quadrada	Tartaria	"Alleviates melancholy, purges the humors, releases wind."

human being, sheep, sparrow, turkey, dog, buzzard, squab pigeon, and fox."[81] In Lisbon, João Curvo Semedo stocked a similar set of medicaments—one that included, as well, "oil of elephant," rattlesnake rattles, Angolan wildebeest hooves, powdered pearls, and artificial, occidental and oriental varieties of bezoar stone.[82] The French Huguenot turned Anglican convert and London drug merchant John Jacob Berlu's *Treasury of Drugs Unlock'd* offered capsule descriptions of hundreds of exotic drugs available for sale in London, ranging from Hudson's Bay, Mexico City, and Peru to West Africa, Java, and Japan.[83]

Although it could be profitable to advertise these foreign origins, drug marketing in Europe increasingly relied on the perception that the substance had been improved and purified by interventions on the part of respectable artisans. The "crude," unmediated forms of a drug had become more threatening than their "purified" counterparts.

Emergence of a Drug Underground?

As drugs like quina, tobacco, and chocolate became global commodities, lines were drawn between the good and the bad, the pure and the impure. The nature of these divisions depended on where drug buyer and seller happened to be standing. Peruvian quina was a miraculous cure in Catholic Madrid or Rome, but the very same bark could become a treasonous poison in Protestant Amsterdam or London. The market value of drugs became so closely tied to matters of identity and status that their names began to incorporate references to famous doctors: "Salmon's pills, which infallibly Cure the Scurvy," "Talbor's Wonderful Secret," Semedo's "Bezoartico Curviano."[84] Drugs like Salmon's pills (Figure 15) numbered among the earliest products to appear in printed advertisements. They were a prototypical example of the concept of a "brand name," using the social status and in-group identity of the seller as a mark of purity for buyers.

The work of commodifying drugs depended not just on these communications of credibility but also on the intentional *failure* to communicate other social and intellectual identities associated with drugs.[85] Some of this secrecy was simply part of a rational business strategy: preserving proprietary trade secrets can, after all, prove essential for maintaining value.[86] In other instances, the drug trade's emphasis on secrets served a deeper function: protection. It could be profitable to emphasize vague exotic origins for novel drugs, but going too far—attributing knowledge directly to non-

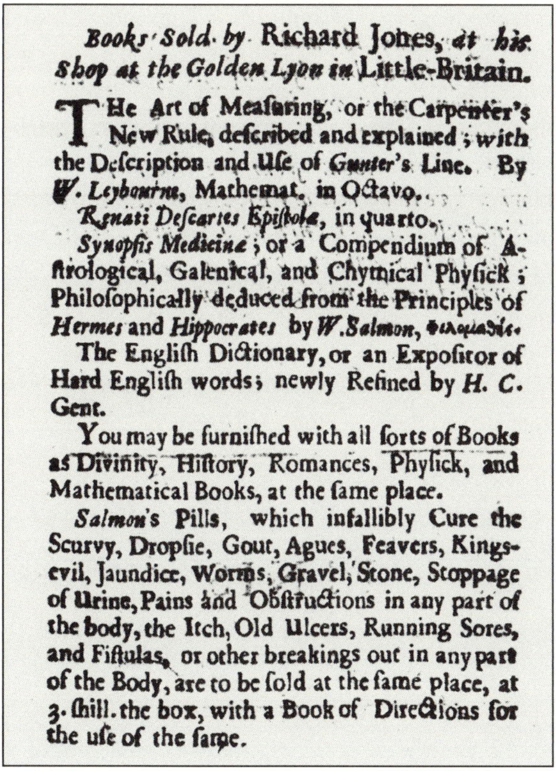

Books Sold by Richard Jones, at his Shop at the Golden Lyon in Little-Britain.

THe Art of Measuring, or the Carpenter's New Rule, described and explained; with the Description and Use of Gunter's Line. By W. Leybourn, Mathemat. in Octavo.

Renati Descartes Epistolæ, in quarto.

Synopsis Medicinæ; or a Compendium of Astrological, Galenical, and Chymical Physick; Philosophically deduced from the Principles of Hermes and Hippocrates by W. Salmon, ϕιλομαϑής.

The English Dictionary, or an Expositor of Hard English words; newly Refined by H. C. Gent.

You may be furnished with all sorts of Books as Divinity, History, Romances, Physick, and Mathematical Books, at the same place.

Salmon's Pills, which infallibly Cure the Scurvy, Dropsie, Gout, Agues, Feavers, Kings-evil, Jaundice, Worms, Gravel, Stone, Stoppage of Urine, Pains and Obstructions in any part of the body, the Itch, Old Ulcers, Running Sores, and Fistulas, or other breakings out in any part of the Body, are to be sold at the same place, at 3. shill. the box, with a Book of Directions for the use of the same.

Figure 15.
Advertisement for "Salmon's Pills" on the final page of William Salmon's drawing manual *Polygraphice; or, The Art of Drawing* (London: printed for Richard Jones, 1672). Courtesy of the Wellcome Library.

European or non-Christian sources, or directly relying on African, Asian, or American experts—was risky. Apothecaries lauded the variety of their wares while minimizing their own connections to suspect or foreign knowledge, lest they face the same condemnation they meted out to the Maria Coelhos of the world.

The practice of trading, preparing, and consuming drugs had, by the early decades of the eighteenth century, emerged as a constellation of activities that was open to slaves, tradesmen, laborers, women and other non-elite figures. For some, this influx of new products and the accompanying hunger for knowledge about them created opportunities for professional advancement: entrepreneurial healer-authors like João Curvo Semedo and William Salmon openly sold drugs out of their own homes and sold sensationalistic tomes that promised to reveal "modern" drugs to ordinary folk. In seventeenth-century Angola, *barbeiros* (barber surgeons) without formal educational qualifications managed to obtain posts as "Chief Physician" (*físico-mor*) because of a breakdown in old systems of medical authority and a hunger for new cures and new practices.[87] In an increasingly competitive marketplace of materials and ideas, drug experts wielded any weapon at hand (judicial, rhetorical, intellectual) to crowd out competitors and establish themselves as guardians of drug purity, authenticity, and effectiveness.

Thus, even as the profession of the apothecary was undergoing tremendous growth, the labors of the drug cultivators in the colonies and of the subaltern figures who moved and sold drugs were frequently hidden. This was nowhere more evident than in early modern sub-Saharan Africa, a region with a vast pharmacopoeia and enormous reservoirs of expertise regarding medicinal drugs. Yet, it was also a region which failed to play a major role in the early modern drug trade due to the same forces of erasure.

CHAPTER 3

Fetishizing Drugs

Feitiçaria, Healing, and Intoxication in
West Central Africa

> We submit to your Majesty that one of the causes of the contagion and sickness that frequently occur in this city has been shown by experience to be an infection of the air occasioned by the great number of cadavers of slaves, which wolves of the night disinter from fields where they are buried.
>
> —CITY COUNCIL OF LUANDA, 1688

So far, this book has focused mainly on Europe and Portuguese America. What about the individuals involved in the drug trade outside Europe and the European colonies in the Americas? In this chapter, we will see how the concept of the *feitiço* (the origin of the English word *fetish*) shaped the early modern drug trade and the course of Portuguese colonization in Africa.

Feitiços and the practice of crafting them (*feitiçaria*) had ancient origins. The word itself derives from the Latin *facticius*, meaning an "artificial" or a "fashioned" object, something made by human artifice. Throughout the Middle Ages, variants of the word described all manner of magical amulets and charms. From the sixteenth century onward, however, Portuguese speakers increasingly applied the concept of *feitiçaria* specifically to sub-Saharan African spirituality, including the use of medicinal drugs and healing objects. In the eyes of some of these observers, the ritual practices of *feitiçaria* relegated the work of African drug experts to the domain of magic and superstition. Yet, sub-Saharan African cultures of drug use were actually quite similar to their early modern European counterparts. Both depended on proprietary mixtures of plants, animals, and minerals, as well as on ritualized spiritual practice, with the aim not only of altering the human mind and body but also of exerting power over the natural world itself.[1]

Fears of *feitiçaria* shaped an emerging global drug trade in the seventeenth and eighteenth centuries. African drugs and drug knowledge were difficult to commoditize because of their entanglement with "fetisheers," and yet both circulated widely along the circuits of the Atlantic slave trade.[2] In particular, the ritualized use of substances like alcohol and cannabis in sub-Saharan Africa had a far-reaching influence. The result of this was another nascent divide in the global drug trade: a division between scientifically approved medicaments on the one hand, and what we might call "fetishized" drugs on the other. Fetishized drugs (incorporated into practices of spiritual healing or ceremonial usage) tended to resist scientific legitimization. And increasingly, over the late seventeenth and eighteenth centuries, scientific legitimacy was necessary for a drug to become a global commodity.[3]

Essential to this process of legitimization were natural philosophers, who sought not only to strip away the "superstitious" elements from drugs but also to isolate these drugs into their constituent chemical parts. This process contributed to a new sense of the supernatural, as these constituents tenaciously refused to yield the mysteries of their unexplainable powers. In these efforts lay the groundwork for the split between substances that passed muster as objects for scientific inquiry—those that would later come to be called pharmaceuticals—and another class of substances that, because of their irreducible entanglement with spirituality, did not pass into the mainstream of Western science, trade, and law.

To better understand this split, we will zoom in on a particular time and place in which social divisions were so heightened as to be a matter of life and death. The place is a hillside in Angola, the year is 1688.

A WHITEWASHED FORTRESS sits in sunlight above a forest valley. Inside the fortress is a chapel. Inside the chapel, two hands lift a surplice and chalice from a chest behind an altar. The man who dons the surplice is an African lord. He is not a Christian, nor a friend to the Portuguese who once controlled this place. Along with the fortress, he has captured a group of slaves destined for Brazil, slaves that he now takes as his own. He brings the com-

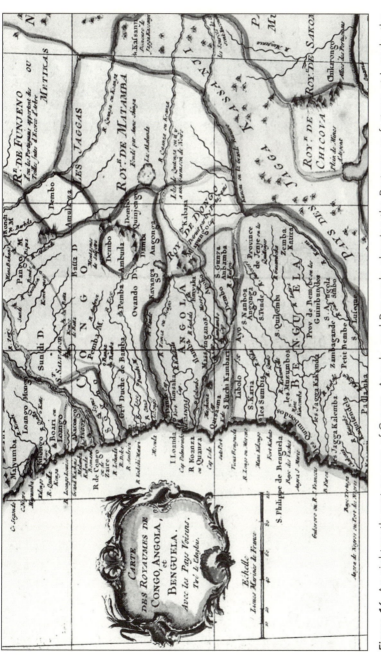

Figure 16. An eighteenth-century map of Congo, Angola, and Benguela, showing the Portuguese fortress at Luanda, the Kingdom of Dongo ("destroyed by the Portuguese"), and Njinga's Kingdom of Matamba to the east, and territories of various jagas, including those of the "Jagga Kakonda" (labeled directly below the "B" in "Benguela"). Jacques Nicolas Bellin, "Carte des Royaumes de Congo, Angola, et Benguela," in François Prévost, *Histoire Générale des Voyages*, vol. 4 (Paris, 1754). Courtesy of the Library of Congress.

munion vessel to his lips and drinks a deep draught of red wine: the sacred blood of the Savior, profaned.[4]

Some version of this scene, the stuff of nightmares for any early modern Portuguese Catholic, took place in the frontier *presidio* of Caconda south of Luanda in February 1688. The captor was a man known to the Portuguese as the Jaga (war leader) of Caconda. Seven years before, the Jaga Caconda had sworn vassalage to the Portuguese Crown. Now, however, Caconda was in open rebellion. The Jaga had already won a number of victories against the disease-ridden battalions of Angola's southern frontier. This chance to consume the communion wine represented another triumph.[5] Word of his "sacrilege" reached the Overseas Council in Lisbon months later, through a letter from Luanda's city council. The council members explained that the Jaga had lured the hundred-odd soldiers of the Caconda presidio into the backlands (*sertão*). The Jaga Caconda's forces were then able to circle back and "invade the Presidio without resistance," taking as prisoners both the remaining soldiers and "the slaves of the whites."[6]

Although the Jaga was eventually expelled from the presidio, it was a disaster for the colonial government, which for decades had sought to subdue the African *principes* (rulers) who surrounded Portugal's colony in Luanda. The dynasty of Queen Njinga of Matamba and Ndongo had been defeated over two decades previously, clearing the way for a Portuguese invasion of the Angolan interior.[7] Yet Portuguese plans for a territorial empire beyond the coast failed to materialize, and rulers like Caconda continued to lead independent polities. Caconda—a "most cruel enemy" as the Luanda city council called him—had, four years earlier, slain the colony's top military officers, the Capitão-mór and Sargento-mór.[8]

Fearing further attacks, the city officials wrote that "munitions, gunpowder and six bricklayers," were now urgently needed in order "to better secure the lands of the blacks." Although the Portuguese officials at Luanda were reticent to elaborate on the Jaga's precise activities in the fortress for fear of "offending the Catholic zeal of your majesty," they wrote that he had "conjured all the Africans against the whites . . . to destroy the fortress, and to kill all of the whites."[9]

This choice of word—*conjurar*—was significant. "Conjurar," in early modern Spanish and Portuguese, could either mean to conspire in a plot or oath or to struggle against evil spirits.[10] Conversely, however, it could mean to *invoke* evil spirits, or to bewitch like a narcotic drug. Francisco Xavier de Menezes used the latter meaning in his 1741 epic poem of the Portuguese empire:

Morfeo contra o mundo se conjura	Morpheus against the world is conjured
De opio lethal no imperio deshumano	From deadly opium in the inhuman empire.[11]

Conjurar, in short, is a word that unlocks new meaning in events that appear on their surface to have been military skirmishes but which were also imbued with both spiritual and pharmacological significance.[12]

The Portuguese tended to interpret West and West Central African herbalists and spiritual healers (*ngangas*) as practitioners of sorcery who were potentially allied with Satan.[13] They believed in and feared the forces African spiritual and political leaders were thought to wield, from amulets granting invulnerability to curses and poisons they could dispatch in secret.[14] One detail of the Jaga Caconda's attack triggered these fears of African spiritual power. "The said Jaga has in his possession images of Christ our Lord, and of the Virgin Mary our Lady . . . and has profaned the sacred vestments that were in the Presidio," the disgraced city officials admitted. Worst of all, the Jaga "sacrilegiously drank of the sacred chalice." In the opinion of the Luanda city council, these acts demonstrated the demonic inspiration of the Jaga and his followers. They confirmed, in their eyes, both his evil intent and his access to the spiritual power of the Catholic communion and vestments.[15]

Drinking communion wine from "the sacred chalice" was a pharmacologically charged act. This was a world, after all, in which wine and alcoholic spirits were not only newly introduced commodities but also becoming part of the ritual practices of African *feitiçaria*. Such drug exchanges shaped a new culture of healing and spirituality both in West Central Africa and in the African diaspora. Intoxicants like high-proof sugarcane liquors (*cachaça* and *gerebita*) and the potent, molasses-soaked tobacco that Luso-Brazilian merchants traded in Africa served both as disruptive novelties and as analogues to existing substances (like palm wine and cannabis) used by *ngangas*. Such drugs—as well as other African cures that will appear later in this chapter, like the "bark of life" endorsed by a Portuguese cavalry officer—played a key role in the creation of vernacular cultures of drug use that mingled European and African elements.[16]

What is especially interesting about this divergence is that the concept of *feitiçaria*, as both term and practice, was actually European in origin.[17] It was a product of the same material and ecological changes—and the same violence—that also enabled the plantation system.[18] When healers and political leaders in Africa and in diaspora sought access to the benevolence of ancestors and gods via offerings of palm wine and mixtures of roots, animal products, and herbs, they did so in a shared framework of *feitiçaria* that was understood as effective by both Europeans and Africans.

Sub-Saharan Africa as Poisoned Landscape

Writing in 1611, the traveler François Pyrard de Laval explained why he had feared to visit Angola during his voyages throughout the Atlantic world. "It is the poorest country in the world," Laval claimed. "No other traffic is carried on but in negro slaves; the Portuguese hold it solely for this, and would not otherwise inhabit it, for the land produces only some fruits and cattle, and but small store of these . . . The cause that more ships go not to Angola is that the air is very intemperate and noisome."[19] French, English, and Portuguese accounts of West and West Central Africa portrayed it as a place of venoms, fevers, and psychoactive powers. This reflected prevailing medical opinion.[20] Europeans who passed into the "Torrid Zone" did so with a conviction in the corrupting effects of tropical nature and tropical stars.[21] Tropical drugs were coveted, but also feared, by Europeans who saw them as necessary evils for surviving in tropical climates. Europeans regarded African cures and the healers who supplied them as a kind of inversion of tropical poisons, miasmas, and demonic influences.[22]

An anonymous English traveler in late seventeenth-century Guinea described a panoply of poisons lurking in African nature. The author's chapter on the fortress of Winnebah spent only a paragraph on the site itself ("it hath 18 Guns, and 50 Europeans besides slaves to defend it") before launching into eleven pages on the "monstrous creatures" in the hinterlands. The account culminated in a vivid translation of Lucan's description of the effects of African venoms. The emphasis throughout is on physical and mental transformations induced by the African landscape, from flesh-eating poisons to venom

> *Which quite drunk up all Moisture that should flow*
> *Into his vital Parts, his Palate now*
> *And Tongue so scorch't and dry, no sweat could go*
> *To his tir'd Joints, from's Eyes no Tears could flow.*[23]

Other venoms performed similarly hideous transformations, distending one unfortunate's body "far / past humane growth" until he became "A Globe deform'd . . . an heap confus'd."

In addition to these descriptions of poisoning, the author emphasized the transformative powers of the landscape itself. The gorilla, for instance, appeared as a human turned bestial by "the alteration and change" of the African jungle: "a monstrous Creature which the Portugals call *Salvage*, that is a Satyr, it hath a great head, a heavy body, fleshy and strong arms, no tail, and goes sometimes upright, and otherwhile upon all four like an Ape. The Blacks affirm it is of the Humane Race, but by the alteration and change of the Woods and Wilderness it is become half a beast."[24] Likewise, the hyena appeared in the text as "another strange Beast which some have thought to be Male one year, and Female another."[25] The implication was clear: the African climate put bodies at risk not only of disease, but also of transformation.

Letters from soldiers and missionaries in Portuguese Angola echoed this belief in the transformative power of African landscapes, and the dangers that awaited bodies incapable of adapting. A dispatch to the Overseas Council by a missionary in 1678 warned that "the climate of this backland, experience shows, is harmful and opposed to the [constitution] of Europeans and white men who enter into it."[26] The report also noted that "horses sent from Brazil and foreign lands . . . [tend to] die, or become incapacitated, due to the change of climate, particularly in the sertão" and described "tests" (*experimenta*) involving attempts to adapt nonnative horses to the climate.[27] However, the missionary concluded, "Horses born as natives of the climate are stronger, and less prone to illness, as has been tested with three or four native [horses] of the land." And just as their European-bred horses succumbed to illness brought on by a "malignant" climate, so too might the Portuguese themselves.

The Capuchin missionary Antonio Zuchelli complained that Benguela had "a climate so malignant and pestilential, that all of the fruit produced by this land communicate a venomous power [*una qualitá venefica*]." As a result, Zuchelli wrote, "those few white men who survive continually have such pale faces, and are so emaciated and exhausted, that it seems that they are in the jaws of death."[28] The African rains also aroused fears. According to the Jesuit Jerónimo Lobo, the Guinea coast's "excessive heat" stirred up hot rains that "as they fell on one's skin, made sores, and in woolen clothing they bred noxious white worms."[29] A French traveler to the Gold Coast, Nicolas Villault, complained in the 1660s of "nipping winds and rains" and

"the Evening dew" that he was convinced bred "worms which grow betwixt
the skin and the flesh," causing "the most violent pain."[30] Villault turned to
an African healer to remove these "venomous" worms, finding European
surgeons inadequate. The Dutch slave-trader Willem Bosman, likewise,
wrote that "green herbs" used along the Gold Coast of Guinea were of "such
wonderful Efficiency, that 'tis much to be deplored that no European Physician has yet applyed himself to the discovery of their Nature and Virtue."
Bosman believed that African treatments were far superior to European
ones in curing tropical diseases, in part because "before [European prepa-
rations] reach us they have lost all their Virtue, and are mostly corrupted,"
but also because European constitutions are "changed [in Africa] by the Cli-

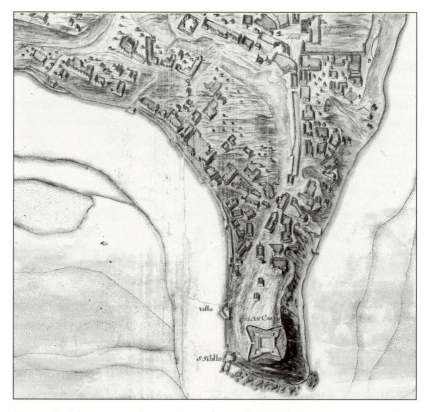

Figure 17. Johannes Vingboons, Map of Luanda, Angola, 1665 (detail). Visible in
this section of the map of the city, created in the aftermath of the short-lived Dutch
conquest of Luanda, are the Jesuit and Capuchin cloisters and a market (to the
north), a section of the port area from which slaves were shipped, and the presidio.
Courtesy of the Nationaal Archief, the Hague, Netherlands.

mate; and therefore this Country's Remedies, in all probability, are better for our bodies that the European ones."[31]

Memoranda sent between the Overseas Council in Lisbon and the leaders of seventeenth-century Luanda vividly demonstrate the failure of European physicians and surgeons to effectively treat the tropical diseases and poisons they encountered in the colony. More than one petition to the crown by a sick or an injured soldier in Africa demanded redress owing to "the lack of doctors" able to "treat illnesses in Angola."[32] It was a failure that left open the possibility of African cures superseding European drugs on the continent. In 1664, during the preparations for the 1665 war against the Kingdom of Kongo, Luanda had been home to an array of Portuguese medical professionals, from a well-paid physician to a surgeon-major, an assistant surgeon, an apothecary, and a barber-surgeon (barbeiro, often the sole medical attendant on slave ships). But even at this high-water mark of medical professions in the colony, they complained about a lack of adequate medical supplies. A visiting French surgeon named Daniel de Sena petitioned the crown in 1666 for an additional 10,000 reis for the purchase of "medicines for the apothecary shop" in Luanda—potentially drugs purchased from African healers. So, too, did Pedro da Silva, the surgeon-mór of the colony's outpost in Benguela (a position that doesn't reappear in later letters), who requested 16,000 reis "to buy purges for the apothecary shop."[33] Neither succeeded.

Portuguese Angola suffered from chronic staffing problems throughout the period. In 1666, the governor of Angola, Tristan da Cunha, reluctantly paid a visit to the Benguela outpost, "despite being very ill from the climate, for which reason no other governor has visited the place."[34] A request for funds in the same year from the surgeon-major Luiz Gonçalves, the apothecary Agosto Ruiz, and the surgeon Alexandre Mugras "to acquire medicaments to make two apothecary boxes [caixas de botica] . . . to cure the infantry that goes off to discover mines [in the sertão]" was likely a reference to this expedition. Tristan da Cunha's letters of appointment as governor had emphasized the dire state of medical care in the colony, and offered funds to spend "in the ways that might cure the aforementioned sick folk."[35] But these funds were insufficient. Da Cunha explained that the soldiers in the interior were not receiving salaries regularly and were instead being paid in "the drugs imported from this land" (drogas da terra importada), a phrase hinting that African drugs may have served as a makeshift currency in the interior.[36] Even chaplains and missionaries received "a limited wage paid in Libongos, and drogas, for the service which they make to God and your Majesty."[37]

Table 3. Salaries of Medical Professionals in Portuguese Angola, 1664-92 (in réis)

	Physician	Surgeon-Mór	Surgeon	Barber	Apothecary
1664	192,000	48,000	33,600	28,800	
1666		40,500	23,000		65,200
1669	70,000		30,000		
1692			60,000		

Source: AHU, cx. 8, doc. 6, April 23, 1664; AHU cx. 9, doc. 151, April 4, 1669; AHU cx. 14, doc. 89, February 15, 1692.

By 1692, the specified wages for surgeons had doubled, perhaps reflecting the shortage of competent professionals in the colony. Meanwhile, the posts of apothecary, barber, and physician went unfilled.[38] In 1684, even the captain of infantry for the city of Luanda, one of the highest military offices in the region, demanded a transfer because his illnesses were deemed incurable in the African climate.[39] This dire situation was driven home in a missive sent by the city council in 1688, which explained why an "infection of the air" was causing "contagion and sickness" in the city: the corpses of slaves had been repeatedly disinterred by *lobos de noite* ("wolves of the night," likely jackals) and the corpses strewn in the street contributed to the poisonous miasmas of the place.[40]

The Paradoxical Powers of Fetisheers

The constant presence of death in the colonial slave trade gave enslaved Africans a paradoxical kind of power.[41] Fear of African nature and African natural knowledge is palpable in the European sources from Angola and the West African slaving ports. One of the most vivid examples of the early modern European fear of African nature comes to us through the travel accounts of the Portuguese Jesuit Jerónimo Lobo (1595-1678). Lobo, on a sea passage from Portugal to Africa, was at first delighted by his sightings of unexplained phenomena like St. Elmo's Fire. Yet he became increasingly concerned as the ship neared the equator. Before long, the "burning of the sun," as he put it, had caused food to spoil, and "malignant fevers" broke out.

Lobo himself fell ill and believed he had only survived owing to well-timed treatments from the two doctors and several surgeons on board, who treated him with bezoar stones.[42] There were so many "extremely pitiful" stories of sailors dying from fever, Lobo wrote, that "I omit [them] . . . in order not to further frighten the reader of this narrative, in case, perhaps, he plans to see and experience for himself these happenings so typical of the India voyage."

Lobo emphasized one consequence of the tropical fever in particular: "This illness caused and causes many to lose their minds," he wrote, "giving way to wild delirium." Lobo described a feverish sailor who attempted to jump into the open water: "When I asked him . . . where he was going, he answered that he was bound for Alcántara [a dockside neighborhood in Lisbon], which must have been where he was from or a place with which he had some connection. But as this was on the coast of Guinea, when I asked him what way he planned to go, he replied, looking at the sea through the gangway which was open, that he was going through that field. And he doubtless would have thrown himself into the water . . . if he had not been held back and confined."[43]

How did Europeans conceptualize this "delirium" caused by tropical fever? Was it simply a physical response to illness? Or was it something more sinister, a kind of curse or conjuring generated by Africa itself? The etiology of diseases—the explanation for their causes—was extremely vague in this period. Lobo sounds surprisingly modern when he blames his own illness on sitting "very close" to a "contagious" sailor. Yet the Jesuit evidently visualized the transfer of the disease as an exhalation of harmful humors, not as a transfer of germs. Elsewhere, Lobo attributed "mortal illnesses" on the African coast to the moon. Shipwrecked on the coast of Mozambique, he observed that "the moonlight, especially that of September, is so harmful that it causes mortal illnesses in those who stay out in it. Its ill effects are such that it damages even the bronze bells and cannon, causing them to crack." Lobo recorded the surreal image of shipwrecked sailors "walking in the streets at night wear[ing] hats," taking "great care against being touched by moonlight and night air."[44] This was not a quirk of Lobo's individual understanding of tropical disease. Letters sent from Angola blamed the moon for hastening a soldier's illness, and Cardoso de Miranda, a physician in Bahia who specialized in treating newly arrived Angolan slaves, speculated that "the repetition of [tropical] fevers is caused by the moon, which has an occult quality or force."[45]

Because early modern Europeans imagined that tropical nature and astrology generated a new set of diseases, they also looked beyond Europe for their cures. The Capuchin friar Jean-François de Rome lamented that "there is no Physician or Apothecary to be found in the whole country [of Kongo], their place being taken by the Sorcerers," but he acknowledged that "nevertheless many others abhor these sacrileges, and are served by natural remedies [such as] . . . decoctions which they make with the juices of herbs and other ingredients that purge benignly," as well as by African "Surgeons" [*Chirurgeons*] who "serve for bleeding."[46] Across the Atlantic but in the same period (1676) William Dampier, the circumnavigator and naturalist, praised the work of an enslaved African-born blacksmith in Jamaica who cured him of worms. This healer applied "a little rough Powder, which looked like Tobacco-Leaves dried and crumbled small," while "mumbling some Words to himself," and drew the worm from Dampier's foot via a silk string.[47] The detail of the healer being a blacksmith may be significant. Working in the Kongo in the 1680s, the Italian missionary Girolamo Merolla had described "blacksmiths, who are sometimes also *feiticeiros* [*fattucchieri*] and are called *Ndè fianzundu*."[48]

The result of such encounters was an intense European fear of African poisoning, accompanied by a fascination with the cures of African "sorcerers" and African drugs. The Capuchin missionary Giovanni Cavazzi described *ngangas* in the Kingdom of Kongo whose cures, performed using powdered plants and animal parts were "something truly marvelous." Yet he regarded these cures as off limits to Europeans because of potential spiritual corruption. "It would be good for healing Europeans also if it did not involve invoking to the Devil," he explained.[49]

The concept of the African *feiticeiro* who could heal or poison at will spread to Brazil as well. In 1706, the Portuguese Jesuit André João Antonil described Fulano slaves on Brazilian sugar plantations who "kill themselves with poison, or with *feitiços*: not lacking among themselves Masters who are expert in this Art."[50] Elsewhere, Antonil wrote of slaves who flee to *mocambos* (hideouts or *quilombos*) in the jungle who, "if caught, kill themselves when the Senhor catches them, or take their vengeance with *feitiço*."[51]

Fetishizing Drugs

In June 1721, a young British ship's surgeon named John Atkins sat down to dine with the ruler of a small independent state in present-day Ghana—a man known to Europeans as John Conny (c. 1670–c. 1725). The year before,

Atkins learned, Conny's forces had ambushed a group of Dutch slave traders, "cut them in pieces" and "pav[ed] the entrance of his Palace soon after,
with their Skulls."[52] Finding the skulls no longer present, however, Atkins
inquired of Conny (whom he called, seemingly unironically, "a man of very
great Civility") "what was become of the *Dutchmen's* Skulls, that lately paved
the entrance of his House." Conny revealed to Atkins that he had forgiven
the Dutch in death, and offered them what he believed to be a fitting burial:
"He told me very frankly, that about a Month before our Ship's Arrival, he
had put them all into a Chest with some Brandy, Pipes, and Tobacco, and
buried them; for, says he, it is time that all Malice should depart, and the
putting up a few Necessaries with the Corps, such as they loved, is our way
of respecting the deceased."[53] The word John Atkins used to describe these
burial practices was "Fetish." As we have seen, *feitiçaria* was a term that
early modern Portuguese authors used to describe African spirituality. But
it was not invented for this purpose. The word originated in medieval Iberia,
where it referred to the crafting of charms and amulets by Christians, Jews,
and Muslims.[54] This catchall term gained new utility when Portuguese slave
traders and missionaries in Africa encountered the practices of the *nganga*
and other herbalists, healers, and poisoners.

From the late sixteenth century on, the word *feitiço* had a wide currency in Portuguese writings about American, Asian, and African cultures.
A cursory sample of early Portuguese mentions of *feitiços* reveals that the
phrase was applied to indigenous Brazilian, West African, East African, and
South Asian contexts. Among the Carijos (a Tupi-Guarani–speaking group
in coastal Brazil) the Jesuit priest Simão de Vasconcellos wrote that "there
are such eminent *feitiçeiros*, and they are so admiring of them, that they give
notice of them by speaking of a River of Magic, and a Valley of Incantations,
and other similar names, no doubt multiplying their numbers by this."[55] Yet
African healing practices and religiosity stood at the core of the concept of
the *feitiço* by the seventeenth century. In his extensive writings about the
feitiçeiros of seventeenth-century indigenous Brazil, for instance, Padre Vasconcellos claimed that the "most detestable type" were those who used their
magic to kill, and that they did so by summoning "a visual apparition of the
demon," which "took the form of a little black African [*Negrinho Ethiope*],
and when they sought to make *feitiços* against any person, they communicated their intentions with the *Negrinho*."[56] The protective pouches and amulets that diasporic African *feitiçeiros* fashioned (called by the Portuguese
bolsas de mandinga) were emblematic of the blended practice of *feitiçaria* by

the seventeenth century. They could contain herbs, shells, tobacco, pieces of animals, fragments of the Quran or Bible, and earth taken from geographic locations with special significance to the wearer and to the wearer's protective deity or spirits.[57]

The *feitiço* thus occupied the interstices of the pharmacological and spiritual traditions of the European, African, and even indigenous American worlds. *Feitiçaria* was a point of both contact and conflict. Drugs, poisons, and healing pouches or amulets literally embodied these mixings, giving them material substance.

Antonio Franco, a Jesuit historian writing about the conquest and conversion of Luanda in 1719, remembered it as a medico-spiritual battle between the sacraments of the Catholic Church and the *feitiços* of the devil. Franco described a padre who "threw the instruments with which they summon the Devil into a fire . . . and the Holy Spirit entered into all of the people, and they threw these things in the fire." All, that is, except "an old woman, who said that Gods would come to visit her, that all of them gave her *feitiços*, that she was the daughter of God."[58] Franco regarded these *feitiços* as offering a chance for the padres to demonstrate God's power by curing sufferers of curses. However, he noted, those afflicted by *feitiços* "listened to the catechism coldly, giving clues that they only desired the health of the body that it brought."[59] In the interior region of Cassanje, likewise, Franco described a padre who braved "the *sertão* of Angola, with its climate extremely poisonous to foreigners" to do spiritual battle with "a famous *feiticeiro*, who all feared because of his great arts." The padre ultimately succeeded in casting "all of the pharmacies of his art" (*todos as boticas da arte*) into a fire. A somewhat similar act was memorialized in Figure 18.[60]

In many cases, the fetish object was, itself, a physical receptacle for medicinal drugs. Writing at the end of the eighteenth century about the interior region of Cazembe, east of the Benguela highlands, Francisco de Lacerda described "hollow idols in which they store their medicines before drinking them."[61] Other documented instances of the fetish object as a container for medicines come from Inquisition trials involving *bolsas de mandinga*, healing pouches featuring medicinal herbs and significant objects.[62] What linked all of the *feitiços* that appear in surviving sources was their functional role: they were material technologies of mediation among the human body, the natural world, and the supernatural world. They offered bodily health but also threatened (from the perspective of the Portuguese) to bring the venomous landscape of Africa to bear on European bodies and minds.

Figure 18. An Italian capuchin incinerates a Kongolese "house of a *feitiçeiro [casa d'un Faticchiero]* filled with diabolical superstitions" in this watercolor from the 1740s. Note the gathered fetish objects in the foreground, including plants, venomous snakes, horns, an idol, and a human hand or sculpture, in Soyo in the Kingdom of Kongo. From Bernardino d'Asti, "Missione in prattica," c. 1750. Watercolor on paper, detail, MS 457. Courtesy of the Biblioteca Civica Centrale, Turin.

The concept of the *feitiço* emerged as a middle ground not only between Portuguese and African epistemologies but also between the concepts of medicine and poison. By invoking supernatural powers to influence bodily health and drawing on physical substances to achieve this, African *feitiçeiros* blurred the lines between cure and curse in a manner that anticipated the later split between licit and illicit drugs.

African *feitiçaria*, then, was a manifestation not only of the emergence of an Atlantic creole culture but also of an emergent division in the early modern drug trade. Within a matter of decades, this trade had marshalled sugar (a medieval Iberian transplantation from South Asia) and *Nicotiana rustica* (from the Americas) along with the technologies of distillation and the agricultural system of the Brazilian plantations in the service of the African slave trade. An unintended consequence of such commercial globalization, however, was that healers and spiritual leaders in West Central Africa co-opted these novel intoxicants. They integrated them into a hybrid medico-spiritual system that was Atlantic in scope, pervading not only diasporic African society but also, increasingly, European society as well. However, it did so outside the realm of elite medicine, in vernacular contexts such as those of the Africans tried by the Portuguese Inquisition who sold their *feitiços* in the marketplace. These figures only entered written sources at the precise moment when they were being silenced.

When Portuguese padres threw fetish objects in the fire and replaced them with crosses, books, and communion wine, they were not only attempting to substitute one set of spiritual beliefs for another—they were competing in this larger, Atlantic sphere of creolized commerce and healing. They succeeded, in part: "fetishized" drugs remained restricted to a regional niche. But the communion wine and wafer, the breviary and the altar also became pseudo-*feitiços*, as did the tobacco and *gerebita* and *cachaça* liquors that the Portuguese carried with them, which became part of a larger, vernacular culture that mixed African ritual with commodified recreational intoxicants and medicines from the Atlantic world and beyond. Turning Marx on his head, we might conclude not that commodities became fetishes under systems of capitalist exchange, but that *feitiços* were a kind of failed commodity.

Brazilian Spirits, African Throats

The rapid adoption of European-traded alcohol and tobacco in West Central Africa added a complex new element to *feitiçaria*. European-traded wine and spirits had a transformative effect on both sociability and spirituality in seventeenth-century Africa.[63] It was Brazilian alcohol traders, above all, who dominated the African experience of spirituous liquors. The significance of this trade is still preserved in the words *gerebita* and *cachaça*, both of which appear to be borrowings from preexisting words for alcoholic brews used in West Central Africa.[64] A 1678 report to the Overseas Council from the city council of Luanda blamed the abuse of newly introduced spirits (*agoas ardentes*) among both Europeans and Africans for the colony's wave of "deaths and illnesses." The authors complained that the new spirits led to "the diminution of industry, and the ruin of the defenses" and advised that the crown "ought to order the prohibition of *agoas ardentes*."[65] A partial ban was ultimately enacted but largely ignored by the inhabitants of the port. Nine years later, the governor of Angola complained that crates of "alcoholic liquors from Brazil which are called *gerebitas* . . . are unloaded and sold, publicly, with notorious scandal," in open disregard of the crown's attempt to prohibit sales to a small cabal of merchants, referred to in this document as the Syndicate (*Sendicato*).[66]

In 1689, officers at the royal treasury in Luanda argued that the ban be lifted entirely because of the "great utility that would accrue to the king-

Figure 19. A French slave trader offering a pipe-holding Alcaty (leader) an exchange of "eau de vie" for water. François Froger, *Relation du Voyage* (Paris, 1698), facing page 7. Courtesy of the John Carter Brown Library.

dom if *agoas ardentes* from Brazil are allowed entrance into this land."[67] A letter from the Overseas Council in response argued that the prohibition be upheld because the liquors "are known to be very harmful to the health of all the white residents and negroes of the Kingdom of Angola, having lost by this means a great part of the infantry of the *presidios* of the entire conquest."[68] Another proposal by the governor of Angola to the city council hedged on the matter, admitting that the illnesses "are partly due to drinking *agoa ardente* from Brazil," but adding "there is no doubt that it also results from the heat of the sun and the malignity of the climate . . . for the climate of this part of Africa has been known by experience to be contrary to the natures of Europeans. Thus, in a little time . . . the malignity of the lands saps their natural powers."[69] Others argued that spirits could actually be medically useful. In 1694, two physicians working at Luanda's sole hospital petitioned the crown to lift the ban. Though some argue "that excess of liquor, being all too common among everyone, can be the cause of various dropsies," they wrote that "after assisting many years in this land, we have never seen either in or outside the hospital any case of *gerebita* causing illness, and indeed up to this point on many occasions we have applied it as a remedy for some infirmities."[70]

In the end, Brazilian spirits were simply too integral to the economics of the slave trade in Angola to be permanently banned. Inland traders called *pombeiros* made healthy livings by venturing into the interior of Angola, Kongo, and Benguela stocked with these imported Brazilian liquors, which were produced cheaply using the cast-off by-products from the sugar refineries of the Bahian coast.[71] *Cachaça* was *gerebita*'s higher-status cousin, a sugarcane rum made from the molasses itself rather than from by-products of the refining process. Along with molasses-soaked tobacco, the two liquors became mainstays of the Portuguese-Africa trade. In the process, they figured in spiritual and medical battles between *feiticeiros* and Christian missionaries. When the missionary Girolamo Merolla first began preaching in the Kingdom of Kongo's Soyo province (Merolla called it "testing" the Bible "against the sorcerers") he described inviting a potential convert into his house "and treating him with alcoholic spirits and roll tobacco, of which they are greedy."[72]

Part of the reason why spirits were so easy to integrate into African cultures of drug taking was that they had a clear correlate with a substance that predated European contact: palm wine. In both West and West Central Africa, the fermented sap of palm trees of the genus *Raphia* had figured prominently in healing and spirituality for centuries prior to the arrival of Europeans. The traveler Nicolas Villault described a funeral in Sierra Leone in which a religious leader takes "Palm-Wine in his mouth, and squirts it upon the most ancient of the Fetiches," then mixes it with herbs and grease and "distributes [it] to the whole company."[73] A similar practice seems to have occurred in the Kongo. The missionary Jean-François de Rome noted that local palm wine (*malavu*) "evoked the tears of mourners."[74] Palm wine was so central to West Central African spiritual and ritual life that, as one historian has noted, belligerents would cut down the raphia trees of their opponents. The act was perceived as a grave atrocity.[75] The introduction of Brazilian sugarcane liquors, which were substantially more alcoholic than even the strongest palm wine, represented a decisive shift in how alcohol functioned in West Central African societies. Yet as high-status alcoholic drinks, they also became integrated into the ritual practices surrounding palm wine.

So, too, did tobacco, a novel intoxicant that nonetheless found a ready consumer base in Africa because of the preexisting use of smoking implements, which were used to consume cannabis.[76] Chewing and inhalation of a potent variety of tobacco—most likely the more intoxicating of the two tobacco species, *Nicotiana rustica*—can be dated in the Kingdom of Kongo to as early as 1611, and the plant soon became one of the most popular crops and trading items throughout Kongo, Angola, and the hinterlands to the east.[77] According to António de Oliveira de Cadornega, writing in the middle of the seventeenth century, aristocrats in the Dembo region of the Kongo were buried "with pipes and tobacco to smoke."[78] The longtime rival of the Portuguese, Queen Njinga, appears with a large pipe in several images of her that derive from the published and manuscript accounts of the Italian Capuchin missionary Giovanni Antonio Cavazzi, who visited her court in 1662 (Figure 20).[79] Tobacco smoking became so thoroughly Africanized in the era of the slave trade, in fact, that the Kimbundu word for pipe (*cachimbo*) was adopted throughout the Portuguese empire. To this day, while Spaniards puff on *pipas* and the French smoke *les pipes*, Lusophones smoke *cachimbos*. The African-style *cachimbo* was a significant marker of social power in Angola and the Kongo, and (as excavations of the grave of an Obeah man buried with a *cachimbo*-like pipe in Barbados hint) it may have signaled spiritual power in diasporic African communities, too.[80]

In both cases—tobacco and spirits—this process of adoption into African practices was not just medical or recreational but spiritual as well. In the context of seventeenth-century North America, according to Peter Mancall, "liquor's ability to alter perception led many Indians to consider it a sacred substance."[81] In one Sioux dialect, brandy was called *mni wakon*, "sacred water," while Ojibwe spiritual leaders "integrated alcohol into healing rituals."[82] A similar process took place across the Atlantic in precolonial Ghana, where alcoholic spirits became "closely linked to conceptions of power" because the intoxication they produced offered a point of contact between the spiritual and material worlds.[83] Likewise in West Central Africa, elites appropriated spirits and tobacco into existing spiritual-medical practices that prized "rituals of rapture."[84] Portuguese-traded wine and sugarcane spir-

Figure 20. Queen Njinga shown smoking a prominent pipe while "venerating the bones of her brother" in an engraving from a French translation of Cavazzi's account of the Kongo. Giovanni Antonio Cavazzi, *Relation historique de l'Ethiopie occidentale* (1732), vol. 4, p. 55, "Veneration de la Reine Anne Zingha pour les ossements de son frère." Courtesy of the Widener Library, Harvard University.

its were being used at the funeral of Queen Njinga in 1663 and rituals in Mbamba during the 1710s.[85] By the early eighteenth century, in short, novel intoxicants like *cachaça* and the potent tobacco of Bahia had become part of the "Atlantic creole culture" of West Central Africa, serving not just as recreational drugs or medicines, but as foundational elements of attaining spiritual power through alteration of ones' consciousness.[86]

To return to where we began, then: the Jaga Caconda was not merely making a mockery of the communion, as the Portuguese believed. He was performing an act of spiritual *and* pharmacological appropriation. By consuming the ritual intoxicant of his enemies, he was gaining access to—and asserting mastery over—the sacramental drug that was one of their sources of power. This assertion of spiritual authority rested upon the consumption of the psychoactive drug we could chose to call communion wine—but which could also justifiably be called the *feitiço* of the Catholic Church.

Buytrago's Bark

The fetishization of drugs thus made certain psychoactive substances spiritually potent in sub-Saharan Africa and its diaspora. However, it also made these substances difficult to integrate into global commodity chains. In 1710s and 1720s Angola and Brazil, a cavalry officer named Francisco de Buytrago offered a glimpse into how Catholic Iberian cultures of healing interacted with African *feitiçaria* and pharmacy. The title of Buytrago's manuscript, "Arvore da Vida, e Thesouro descuberto" (*Tree of Life, and Discovered Treasure*), evoked both the Garden of Eden and the obsession with making profitable "discoveries" in the *sertão*.[87] The structure of his text reflected a dual concern with "treasure" and spirituality: the first half narrates the "miraculous" cures of demon-possessed people (*demoninhados*) in Angola, Brazil, and Portugal that Buytrago attributes to the medicinal bark of the "Arvore da Vida," and the second half transitions into a more workmanlike descriptive list of "the names of the most unique things which are found in the Kingdom of Angola, and their virtues."[88]

From the opening pages of his text, Buytrago argued emphatically for the medical value of African nature: "In the Kingdom of Angola and in the provinces and neighboring lands of that region," he wrote, "there exists such a profusion of barks, and herbs, and other things of such singular virtue and efficacy . . . that they exceed those of all of the world in power, and in the greatness and variety of the plants and herbs that these folk employ."[89] Unlike his compatriots, Buytrago unreservedly praised the skills and honesty of African healers, lauding the transparency of their "surgeons and physicians, who do everything in the sight of the Sick, in order to free them from any ill suspicion." For Buytrago, the *botica* (pharmacy) used by these healers was indeed nothing short of "perfect": "They have for their *botica* the barks, roots, herbs, leaves, fruits and other *materia medica* that exist in these lands, bestowed by divine Providence with singular virtues, as also are teeth, bones and skins of a great variety of animals, giving them remedies to serve for their infirmities which are so easy and perfect."[90] In order to understand Buytrago's manuscript, we need to consider its dual contexts as an early modern European medical text and an artifact from the Africanized world of the South Atlantic slave trade.[91]

In many ways, of course, Buytrago's rhetoric regarding the powers of his "Arvore da Vida" was typical of an early modern Christian. When Buytrago called its cures miraculous and used language connecting the tree to Eden, he was following a medieval precedent of associating tropical drugs and spices with the biblical Paradise.[92] In the Portuguese context, this link was drawn in 1650 by the physician Duarte Madeira Arrais, whose treatise on the *Arbor vitae* (Tree of Life) was one of the few medical texts from seventeenth-century Portugal to be translated into a foreign language.[93] Arrais's inquiry into the physical nature of the Edenic tree of life concluded that the plant functioned both "as Aliment, and as Medicament."[94] He believed that its medical virtues were connected both to its anti-poison ("alexipharmic") properties, and to its ability to intoxicate, or "stupefy the Sense . . . as Narcotick Medicines do."[95]

For Arrais, the Tree of Life was no metaphor. It was an actual plant, yielding a medicinal drug of seemingly great power. Arrais had been vague about precisely where he thought the Tree of Life had grown. Buytrago, however, was specific. He described his *Arvore da Vida* as a "a small and skinny tree, numerous in the Kingdom of Kongo, called *emcassa* or *cassa* by the local folk," which was "very good against worms and the most singular antidote for poisons (*contraveneno*) in the entire world." Above all, Buytrago wrote, this "bark of life" was "most singular and miraculous in combating *feitiços* . . . and demon possession."[96]

To be sure, Buytrago was not the only European writer in the early eighteenth century to acknowledge the medical skills of African healers or the "virtues" of African drugs. Indeed, at least two other Europeans in Africa appear to mention his bark of life in passing.[97] But what is unusual here is that whereas other European accounts tend merely to *describe* the techniques or drugs in use, Buytrago went into considerable detail describing the cures that he *himself* had performed using skills he learned from Angolan "physicians" (*medicos*). Compared to Buytrago's effusive account, two other mentions of "*ncassa*" from the seventeenth century are short and unfavorable. For instance, the missionary Giovanni Cavazzi described *ncassa* as a bark "used to discover those who are suspected of being *feiticeiros* [*fat-*

tucchieri] or witches." He did briefly praise certain "stupendous" healing effects of the bark but believed that, overall, it had "a venemous and malign quality"—one, indeed, that was so potent "that birds, when passing over [the *ncassa* trees], fall to the ground and immediately die."[98]

As Buytrago explained, his introduction to the bark came during a bioprospecting mission along with a more experienced comrade to investigate the properties of a cure "much used and esteemed among all of the [Angolan] folk and many of the whites" early during his time in Africa:

> Since I have always been very curious and inquisitive in everything I did in all my years, and having no knowledge of [Angola] before being sent to this Kingdom, a friend of mine, being diligent in these matters, introduced me to another fellow, who I observed going continually to the blacks of this Kingdom, asking that I likewise go and see [this bark] in quantity. This sufficiently persuaded all of them, such that they purchased it, declaring its virtues, it being preeminent for the treatment of *feitiços*, poisons and wounds, [this last] the sole virtue which it was known to confer when it was discovered in the year [16]66.[99]

The drug, of course, was not "discovered" in 1666. Buytrago was likely referencing the earliest description he could locate among other European sources.[100] The economy of Portuguese Angola increasingly relied on local go-betweens in the late seventeenth and the eighteenth centuries, and Buytrago's guide who he observed "going continually to the Blacks" may well have been a mixed-race *filho da terra* (a term used both for African-born Portuguese and children of Portuguese soldiers and local women).

Significantly, however, Buytrago claimed that his "first experience" of healing with the bark occurred not in Africa but in Brazil. In Bahia, he related, he had used it to cure "the slave of a relative, who was dying . . . from what I perceived to be *feitiços* that had been cast on her."[101] Buytrago then proceeds to describe a number of case studies of different maladies and enchantments performed by the bark, including the cure of an entire family suffering from *feitiços* had which prevented them from attending Mass. This was performed by a man identified only as "the Blessed Antonio" in Bahia, who "knowing that I, for love of God, sold this remedy, came to my house to buy some." Antonio also "burnt the *botica* [drugs]" that a malevolent *feiticeiro* was said to have been adding to the family's food.[102]

Buytrago's conviction that *casca da vida* was a "miraculous" drug gifted by God to restore victims of *feitiçaria* helps explain his unusually receptive attitude toward African healing. The actual substance he was using in his cures (likely *Erythrophleum suaveolens*, sometimes known as *nkasa* or *cassa* in the Congo Basin) was widely used throughout West and West Central Africa to drive away evil spirits.[103] Buytrago seems to have simply adapted this widespread cure into an explicitly Catholic context. However, given the Congo's long history of Christianity, it is possible that even this was not his own innovation.[104] It is also important to remember that this dual role of a substance (as both medical and magical) was not unfamiliar to Buytrago's European audience. In fact, it was common. A Portuguese contemporary of Buytrago wrote, for instance, that diabolical curses could be cured not only by herbs such as artemesia but also by performing acts involving blood and excrement that used material properties to fight supernatural ones. "If one suffers from a curse," wrote one respected Portuguese physician in 1713, "take the manure of the person who you love, and put it in the right shoe of the loved one, and they who first notice the stench dissolve the curse . . . if one streaks the walls of one's house with the blood of a black dog, it will break a curse upon the house or those in it. The gall of a crow mixed with sesame oil can also dissolve curses."[105] In early modern African and early modern European contexts, cures involved a mixture of performative acts (such as anointing with blood, oil, or wine) and the application of drugs, such as powdered herbs and roots. As historian William Eamon has noted within the context of late medieval Europe, the blurred lines between demonic possession and disease "made it possible for popular healers to appropriate the role of exorcist, and for exorcists to play the role of doctor"—a state of affairs that was not unfamiliar in early modern Africa or elsewhere in the early modern world.[106]

In short, a mixed medical culture based on Africanized *feitiços*, tropical drugs, and spiritual rituals was beginning to emerge by the first decade of the eighteenth century. It operated in African-dominated social spaces, and while it never made its way into elite European medical and scientific practice, it made a mark on the slave societies of the Atlantic world. Around 1710, for instance, a missionary priest named Alberto de Santo Tomás attacked the *feitiçaria* that he observed in the plantation societies of Bahia and Pernambuco, warning that Christians "should not consult the Negro *feitiçeiros*, nor any other person they might believe had dealings with the devil," and instead, they should restrict themselves to the traditional "exorcisms of the

Church."[107] Yet Father Alberto himself practiced "Africanized" techniques (such as crafting *bolsas* to sell to *demoninhados* and others with spiritual afflictions) in order to compete in the changing medical marketplace of colonial Brazil.[108] Likewise, a man who called himself Padre Januário wandered 1730s Brazil posing as an official of the Portuguese Inquisition, toting a magical stone he called *pedra d'ara* as he went. The *pedra d'ara* was usually carried in a bag (*bolsa*) and became tied up with the concept of the *bolsa de mandinga* as a "consecrated object" (in short, a *feitiço*) with "magical powers."[109] Januário's actions conform to those of the African healers in Lisbon reported in Inquisition trials from the same period: he traveled the *sertão* and demonstrated the healing powers of his amulet and *bolsa* by inviting a crowd to shoot a stray dog with a gun.[110] When the dog was touching the *bolsa*, Januário said, it would be uninjured. It was a claim borrowed from the magical toolkit of the African *nganga*.[111]

Early eighteenth-century slave entrepôts were sites of brutal assertions of European power over African bodies. But they were also places where African ways of *healing* bodies flourished. In 1720, the British naval surgeon John Atkins complained that James Phipps, a veteran captain-general of the Cape Coast Castle in present-day Ghana, had "give[n] the preference of *Fetishing* to any Physical Directions of mine, wearing them on his wrists and neck." Atkins ascribed what he called this "silly custom, created by our fears [of disease]" to Phipps's marriage to "a *Mulatto* Woman" who was "a strict Adherer to *Negrish* Customs."[112]

Despite the brutality of the Middle Passage and the plantation system, many localized healing traditions from West and West Central Africa survived intact among ethnolinguistic enclaves of slaves in Brazil. For instance, a variant on the *asen* (a sort of portable altar used in healing by the Gbe peoples of Dahomey) was used by Gbe speakers in 1740s Minas Gerais. One, a healer named Francisco Axê, used the *asen* in a complex series of disease-curing rituals involving an invocation of "the father of the *feitiços*," verbal exhortations directed at the *asen* itself, the creation and burial of a clay figure of a man along with the patient's hair, ritual sprinkling of *cachaça* over an iron altar, the sacrifice of a white rooster, and the use of a healing root known as *melão de São Caetano*.[113]

Throughout the seventeenth and eighteenth centuries, then, a shared vocabulary of healing, which heavily featured psychoactive drug use, began to emerge from this ferment of African knowledge, techniques, and material culture. These practices were continuously reshaped by the changing demographics of colonial Brazil and by the needs of patients, but we can identify a few common threads: the sacrificial animal was a common trope, as was the creation of a clay doll, the exorcism of *feitiços*, and the burial of an item from the patient's body, like hair. So, too, was the sacramental use of alcohol and tobacco. These practices were malleable. While healers like Axê used *cachaça*, a century later, wielders of the *asen* were demanding that patients make a sacrificial payment of gin. By the early twentieth century, gin had largely replaced Brazilian sugarcane liquors as the preeminent high-status drink of West and West Central Africa—and, tellingly, "became strongly associated with rituals" in the process.[114] Ritual uses of intoxicating drugs were a common thread linking early modern African and Afro-Brazilian healing practices—but the special *type* of intoxicant shifted, from palm wine to *cachaça* to gin. European-traded drugs were repurposed in the service of healing practices that offered diasporic Africans a degree of agency and connection to a continuous tradition.

Buytrago's manuscript shows the other side of this equation: a European adopting the *materials* of West Central African medicine, while packaging them using demonological concepts that would have been familiar to a medieval European Catholic. Buytrago's attempt to bridge the gap was unsuccessful. His contemporary, João Curvo Semedo, did prescribe a number of similar remedies from Angola, including "Mubamgo, a tree with a white bark from Embaça" whose root, when powdered and mixed with tobacco, aided "the accidents of the mother."[115] The Angolan drug that Semedo elaborated in the greatest detail was the "Minhaminha" or "Quiminha" root, which exhibited a miraculous ability to "swallow up the virtues of poisons." He described "a root [with] such a virtue against venom as to equal or exceed the *pao Cobra*.[116] These substances did not appear in any other printed medical texts of the period. Buytrago's text stands as clear evidence for the use of African drugs and pharmaceutical knowledge within a distinctively Atlantic material and cultural framework. But it also evidences the failure of that knowledge to take hold in European pharmacy.

In the end, it is misleading to label remedies like Buytrago's bark as either African or European. As with other "fetishized drugs," it was both. Substances like the Casca da Vida operated at the nexus of European, Central West African, and Brazilian influences. These included the long tradition of Catholicism in the Kongo, the medieval Iberian concept of *feitiçaria*, the knowledge and ritual practices of *ngangas* in Angola, and the boundary-crossing eclecticism of the early modern medical marketplace. The case of

Buytrago's bark exemplifies how some colonists embedded their healing practices in explicitly spiritual frameworks, like the exorcising of demons, and moved fluidly among the realms of African, American, and European healing. It also shows how the drug trade was not *just* a trade. It was (and remains) a commerce freighted with powerful spiritual beliefs as well.

The Fetish in World History

Today, the term "fetish" has two prominent meanings in popular consciousness: Marx's "commodity fetishism," and the word's sexual connotations, which appear to derive from Marx's use of the term. Marx's altered concept of "fetish" to denote the invisible power relations involved in capitalist systems has, in effect, drawn a line between the word as used in its original Iberian and African context and "fetish" as a metaphor for a distinctive feature of modernity. This sets up a false opposition, as Roger Sansi notes, "between magic, *feitiçaria* and traditional practices on one side, and modernity, science, and rationality on the other."[117] The fetish was more a product of an emerging, globalized modernity than a relic of "traditional" cultures. The rise of the African fetish was a manifestation of the same globalization of healing and consumption that drove the drug trade.

It is for this reason that novel intoxicants such as tobacco and alcoholic spirits were so readily integrated into long-standing techniques of *feitiçaria*. Ritual practices that might once have included palm wine were, by the eighteenth century, featuring European-traded liquors like *gerebita*. Some Europeans balked at these practices and regarded them as evidence of African "barbarism." Yet many others availed themselves of the pharmaceutical and healing knowledge of Africans. This dichotomy of Africans as demonically inspired "sorcerers" or as miraculously gifted healers continued to persist in the Atlantic world, as it had in Portuguese Africa.

From one perspective, a similar binary emerged in colonial Mesoamerica. Spanish commentators on the natural wonders of New Spain debated whether the healing plants used by the indigenous peoples of Mesoamerica had a "demonic" essence—that is, whether their medical or psychoactive effects were directly implanted by Satan. Others argued that their supposedly malign effects simply came from their use in "barbarous" healing practices.[118] The question hinged on whether a non-European cure, unknown to the traditional authorities, could be repurposed as a tool of Christian bodily and spiritual health. This question was faced by Buytrago, too. But there was an important difference between these two cases. The Kingdom of Kongo was, nominally, a Catholic society of long standing. By the time Buytrago reached the Kongo, it had been officially Catholic for well over two hundred years. It is thus unclear from Buytrago's account whether Buytrago adapted the Casca da Vida into a Catholic exorcism framework or whether the experts who taught him the cure had already made the shift from invoking *voduns* to expelling Satan.[119]

In theory, the Catholic legacy of the Kongo would, perhaps, have made cures from that region easier to integrate into the European drug trade than those of the indigenous Americas. Yet this existing framework for understanding the action of African cures did not translate into a widespread adoption of African drugs on a global stage.[120] Fetishized drugs like Buytrago's bark became tarnished by association with enslaved healers and colonial mountebanks, and with fears of poisoned landscapes. While some fetishized drugs thrived in the Africanized spaces of the South Atlantic world, they did not become enduring elements of the elite-level knowledge and trade in drugs that would come to be known as the realm of *pharmacy*.[121]

In Part II we will explore how these factors contributed to the emergence of a legal and an epistemological division between pharmaceuticals and "narcotics."

PART II

Altered States

CHAPTER 4

Occult Qualities

British Natural Philosophers and Portuguese Drugs

The Indians say this Plant agrees
With ours in all its qualities
Our European old wives say
This herb is sacred: so say they
And both their dotages agree
It drives away all witchery . . .

—JAMES PETIVER, "OF INDIAN VERVINE"

As he grew old, the Portuguese diplomat Duarte Ribeiro de Macedo (1618-1680) became increasingly obsessed with his nation's loss of status among the powers of the earth.[1] Late in life, Macedo began to cultivate a plan for Portuguese renewal that hinged on an alliance with the English, specifically a new organization known as the Royal Society of London. In 1675, Macedo wrote to King Alfonso VI of Portugal with an idea that he claimed had been inspired by King Charles II of England, passed along to him by the Royal Society's patron Lord Montagu.[2] "During our conversations, in which we spoke vaguely about both the English colonies in Virginia and those of the Portuguese in Brazil, [Montagu] remarked to me that the first time that the King [of England] saw the powder that we call *Cravo*, the King remarked in the presence of various subjects of his court that only his brother, the King of Portugal, had the means to destroy the Dutch."[3] In the "Discourse on Transplantation" that Macedo attached to this report, he argued that the Portuguese crown should finance attempts to transplant spices and drugs from the East to the West Indies. For Macedo, Portugal's "captivity" under the Spanish Hapsburgs (1580–1640) had set the Portuguese empire in an artificial opposition to "the nations of the North, with whom we had formerly enjoyed friendship and useful exchanges."[4] When the Portuguese became "vassals of the Kings of Castile," he explained, they were forced to become "enemies of England, of Holland, and of France, and this evil resulted in the greater part of the losses of our conquests." Macedo continued: "When we were ruled by our own Kings many nations came to our ports in search of the drugs of the Orient [drogas do Oriente] . . . but after we became subject to Castile they ceased their commerce."[5] In Macedo's vision, Portugal and her "conquests" possessed immense natural resources but a poverty of technical expertise necessary to benefit from control over drogas.

Macedo derided the Spanish for having squandered the riches of their American empire by failing to develop technical and scientific skills. "Charles V liked to say that the Spanish seem prudent but are mad," he said, "and that the French seem mad but are prudent." Macedo explained that this was because "the Spanish had all of the materials, and disdained the Arts; and the French had no materials, but esteemed the Arts. The Spaniard thus sells raw materials to the Frenchman and buys finished products from the same, but at a greatly increased price. Who could not say, therefore, that one nation is barbarous and the other civilized, one insane, and the other wise?"[6] Macedo returned again and again to the question of drogas, for drugs were the most unique and valuable of the commodities to which the Portuguese could lay claim. Following the lessons of the French, Indies drugs could be rendered more valuable by the proper application of "art." East Indian cinnamon and cloves, Macedo explained, "are the greatest drugs, from which the Dutch receive enormous wealth." Producing these crops in the Maranhão, "with its short and easy navigation to Europe, at the same prices" would lead to the collapse of the commercial advantage upon which Dutch power rested.[7]

Macedo's plan was ambitious, but it was no fantasy. He shared his hopes with one of the most influential figures in the empire, the Jesuit padre António Vieira.[8] Vieira had been arguing for a strategic shift in priorities away from defending the failing Éstado da India and toward ecological projects that would effectively turn Brazil into a replacement of India. In a series of letters sent in 1675, Vieira reminded Macedo that spice transplantation had technically been banned by the royal decree of King Manoel in the 1510s, who sought to retain monopolistic control over goods like nutmeg and cinnamon by limiting their cultivation zones on pain of death.[9] The Jesuit advocated for abandoning this approach. He declared himself and Macedo to be "the true alchemists [*chimicos*] of Portugal" because "it seems to me that we have both discovered the Philosopher's Stone [in Brazil]." However, Vieira added sardonically, "like alchemists, we have profited little from it."[10]

In his memorandum, Macedo repeated Vieira's "philosopher's stone" language: "It seems to me we have discovered the Philosopher's Stone [*Piedra Filizophal*], for there is no doubt that if Brazil produces cloves, peppers, cinnamon, and all the most [valuable] plants that Nature yields, and which are cultivated in the East, then Brazil will come to provide greater riches, and fewer costs, than the Mines of Peru or Sofala."[11] These references to alchemists and philosophers' stones were more than metaphors. They reflected a direct connection between the colonial drug trade and the alchemical experimentation of the period. In this case, the key go-between was Ralph Montagu, who had recently become Queen Catarina's master of the horse after his elder brother had been dismissed from the post for "making amorous advances."[12] Montagu was a prominent patron of the Royal Society who maintained relationships with pivotal figures in the history of science, such as Robert Hooke and John Locke.[13] It was Montagu who had given Macedo a French translation of Thomas Sprat's *History of the Royal Society* (1667), which Macedo described as "a History of this Academy . . . whose mission is the discovery of secrets of Natural Philosophy via Chemical experiments, and to search out the reasons for all natural phenomena, which seem to us to come from occult causes [*causas occultas*]."[14]

This emphasis on discovering and explaining "occult causes" was a key point of contact between the history of drugs and the history of early modern science. Here, I hone in on links between members of the Royal Society of London and individuals in the Portuguese Empire to demonstrate the degree to which novel drugs from places like Brazil, Angola, and India served as catalysts for new developments in experimental science and medicine. Crucial aspects of the Scientific Revolution relied upon the convergence of new technologies (like the microscope) with cross-cultural exchanges of knowledge and materials, many of them drugs.[15] In arguing for the importance of drugs in early science, I am also highlighting the importance of individuals from the "drug underworld" (both Europeans and non-Europeans) in the mainstream narrative of the history of science. There is no group more emblematic in that history than the Royal Society. In the period we are dealing with, the Royal Society's presidents including Isaac

Newton, and their membership discovered the first cell and published what were, arguably, the first peer-reviewed articles.[16]

Medical experts from the Portuguese world played a vital role in contributing to a new culture of empiricism and experimentation around drugs.[17] But this was a role that Protestants, particularly in Britain, sought to conceal. If Protestant natural philosophers openly acknowledged their debts to Catholic, Iberian, or indigenous knowledge and materials, they exposed themselves to charges of credulity, impiety, and "Jesuitical" methods. On the other side, Jesuits, physicians, apothecaries, and traders in the Iberian empires risked inquisitorial and royal scrutiny if they publicly avowed "Northern" scientific doctrines.[18] Moreover, for Iberians and Britons alike, scientific engagement with drugs remained limited by fears of physical and mental harm resulting from the indigenous or "heathen" origins of novel substances from the Indies. By better understanding how natural philosophers like the members of the Royal Society of London encountered both inspiration and competition in the colonial drug trade, we also find that the Scientific Revolution was more global—and more druggy—than we once thought.

"A Very Speedy Way to Be Besotted"

Not long after he arrived in Machilipatnam, Thomas Bowrey began to wonder what it was the Machilitipatnamese were smoking.

The bustling port city on India's Coromandel Coast felt fantastical to the young East India Company merchant. During the first days of his visit in 1673, Bowrey marveled at wonders like "Venomous Serpents [which] danced" to the tune of "a Musicianer, or rather Magician," and "all Sortes of fine Callicoes . . . curiously flowred."[19] Above all, Bowrey was most fascinated by the effects of an unfamiliar drug. The Muslim merchant community in the city was, as Bowrey put it, "averse [to] . . . any Strong drinke." Yet, he noted, "they find means to besott themselves Enough with *Bangha*." They consumed this "Soe admirable herbe" in many forms, "but not one of them that faileth to intoxicate them to admiration." It could be chewed, made into a tea, or mixed with tobacco and smoked (this last technique, as we'll see in Chapter 5, was a recent innovation with far-reaching impact). Whatever the route of administration, Bowrey noted, this *bangha* was "a very speedy way to be besotted."

Bowrey initially compared the effects of the drug to alcohol. Yet it seemed that *bangha*'s properties were more complex, "Operat[ing] according to the thoughts or fancy" of those who consumed it. On the one hand, those who were "merry at that instant, shall Continue Soe with Exceedinge great laughter," he wrote, "laughinge heartilie at Every thinge they discerne." On the other hand, "if it is taken in a fearefull or Melancholy posture," the consumer could "seem to be in great anguish of Spirit." The drug seemed to be a kind of psychological mirror that reflected—or amplified—the inner states of consumers. Small wonder, then, that when Bowrey resolved to try it, he did so while hidden in a private home with "all dores and Windows" closed. Bowrey explained that he and his colleagues feared that the people of Machilipatnam would "come in to behold any of our humours thereby to laugh at us."[20]

Bowrey's account of the resulting effects is worth quoting at length:

It Soon tooke its Operation Upon most of us, but merrily, Save upon two of our Number, who I suppose feared it might doe them harme not beinge accustomed thereto. One of them Sat himself downe Upon the floore, and wept bitterly all the Afternoone; the Other terrified with feare did runne his head into a great Mortavan Jarre, and continued in that posture 4 hours or more; 4 or 5 of the number lay upon the Carpets (that were Spread in the roome) highly Complementinge each Other in high terms, each man fancyinge himselfe noe lesse then an Emperour. One was quarralsome and fought with one of the wooden Pillars of the Porch, untill he had left himself little Skin upon the knuckles of his fingers.[21]

Reckless self-experimentation with drugs is sometimes assumed to be a modern practice. Accounts like Bowrey's quickly disabuse us of this notion. Bowrey and his merchant friends were plainly interested in *bangha* (cannabis) as a recreational intoxicant, even if three of Bowrey's group seem to have found the experience to be less than optimal—to put it mildly.

Bowrey, who would later author the first English dictionary of the Malay language, was what his contemporaries called a "philosophical traveler."[22] His interest in *bangha* lay not only in its recreational value but also in its "curiosity" as a wondrous substance with hidden properties. He was also keenly interested in discovering substances with the potential to become commodified. However, converting a drug like *bangha* into a global commodity was not easy. As with Buytrago's bark, this drug was embedded in a local spiritual and cultural framework—Bowrey seems to have viewed it as a distinctively Muslim substance. In addition, Catholics and foreigners were becoming increasingly persecuted in the England of Bowrey's time, in part because of Catarina, the kingdom's deeply unpopular Portuguese Catholic Queen.[23] Portuguese and Muslim go-betweens nevertheless remained essential for British merchants seeking a foothold in the East Indies. Bowrey's primary contact in Machilipatnam had been "Petro Loveyro, an antient Portuguees," who Bowrey said he came to "[know] very well" and who may have played a role in Bowrey's introduction to bangha, along with Bowrey's Muslim bodyguard.[24]

Even if these racial and religious biases were overcome, a final challenge was in store for a drug like *bangha*. How to prove, conclusively, that it worked? As we'll see, assessing the "occult causes" of a drug's virtues became a signature goal of the Royal Society and of early modern natural philosophy as a whole. It was a goal buoyed by Iberian-mediated links to pharmacological knowledge in the colonies. But it was also one that depended on the *erasure* of these links. The sorts of witnesses that the Royal Society deemed trustworthy, after all, tended to be elite, Protestant, and British. Too strong a reliance on figures like Petro Loveyro, or Bowrey's unnamed bodyguard, was epistemologically unacceptable. On both a cultural and a chemical level, British scientists sought to "purify" pharmaceuticals of their Iberian, indigenous, tropical, colonial roots.

Medieval Christian and Muslim travelers such as Marco Polo and Ibn Battuta expected to find marvels along the edges of their mental maps, spinning tales of roc's eggs, "mellified man," or elixirs of life. Some medieval commentators even speculated that tropical drugs and spices were fragments from the Garden of Eden, making them both items of everyday commerce that were somehow also imbued with an aspect of the sacred.[25] In the sixteenth century, however, we encounter a new emphasis on the experimental investigation of Indies drugs, one spearheaded in the Portuguese empire by Garcia da Orta and in the Spanish by the physicians Nicolás Monardes and Francisco Hernández.[26]

As with the simultaneously occurring transformations in cosmology and physics, these works demonstrated a newfound interest in "explaining the appearances" of how wondrous tropical phenomena worked—not just reporting marvels, but seeking to demystify them. Francisco Hernández, for instance, lavished attention on describing the wonders of the drugs, poisons, and antidotes he encountered in the colony of New Spain. His was a totalizing mission—to document the natural history of Mexico in its entirety, and, by seeing the thousands of discrete naturalia involved as part of a larger system, to understand it in a new way.[27] Others focused on phenomena that broke down the boundaries of existing European epistemologies.[28] They fixated on fruits that could dissolve the iron in a knife, leaves with "miraculous" powers to poison or heal, and woods and stones that glowed in the dark.[29] Scientists today hunt for particles that disprove their theories of the fundamental laws of nature; early modern natural philosophers searched for drugs that did the same.

The key point of contact for introducing the mysteries of cannabis to England appears to have been not Bowrey but another English East India Company merchant, Robert Knox. In the 1670s, Knox fled from years of captivity in the kingdom of Kandy in the interior of Sri Lanka by piloting a stolen sloop along the Dutch-controlled coast. Parched with thirst and floating through hostile territory, Knox and a fellow escapee were forced to drink "[p]onds of rain water . . . so thick and muddy, that the very filth would hang in our Beards . . . by which means . . . we used often to be Sick of violent Fevers and Agues." Remembering his brush with death, Knox concluded that he would have died were it not for the anti-nausea effects of a certain South Asian antidote, the true identity of which—cannabis—the reader has perhaps already been able to guess. "At length we learned an Antidote and Counter-Poyson against the filthy venemous water, which so operated by the blessing of God, that after the use thereof we had no more Sickness," Knox would recall. "It is only a dry leaf: they call it in *Portugueze Banga* . . . and this we eat Morning and Evening upon an empty Stomach. It intoxicates the Brain, and makes one giddy."[30] *Banga* was a Sanskrit word, not a Portuguese one—hence Knox, like Bowrey, seems to have been drawing on a Lusophone go-between. After Knox reached London safely in September 1680, he retained a taste for this intoxicating "Counter-Poyson" and found a source able to procure it back home. We know this because, on November 7, 1689, Robert Hooke met with Knox at a London coffee house to obtain a sample of what Hooke called the "intoxicating leaf and seed, by the Moors called *Ganges*, in Portug[uese] *Banga*, in Chingales *Consa*." Hooke added in his diary that the drug was "accounted wholesome, though for a time it takes away the memory and understanding."[31]

On December 18, 1689, Hooke delivered a lecture to the Royal Society, describing his administration of the drug to an unnamed "patient" (perhaps Knox, or even Hooke himself).[32] "The Dose of it is about as much as may fill

a common Tobacco-Pipe," Hooke explained, although the route of administration he tested was to grind the leaves and seeds into a fine powder, then
chew and swallow them. The result, "in a short Time," was to "take away
the Memory and Understanding; so that the Patient understands not, nor
remembereth any Thing that he seeth, heareth or doth, in that Extasie but
becomes, as it were, a mere Natural, being unable to speak a Word of Sense;
yet is he very merry and laughs and sings and speaks . . . yet he is not giddy
or drunk, but walks and dances and sheweth many odd Tricks."[33] Despite
emphasizing this loss of "Understanding" and "Sense," Hooke's assessment
was positive. The drug, he explained, "is so well known and experimented
by Thousands, and the Person that brought it has so often experimented
with it himself," that "there is no Cause of Fear, 'tho possibly there may be
of Laughter." Hooke concluded by noting that he was currently attempting
to grow the seeds in London, and that "if it can be here produced" the plant
could "prove as considerable a Medicine in Drugs, as any that is brought
from the Indies."[34]

Hooke's note served as a terminal point for the colonial intellectual networks that carried drugs like cannabis into (and, at times, out of) the realm

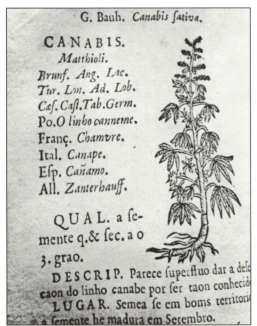

Figure 21. The entry for
Cannabis sativa in João
Vigier's *Historia das Plantas
da Europa, e das mais uzadas
que vem de Asia, de Affrica,
e da America* (Lyon, 1718). "It
seems superfluous to give a
description of *linho canabe*,"
Vigier writes, "because it is
so well known." However,
he mostly prescribes it
as an external treatment,
and doesn't describe it as
psychoactive. Courtesy of
the New York Academy of
Medicine Library.

of the "scientific." The first step in the chain was Hooke himself. As a commoner who served as an "experimentalist" for the more elite members of the Royal Society, Hooke was an "invisible technician" who worked in the shadow of scientific elites like Boyle and Newton.[35] Next in the chain were even more non-elite figures like Knox, who was noted by name in Hooke's diary but anonymized in the printed account. Then the Portuguese go-betweens like Pedro Loureiro, the "antient Portuguese" who guided Bowrey through the bazaars of Machilipatnam. And finally, the inhabitants of societies in which drugs like *Cannabis indica* and *Datura* were parts of everyday life—the people with the most to offer in terms of firsthand knowledge, but also the least likely to appear in the annals of science.

Amplifying the Virtues of Drugs

Hooke's excited remarks about *bangha*'s psychoactive effects reflected the high stakes of the search for how drugs worked. If powers to heal, cause sleep, alleviate pain, or cure melancholy could be *explained*, then who was to say that they couldn't also be *amplified*? Just as the microscope and telescope had expanded the natural limits of human vision, was it possible that the technological modification of psychoactive drugs could allow an expansion of other human senses and faculties? Francis Bacon, for one, devoted considerable time to questioning the nature of what he called the "secret virtue" that made drugs effective. His understanding of how medicines work is useful to us because it offers an illustration of a typical (and influential) seventeenth-century view.

For Bacon, both diseases and their cures could be transmitted, invisibly and at a distance, by a hidden force called "sympathy." Sympathy caused a mysterious entanglement between a substance's physical characteristics and its effects on body and mind. For instance, Bacon believed that roasted rabbit brains dissolved in wine could "strengthen the memory," that "the juice of a hedge-hog" was inherently "harsh and dry" owing to the prickles that had once adorned the deceased creature, and "that the heart of an ape worn near the heart, comforteth the heart . . . and that the same heart likewise of an ape, applied to the neck or head, helpeth the wit."[36] (Bacon, ever the impractical theorist, neglected to walk his readers through the logistics of how they might go about obtaining an ape heart or reliably secure it to their head.)

How were these sympathetic powers or virtues transferred? Some believed that invisible particles, or "atoms," radiated from disease- or health-giving substances and entered the body from a distance. For instance, Bacon argued that peony root, worn around the neck, could cure epilepsy because the particles comprising peony worked "by extreme and subtile attenuation" to lessen "the grossness of the vapors which rise and enter into the cells of the brain." Bacon also speculated about the inherited cognitive effects of excessive intoxication, noting that when a pregnant woman consumed tobacco or "strong drink immoderately," it "endangereth the child to become lunatick" because the intoxicating principles inherent in tobacco or alcohol were passed along to the child in her womb.[37] This, too, was an effect of sympathy.

Later in the seventeenth century, Paracelsans stressed the physical nature of qualities, including those associated with psychoactive drugs.[38] They envisioned these qualities as the invisible causes laying behind the "forces" that it was possible to observe directly. The chemical physician Daniel Sennert cited poisons and purgative drugs (of which the most famous in the seventeenth century was Brazilian ipecacuanha) as the prime examples of what he called "occult qualities." These, he wrote, "are not immediately known to the Sences." Instead, "their force is perceived mediately by the Effect, but their power of acting is unknown."[39] A drug could be known by its *end result* (effect) but might not be understandable or even perceivable through the senses. Sennert listed opium, peony root, and "the Nephritick Stone" as substances possessing "occult qualities" that were "known by experience to be really true."[40] An intoxicating and unexplainable drug like *bangha* or *dutra* became an object of natural philosophical interest because it possessed these same occult qualities, with a perceivable effect but mysterious mode of action.

Many writers seeking to understand the occult qualities referenced a the drug *mumia*, from which the contemporary English word "mummy" derives. In many (but not all) cases, this drug actually does appear to have included mummified human flesh.[41] Medicinal mummies sometimes hailed from Egypt—but also, as early modern druggists recorded, from Persia and Arabia. Other commonly cited substances with occult qualities included oriental and occidental bezoar, Peruvian balsam, and Indies ambergris. Many of the natural substances that most demanded scientific explanation, in short, hailed from places with an Iberian colonial footprint. As a result, some British merchants and philosophers who were interested in occult virtues established ties with Lusophone merchants, physicians, and apothecaries in the East and West Indies.

At the same time, medical practitioners in the Iberian colonies emulated the new trends of chemical medicine in Europe.[42] One of the most famous of these was the *Lapis de Goa*, an "artificial" version of a bezoar stone, which was invented by the Portuguese apothecary Gaspar Antonio in Goa in the middle decades of the seventeenth century. Semedo presented the drug as a "modern" innovation that was distinct from classical and medieval compound drugs like theriac: "These stones are not created by nature in the entrails of animals, but are artificially created from various ingredients, all of them chosen and known to have great cardiacal and bezoartical virtues."[43] These virtues, Semedo wrote, "proceed from the artifice with which these stones are created by a member of the Society of Jesus living in India . . . the stones being made by the hands of this Jesuit have singular virtues." In 1691, the Jesuit brothers who ran the Royal Hospital in Goa (which employed Gaspar Antonio as a lay apothecary) attempted to restrict sale of these bezoar-like "cordial stones" and license them using certificates of authenticity.[44] The stones were frequently counterfeited and sold in London in the 1680s and 1690s.[45] In his *Treasury of Drugs Unlock'd* (1690), John Jacob Berlu wrote of "*Goa Stones* (by some, not rightly called *Lapis Jasper Antonicus*)" composed of "seed-pearl, *Bezoar*, Gold, and other Ingredients.[46] The merchant John Ovington's report of his 1689 voyage to Surat included a substantial description of two different cordial stones produced by the Portuguese in India: the "Snake-stone," made of "Ashes of burnt Roots, mixt with a kind of Earth, which is found at Diu, belonging to the Portuguese" and the "deservedly fam'd Gasper Antoni, or Goa Stone." Ovington claimed that Europeans he met in India "carry always about them one of these Stones inclosed in a Heart of Gold . . . which hangs about their Necks."[47]

Drugs from the Portuguese world—both "simples" and compound remedies like the Lapis de Goa and the "Snake-stone"—emerged as a special interest of Robert Boyle and his circle in the years following the 1662 marriage alliance of Queen Catarina de Bragança and Charles II. The London physician Richard Griffith noted that his research arose out of his "being frequently importuned by Esq *Boyl* to make Experiments upon *Indian Simples*, and to give an Account of my Observation and Success to some London Physitians."[48] Hans Sloane also took a strong interest in ipecacuanha, the introduction of which into European medicine he credited to "an anonymous Portuguese, who lived in Brasil" and "whose book [fell] into the hands of the English."[49] In his work on hydrostatics, Boyle described a series of experiments on bezoar stones, nephritic stones, and "calculi humani" (concretions found inside human bodies). The work, Boyle explained, was inspired by Garcia da Orta, who he called "a famous physician, who practiced long in the East Indies, and who had better opportunity that any European had before him, to try the virtue of bezoar."[50] Boyle also described being approached by a London drug merchant to test the legitimacy of an artificial bezoar, which was likely a Goa stone: "I have seen a fair adulterate bezoar-stone so resembling the genuine, that a great price was set upon it," Boyle wrote. "But by being brought to me for my opinion, I made no doubt of it being counterfeit, from its appearing as heavy, as a mineral stone of the same bulk."[51]

Boyle was later tasked to "try ye goodness of a snakestone" from Queen Catarina herself. The queen had been given the medicine by the emissaries of the king of Siam during their 1684 visit to London. Boyle tested the stone's antidote effects by administering it to a dog that had been bitten by a viper but found it "void of virtues." However, the queen, "being not discourag'd at this disappointment was pleas'd to send me another of these Antidotes that came from ye same parte of ye East Indys." This time, the antidote worked, and Boyle recorded his "great satisfaction" at being able to report to Catarina that her drug was the genuine article.[52]

Buoyed by novel or intoxicating substances that flowed in from the Portuguese world, a kind of drug utopianism began to take hold in Restoration London. Boyle's private list of "desiderata" that he hoped natural philosophers might discover in the future is telling in this regard. The list included both "Potent Druggs to alter or Exalt Imagination, Waking, Memory, and other functions" and drugs that would allow "Freedom from Necessity of much Sleeping [as] exemplify'd by the Operations of Tea"—the same drug that, in Boyle's lifetime, had been introduced to England by Portuguese merchants.[53] Some have argued that the early Royal Society was hostile to the supposedly "medieval" notion of occult virtues. But, in fact, the meaning of "occult" shifted markedly in the seventeenth century.[54] Occult qualities had been regarded, in a medieval Aristotelian framework, as unknowable by mortal minds. They were "insensible," unobservable using the tools and senses of the sublunary realm.[55] The triumph of the microscope and the telescope upended this worldview.[56] So, too, did the global drug trade, which brought the preternatural substances of the Indies into the ambit of natural philosophical observation and experiment. Figures like Newton, Hooke, and Boyle may well have been hostile to an older definition of *occult* as insensible. But they were committed to a revised conception of occult virtues as forces hidden in nature that, though currently unintelligible, could be

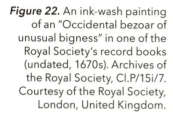

Figure 22. An ink-wash painting of an "Occidental bezoar of unusual bigness" in one of the Royal Society's record books (undated, 1670s). Archives of the Royal Society, Cl.P/15i/7. Courtesy of the Royal Society, London, United Kingdom.

subjectively sensed and potentially transformed into matters of fact through experiment and instrumental observation.

It is a coincidence, but a fitting one, that the "occidental bezoar," which appeared in Boyle's notes (Figure 22) resembles a telescopic view of a moon. In both cosmology and pharmacy, new technologies of analysis were making the previously invisible visible. In a memorandum on "specific medicines," Boyle wrote, "I am apt to think, that the future industry and sagacity of men, will be able to discover intelligible causes of most of those qualities, that now pass for occult."[57] Yet he also believed that many of the "specific virtues ascribed to medicines" were of such "uncommon textures" and "irregular motions" that even the most sensitive instruments might be incapable of detecting them. Instead, they would have to be theoretically deduced.[59] Boyle associated these "uncommon" qualities with Indies drugs, as a list of the specifics he mentions by name following this passage makes plain: Virginia snakeroot for poisons, Peruvian bark for fevers, a curious "stone" (an artificial bezoar?) that cured hemorrhages, Javanese scorpions, the Mexican "blood-stone" described by "the experienced Monardes," a mysterious "mortal poison" dispatched by "a young Negro woman of quality" in Africa, and even "the tooth of a true hippopotamus, or river-horse" that a former housemate of Boyle's wore around his neck to relieve "violent cramps."[59] Unlike the other occult qualities that fascinated figures like Boyle and Newton—the invisible powers of the lodestone, the force of gravity— these exotic *materia medica* were not always easily obtainable, and their legitimacy was difficult to verify.[60]

To probe the mysteries of exotic drugs, natural philosophers in London also had to tap into what was, to them, another variety of "occult" or concealed knowledge: the Catholic and indigenous pharmaceutical networks of the Iberian tropics.

Jesuits on Drugs

Explaining the changes in the revised second edition of his *Pharmacopea Lusitana* (1711), the Lisbon apothecary Caetano de Santo António noted a recent shift in his thinking about medicine: "Since the Northern nations have introduced chemistry it is evident that this important art [of pharmacy] is now very different than it was in earlier times." Thus, he wrote, "I have resolved to revise my *Pharmacopea Lusitana*, increasing the number of *receitas*, and modern theories, that may not have reached your notice owing to an incomplete knowledge of the different languages that the foreigners write in."[61] Santo António may have been trying to catch up with his rival, João Curvo Semedo, who cited "Roberto Boyle" six times in the revised second edition of his popular *Polyanthea Medicinal* (1704). Semedo even included quotations from Boyle in a section on "remedies which work by occult virtues or qualities."[62] By 1733, the Portuguese physician José Rodrigues Abreu was citing Francis Bacon to argue that coffee was a "stupefying" drug. And in 1728, the Lisbon physician Luis Caetano de Lima demonstrated his bona fides as a proponent of the new chemical medicine by compiling an exhaustive, three-volume "epitome" of the works of the controversial English physician (and Royal Society founding member) Thomas Willis.[63] Even as British natural philosophers were relying on Portuguese material networks to study the properties of novel drugs, their Portuguese counterparts were beginning to embrace the "Northern" chemical methods of the Royal Society.

In the decades following the Anglo-Portuguese alliance, Portuguese and British experts engaged in an intensive but largely hidden set of knowledge exchanges. These exchanges usually occurred through personal meetings and manuscripts rather than in print, due both to pressure from the censors of the Inquisition and anti-Catholic bigotry in England. Just as English chemistry was influencing medical writers in Lisbon, knowledge and materials from the Portuguese tropics were shaping natural philosophy in England. In August 1671, for instance, Henry Oldenburg, the secretary of the Royal Society of London, dispatched his "Inquiries for Brazil" to the Jesuit astronomer Valentin Stansel, an informant in Bahia who remained anonymous in the official Royal Society account.[64] The questions (collectively composed at a meeting of the Royal Society) highlighted the members' eclectic curiosity about tropical nature, inquiring about poisonous jellyfish, plagues, glow-worms, "fiery flying dragons," and native Brazilians who, "moved by affection," were reputed to "seize the bodies of parents not killed by poison and, having dismembered them, bury them inside themselves." Native knowledge of medicinal drugs was a central focus: "Are the older Brazilians excellent botanists," one question asked, "able with ease to prepare every kind of medicine," and to "seek after knowledge of diseases . . . according to some common intellectual principle?" Does the *murucuia-miri* plant "expel the afterbirth in a safe and pleasant manner?" What of ipecacuanha, already famous in England for "combating strongly every kind of poison"? Many drugs from South America had by this time been publicized through a series of treatises ranging from André Thevet's *Les singularitez de la France Antarctique* (1557) to Piso and Marcgrave's *Historiae Naturalis Brasiliae* (1648), and Arnoldus Montanus's *De Nieuwe en Onbekende Weereld* (1671). Much of the "Inquiries for Brazil" effectively sought to fact check the assertions made by earlier Dutch and Portuguese accounts of tropical nature.

Jesuits, merchants, and non-European informants from the Portuguese empire became important—albeit largely invisible—contributors to the Royal Society's mission. The Anglo-Irish diplomat Robert Southwell (Figure 23), was a specialist in forging these connections. In the 1660s, a now-septuagenarian Jesuit named Jerónimo Lobo (who we previously encountered, in Chapter 3, as a young missionary, nursing a fevered sailor off the coast of Africa), struck up an unlikely friendship with the gregarious Southwell. This was typical. Southwell seems to have made a habit of befriending Catholics with access to knowledge and encouraging them to exchange what he called "secrets" with Boyle and Oldenburg, the Royal Society's secretary.

In the fall of 1660, Southwell paid a visit to "a meeting of the *virtuosi*" in Florence (the Accademia del Cimento) and forged an acquaintance with the Accademia's eminent patron, the Cardinal Leopoldo de Medici. Southwell wrote to Boyle informing him of the Accademia's experiments, promising that "I am sure there will pass communication of great secrets between you."[65] As a taste, Southwell described a recent series of experiments attempting to extract and observe the "salts from all things" with the aid of a very early microscope ("by the help of glasses"). The Accademia had found, according to Southwell, "that [drugs] which afford the most sharp and edged salts, are of the fiercest operation in physic," a finding which may well have influenced Boyle's thoughts about the "uncommon textures" of certain psy-

Figure 23. A portrait of Robert Southwell still hangs in the manor he bought on his return from Lisbon. Geoffrey Kneller (c. 1680), Kings Weston House, Bristol. Courtesy of Wikimedia Commons.

choactive drugs. Southwell also referred to a box of Italian curiosities that he had earlier sent to Boyle, purchased from a curiosity cabinet owner in Bologna.[66]

In a subsequent letter from Rome the following spring, Southwell happily reported that "Father [Athanasius] Kircher is my particular friend, and I visit him and his gallery frequently. Certainly he is a person of vast parts. . . . He is likewise one of the most naked and good men that I have seen, and is very easy to communicate whatever he knows."[67] Although Southwell admitted that Kircher "is reputed very credulous, apt to put in print any strange, if plausible, story, that is brought unto him," Southwell deemed him to be "philosopher enough" and promised to give Boyle a detailed report of Kircher's answers to "all the questions you bid me ask him."

Southwell's friendship with the well-connected Kircher gave the Royal Society access to a global network of learned Jesuits. In late 1665, King Charles II sent Southwell to Portugal to negotiate a peace with Spain, and as he resided in Lisbon for the following three years Southwell continued to develop ties to the Society of Jesus and Portuguese imperial agents. During this time, Southwell encouraged Lobo to write in greater depth about the natural curiosities of east Africa, and by 1667 Southwell possessed a complete set of natural philosophical treatises written by Lobo and annotated by another Royal Society member and junior diplomat who worked alongside Southwell in Lisbon, Peter Wych.[68] These five treatises were decontextualized fragments from Lobo's extensive travels that carefully avoided extensive descriptions of Lobo's missionary activities. Instead, they emphasized the impartial relation of tropical naturalia, like unicorns and palm trees.[69]

Wych and Southwell nurtured clandestine contacts with the Jesuit community in Lisbon. Wych, for instance, reported to Oldenburg that he'd "engaged for a Correspondent in Philosophical Matters, the Professor of the Mathematicks at Lisbon, called Father John Marks, an English Jesuit." Marks facilitated the Royal Society's ties with Valentin Stansel, the Jesuit astronomer to whom Oldenburg would later direct his "Inquiries for Brazil."[70] By March 1668, Southwell had sent Lobo's manuscripts to Henry Oldenburg, along with two boxes of "divers curiosities" from Portugal, Brazil, and Angola, which Oldenburg wrote of excitedly to Boyle.[71] A year later, Southwell dispatched a letter from the German-Portuguese apothecary Gabriel Grisley proposing a plant exchange; the letter was accompanied by a bottle of Amazonian *copaiba* balsam, a Portuguese manuscript titled *Varias Receitas et Segredos da Medicina*, and an even larger set of medical and botanical curiosities from the Portuguese tropics.[72] At the May 20, 1669, meeting of the Royal Society, some of Southwell's finds were presented. They were likely from the same cache of artifacts documented in Nathaniel Grew's 1681 compendium of the belongings and curiosities of the Royal Society (*Musaeum Regalis Societatis*), which Grew had described as medicines of "the Portugal Negros" sent by Southwell from Lisbon. The cache included "Sagu"; "the Mallaca gum"; Poco Sempie, "a Golden Moss . . . accounted a great Cordial"; and Rizagon, a "root brought from Bengala, of good use."[73] As was often the case in early modern drug descriptions, the labels were hopelessly ambiguous: Precisely what "good use" did the root have? And was it from Bengala (i.e., Bengal) or from Benguela, the African slaving port? Likewise, it is entirely unclear what was meant by "Portugal Negros" as a descriptor. English travelers increasingly viewed Portuguese colonial spaces in racialized terms, and the term could just as easily have referred to the inhabitants of Malaysia or São Thome as it did of Africa.

We do, however, have more clarity on the origins of four drugs from Southwell's cache that were clearly identified as originating in Angola. The source for these may have been the Lisbon apothecary João Curvo Semedo, or, perhaps, one of Semedo's suppliers in Lisbon's Chiado district or the Alcântara docklands. (Semedo had boasted of his close ties to participants in the African slave trade, and he appears to have been the only seventeenth-century Iberian author to mention Southwell's "tooth of the beast emgala.")[74] These dispatches from Southwell and his Lusophone informants like Grisley, Lobo, and the anonymous apothecaries of Lisbon evidently drummed up an interest in the drugs of the Portuguese empire in London. Later that year, four apothecaries, including Hans Sloane's associate James Petiver and the queen's botanist Leonard Plunket, gathered at the Temple Coffee House in London to plan a newly updated subscription edition of Grisley's *Viridiarum Lusitanum*.[75]

In the earlier decades of the century, Lobo and Grisley had labored in the service of the Portuguese crown, with Lobo attempting to win converts and Grisley repeatedly petitioning King João IV to grant him funds to collect and grow "medicinal plants . . . for the good of the Kingdom."[76] Yet by the 1660s, both of these lifelong imperial servants found themselves working clandestinely with a charismatic Anglo-Irishman to send valuable natural knowledge of tropical drugs to the philosophers of London.

Decontextualizations of the Drug Trade

The Anglo-Portuguese exchanges explored here were obscured in the eighteenth century by both confessional antagonism between Protestants and Catholics and by emerging notions of racial difference. Duarte Ribeiro de Macedo had met with English natural philosophers and political leaders as an equal. Montagu was interested in how the Portuguese had managed to transplant oranges; Macedo was interested in English efforts to produce silk in Virginia. Both had a keen interest in transplanting drug and spice crops from the Old to the New World. Figures like Macedo, Southwell, Montagu, and Valentin Stansel moved within a cosmopolitan, "Republic of Letters" framework in which religious and national differences were, by and large, politely ignored. A mere generation later, the gap between British and Portuguese spheres of knowledge had widened considerably.

The anti-Catholic elements of the shift were already evident in the generation of Macedo and Southwell. The manuscript owned by the Royal Society identifies Lobo by name and calls him a "learned Jesuit." The members of the Royal Society even decided to send the "good old Jesuit Heironymo Lobo" (as Southwell referred to him) a formal letter of thanks.[77] Yet when Lobo's work reached print in November 1668 under the title *A Short Relation of the River Nile . . . and of Other Curiosities,* his name did not appear on the title page. Instead, the author was listed simply as "an eye-witness."[78] In his dedicatory epistle, Wych stated that the manuscript was procured "by the curious Sir Robert Southwell from an inquisitive and observing Jesuit at Lisbon" who offered a "candid relation of Matter of Fact . . . and Naturall Curiosities." But Lobo's identity had become anonymized, perhaps because of the Jesuit's fear of reprisals from either the Portuguese court or his own Order.[79] Even this carefully neutral packaging exposed the book to dismissal: an eighteenth-century British traveler to the same region of Ethiopia dismissed the author as "a lying Jesuit." As one historian has noted, in 1769 England, this epithet amounted to a "conclusive argument."[80]

From at least the early seventeenth century onward, European writers on foreign drugs had begun to express their disapproval in racialized terms. Although modern understandings of race did not yet exist at this time, there were already strong associations between blackness, corruption, enslavement, and heresy.[81] Writing in 1606, the French alchemist Joseph Duchesne attacked the newly imported medicine known as sugar by saying that it caused harmful heating of the blood, corruption of the teeth, and a "perpetual thirst" in those who used it "immoderately." "Even if sugar is white, beneath the whiteness it hides a great blackness of its own," he wrote, "just as there is beneath the sweetness a vast bitterness." It was a telling metaphor for an attack on a substance made by African slaves. Europeans began to think about mixed-race groups in the tropics in newly racialized terms. These individuals were increasingly imagined as having been "blackened" not only by the climate but by the results of rape and intermarriage between European and non-European ancestors. The Portuguese, being the most "antient" European colonists in Africa and the Indian Ocean—and among the most committed participants in the global slave trade—became a natural target for these early modern fears of a black planet.

The experience of the buccaneer William Dampier, who circumnavigated the world three times in the decades bookending 1700, is a good example of this shift. Dampier relied heavily on informants from the Portuguese world to gather knowledge of local medicinal drugs and safe anchorages, as well as linguistic and navigational expertise. But increasingly, he cast doubt on the status of these informants as Europeans, and hence as reliable witnesses. In the Philippines, for instance, Dampier met a local informant, who he "entertained for the sake of his knowledge in the several Languages of these Countries" but who he dismissed as "a kind of bastard Portuguese."[82] In the eastern Indian Ocean, likewise, again Dampier mentioned what he called a "mongrel Portuguese" who had joined the crew. Dampier's colleague Captain Cowley wrote similarly in his own travel account that he encountered at the Ilha do Sal in the Cape Verde archipelago off the coast of Africa "five Men upon the Island, *viz.* 4 Officers and one Boy to wait on them: One being a Governor, who is a *Mullatoe*; two Captains and one Lieutenant." To Cowley's eyes, "They were all black," but he noted that they "scorn to be counted any other than *Portuguese*; for if any Man call them *Negro's*, they will be very angry, saying, That they are white *Portuguese*."[83] Cowley did not agree.

In one of the most telling moments in Dampier's travels, a man on the same Ilha do Sal—which Dampier described as inhabited by "Portuguese *banditti*"—approached one of Dampier's crewmates with what he claimed was a lump of ambergris. Early modern doctors attributed compelling properties to this valuable substance, from an "alexipharmic" (anti-poison) power to the ability to intoxicate and cure melancholy.[84] Dampier's crewmate was intrigued and purchased the lump for "more than it was worth." "We had not a Man in the Ship that knew Ambergriese," Dampier confessed, "but I have since seen it in other places, and therefore am certain it was not right." (True ambergris, as Dampier later learned, is "very hard," odorless, and "of a lighter color.") Dampier realized that his friend had been tricked. The Portuguese *bandito* hadn't been selling ambergris at all: "Possibly 'twas some of their Goats Dung," the sea captain pondered.[85] As with the "impure" apothecaries like Maria Coelho, these inhabitants of the Portuguese tropics became increasingly invisible go-betweens in the drug trade.

In the 1630s British imperial theorists could see themselves as walking the same path to empire as the Portuguese. And in the 1660s, British consumers had adopted Portuguese tastes for tea and other Indies drugs. However, the anti-Catholic mania of late seventeenth century and early eighteenth-century Britain cast a pall over the prospect of directly engaging with Iberian and Catholic pharmacological knowledge. The British-Virginian physician John Tennent's treatise on "Northern People" in "Southern Climates," for instance, equated the dangers of tropical nature with the dangers of southern European Jesuits. This segued into an attack on a "Quack" who "in *Paris* became posses'd of two *Arcana*, which he stiled his *Pill and Drop*." Tennent wrote suspiciously that "there are many Conjectures about his getting them, amongst which the most probable one is, that a *Jesuit* there communicated them to him."[86] The implication was that a Jesuit origin for the quack's "Arcana" would automatically invalidate them as proper medicines for "Northern" bodies. In other words, if a tropical drug were going to be able to make the jump into European science, it needed to be carefully repackaged. As we will see in the next section, this was a process that combined scientific manipulation with a kind of proto-rebranding that often involved the erasure of a drug's origins. This practice became a key trait of the drug trade. Indeed, the legacy of these early efforts to "rebrand" a drug for new audiences continues all the way up to the present day, as claims to scientific legitimacy and of quackery continue to fixate on themes of purity, indigenous origins, and reliable witnessing.

The English Water of Doctor Mendes

Gathering medical knowledge from the Portuguese world meant associating oneself with Catholics, mestizos, and indigenous groups: associations that threatened the scientific credibility of the Protestant natural philosopher. The solution to this problem was to tacitly maintain ties to the global drug trade but to allow these ties to disappear when presenting to scientific publics. Medicines from the Goan apothecary Gaspar Antonio became merely "Antonios" or "stones" stripped of their specific pharmaceutical context, but retaining the "Indies" origin that made them fashionable.[87] The Portuguese world was key to British natural knowledge, but it was also critical (from the perspective of British merchants and authors) to obscure these origins.

A prime example of this process was the *Água de Inglaterra* ("English water"), a proprietary remedy for tertian (i.e., malarial) fevers developed by Fernando Mendes, a Portuguese-Jewish physician who traveled with Queen Catarina to England as part of her courtly entourage.[88] The preparation was derived from the Peruvian bark (*Cinchona officinalis*), which we encountered in Chapter 1. Although Peruvian bark commanded high prices, anyone who dared to sell so distinctly Jesuit-flavored a remedy in 1670s England exposed themselves to public suspicion. In his *Conclave of Physicians*, Gideon Harvey annotated Latin drug prescriptions with ribald commentary that compared the Indies drug-prescribing physicians of London to Jesuits, Cardinals, and Inquisitors. "Despair, despair, all is like to be lost. The Vessel is overloaden with Bark," Harvey wrote beneath one receipt that included quina, comparing the patient's body to an East India vessel. "The mischief is, there is no opening the hatches by a Purge, to let out the *Jesuit*."[89]

John Evelyn speculated in his diary that such negative opinions of quina arose "out of envy" among elite physicians because "it had been brought into vogue by Mr. Tabore, an apothecary."[90] Evelyn was referring to the treatment of King Charles II's 1685 malarial "ague" (which led to his death) by an obscure young apothecary named Robert Talbor who employed the use of quina despite protestations by some physicians that it was a dangerous Catholic medicine.[91] Talbor was a skilled self-mythologizer, and his narrative has shaped how later historians have written about the early history of the Agua da Inglaterra. But the Portuguese side of the story complicates matters. Although Fernando Mendes sent a now-lost set of *Reflexões sobre a virtude da água de Inglaterra* to the Portuguese crown in the early 1680s, the drug appears to have been popularized in Iberia by João Curvo Semedo.[92] Semedo's most popular work, *Polyanthea Medicinal* (first printed in 1697) recommended the drug no less than seventeen times, and he included several case studies detailing the drug's success with patients in his later *Medical Observations of One Hundred Extremely Serious Cases*.[93] Semedo even reformulated the drug with a patriotic twist. Among the proprietary remedies that he dubbed the "Curvian secrets" (*secretos Curvianos*) and sold from his house, Semedo included a remedy against "tertian" fevers that he called "Água Lusitana," which he admitted elsewhere was a tweaked version of the formulation of Mendes.[94]

Mendes is almost entirely forgotten in English-language scholarship and didn't appear in any contemporary printed works by British physicians. Yet Semedo seems to have regarded the Jewish physician, and not Talbor, as something of a medical celebrity and as the true inventor of the preparation.[95] In a ten-page "Manifesto . . . directed at lovers of health" that may have circulated as a pamphlet in Lisbon and was also often bound with Semedo's other medical works, Semedo defended his choice not to reveal his "Curvian secrets" because he was not yet as famous or rich as Fernando Mendes: "To those who complain that I have not revealed the composition of my sixteen secrets, as certain other Physicians have revealed their own: I reply that while it is true that they have revealed them, they only did so after being rewarded with great honors and praise: for instance, Fernão Mendes, for revealing his *agua das cezões* [i.e., Agua de Inglaterra] the Kings Dom Pedro II of Portugal and Louis XIV of France gave him sixty thousand cruzados."[96] Semedo was mistaken. Although Mendes may have received a cash gift from Pedro II, it was the Englishman Robert Talbor—and not Mendes—who Louis XIV showered with riches.[97] Today, Mendes is forgotten, whereas the colorful Talbor tends to have a prominent walk-on part in the numerous popular histories of malaria, quinine, or tonic water.[98]

In truth, neither Talbor nor Mendes can be credited with any major innovation. Quina bark taken as a powder was already in wide use as a treatment for tertian fevers in Europe by the 1650s and 1660s. What made the Água de Inglaterra and Talbor's "English remedy" different is that both preparations called for the bark to be infused within wine or spirits. Because quinine, like many alkaloids, is soluble in alcohol, this practice likely increased the bioavailability of the drug and gave it a longer shelf life.[99] But this was hardly a stroke of genius: infusing a plant-based remedy in spirits or wine was among the most common preparations used by early modern apothecaries. An anonymous flyleaf annotation by a French nobleman who claimed to have taken the cure direct from Talbor in Flanders described him as "a very poor man" who had simply administered a "powder steeped in a

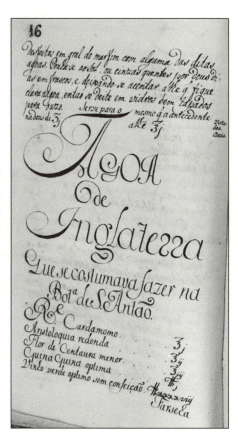

Figure 24. A 1750s recipe for "Agoa de Inglaterra" as was "customarily made in the apothecary shop of San Antonio," from "Collecção de varias receitas de segredos particulares des principaes boticas da nossa companhia de Portugal, da Índia, de Macao e do Brasil" (1766), Manuscript Opera Nostrorum, 17, ARSI, Rome. Courtesy of the Archivum Romanum Socictatis Iesu, Rome.

large glass of white wine." The annotator added: "It was very surprising to find out that it was nothing more than Quinaquina well disguised. . . . One cannot imagine the confusion of the King's physicians, whom he had made great fun of, as was his way."[100]

Talbor's rhetorical flourishes were more original than his cure. In his book *Pyretologia* (1672), the apothecary wrote mysteriously of his remedy containing "three Herculean Medicines," each "requiring twelve . . . labors in their preparations" and shrewdly warned his readers away from "Jesuits Powder . . . for I have seen most dangerous effects follow the taking of that Medicine."[101] Talbor intentionally obscured the fact that his *own* recipe depended on consuming very large quantities of "Jesuit's powder." This fact only became widely known in the final year of his life, when his so-called *remède Anglois* was published—initially at the behest of Louis XIV and thereafter by a number of printers capitalizing on the cure's popularity—in a confusing profusion of editions attributed to at least four authors and involving an array of different ingredients. (See Figure 24 for an example of one recipe.)[102]

It is reasonable to assume that Mendes adapted his recipe for Agua de Inglaterra from this printed source.[103] Yet Mendes's position as one of the royal physicians raises the possibility that the reverse was true. It is possible that Talbor obtained knowledge of quina from Mendes or perhaps from another émigré Iberian physician at the English court, then appropriated it as a secret preparation sold not by a Catholic foreigner but by a homegrown Anglican apothecary. It would not be the last time that a controversial drug was successfully "rebranded" in this way.[104]

In Portugal, likewise, it was not Mendes but the more well-connected physicians João Curvo Semedo and, still later, the Royal Society member Jacob de Castro Sarmento who would transform Agua de Inglaterra into the blockbuster remedy that it became in the eighteenth century.[105] The mingled character of the "English water"—which combined a tropical drug from the New World with clever drug marketing and the veneer of scientific authority—stands as an example of the ways that science, race, and consumer demands allowed early modern drugs to be rebranded, their original identities altered. These erasures associated with the scientific study and analysis of drugs had far-reaching influence. With the benefit of hindsight, we could say that it marked the beginning of a process that leads directly to the transformation of Bowrey's "Muslim" bhang into Mexican marijuana, or California cannabis.

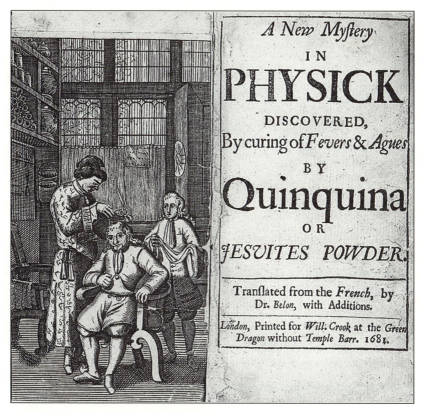

Figure 25. The frontispiece engraving of the English translation of one of several quina-promoting books inspired by Talbor's in 1681, which may depict a barber in an East Indies locale, despite the drug's South American origins. Courtesy of the John Carter Brown Library.

From Apothecaries to Pharmacies

This pattern continued to play out throughout the eighteenth and nineteenth centuries. "Quina-like" anti-fever drugs originating in Portuguese America had become common by 1800.[106] However, it was not until the 1810s and 1820s, with the rise of chemical processes designed to isolate the active principles of drugs, that savants began to draw conclusive distinctions between Peruvian quina and quina from Brazil.[107] Breakthroughs in chemistry allowed scientists of the 1820s to isolate a certain class of bioactive chemical compounds present in many plants—called alkaloids— that conferred their medicinal or psychoactive properties. By measuring the alkaloidal content of different plants purported to be quina, chemists of the

1820s were finally able to determine conclusively whether a plant sample was "true" quina (*Cinchona officinalis*) or a related species. Although two French chemists are popularly credited with synthesizing quinine in 1820, the Luso-Brazilian surgeon Bernardino António Gomes identified the same alkaloid in 1811, calling it *cinchonin*. His discovery was the culmination of two decades of close observation of how Brazilian fever patients responded to Peruvian, Brazilian, and other varieties of quina.[108] Given the prolonged research surrounding the identification of the alkaloid, it is no coincidence that this, one of the first alkaloids ever isolated, was derived from the quina plant—nor that the discoverer was a Portuguese naval surgeon with long experience in the Brazilian tropics.[109] It is also not surprising that Gomes, the colonial surgeon, became forgotten in place of two scientists based in Paris, an imperial metropole.

The Royal Society, as a preeminent scientific institution of the era, has typically been portrayed as a conduit by which "science" flowed to Portugal.[110] It is true that by the mid-eighteenth century the Portuguese state (now under the control of the Anglophilic Marquês de Pombal) made concerted attempts to reform Portuguese medicine along the empiricist lines originally articulated by British, French, and Dutch scientists and physicians—and by Macedo. Yet these exchanges went in both directions. Robert Boyle eagerly collected, experimented upon, and wrote about *drogas* from Brazil, Africa, and Goa. Henry Oldenburg solicited the botanical knowledge of a Jesuit in Brazil. Philosophical travelers from Bowrey to Dampier relied at every turn on the local knowledge of Lusophone creoles and *mestiços*. British medical consumers eagerly sought out "stones" that were the invention of a Jesuit apothecary in Goa, while a Portuguese Jewish physician's tinctures of South American quina emerged as a cure fit for kings.

Like the hidden virtues in drugs, the connections explored here were difficult to quantify, productive of scientific knowledge as well as of scientific confusion. Unstable and unreliable though they were, exchanges among natural philosophers, apothecaries, and drug merchants in the British and Portuguese worlds played an important role in turning drugs from curiosities and commodities into objects of scientific interest. By the middle decades of the nineteenth century, using methods not dissimilar from those of Boyle, chemists could perform mass extractions of quinine and repackage it as a pill or clear liquid (or, indeed, as a cocktail, the gin and tonic) rather than as a bitter, unreliable, and indigenous tropical bark.

The goal was the reformulation of an Indies drug into something new, a proprietary remedy with a memorable brand name: in short, a pharmaceutical. The result, ultimately, was the formation of a truly massive commercial force that would come to be known, collectively, as the modern pharmaceutical industry. It marked a revolution not just in the business but in the epistemology of drug taking. From a chaotic world of stuffed alligators, Venetian treacle, curiosity cabinet-like shops, and enslaved plantation laborers, we now begin to approach the pristine sterility of the pharmacy.

CHAPTER 5

The Uses of Intoxication
in the Enlightenment

Oh Tom! such a Gas has Davy discovered! the Gazeous Oxyd! oh Tom!
I have ha[d] some. it made me laugh & tingled in every toe & finger tip.
Davy has actually invented a new pleasure for which language has no
name. oh Tom! I am going for more this evening . . . Tom I am sure the air
in heaven must be this wonder working gas of delight.

—ROBERT SOUTHEY TO THOMAS SOUTHEY, JULY 12, 1799

Intoxication is universal. Or, at least, altered mental states are. As philosophers of consciousness like to point out, our experience of our own continuous mental awareness—our sense of *me*-ness—is an illusion.[1] Every night we experience a break in our train of conscious experiences, or "qualia," as we confront the final, hypnotic moment before sleep. Even in waking life, our consciousness ranges across a vast landscape of potential states.[2] We experience something akin to intoxication every time we have a feeling of terror, or sublime beauty, or deep love. Our sense of our own conscious experiences may be utterly transformed by illness. Indeed, it can change when we simply skip a meal or two.

Humphry Davy, an aspiring chemist from the West of England just out of his teens, prized his reason above all other things. But, paradoxically, it was Davy's discovery of a novel source of *irrationality*—"a new pleasure for which language has no name"—that first gave him entry into the realm of elite science.[3] The "Gazeous Oxyd" that Davy studied in the final year of the eighteenth century was so different from other intoxicants as to be a revelation.[4] It seemed impossible that a mere gas, invisible and odorless, could induce such profound mental transformations (Figure 26).

Nitrous oxide, as the gas came to be known, would only later become a prosaic tool of dental appointments. In Davy's laboratory in Bristol, as the Age of Reason morphed into something else, the drug seemed like a profound discovery, a substance that opened terrifying new vistas of the mind. It was in some ways the fulfillment of what the alchemists had long sought: the transformation of matter into something that transforms the soul.

This, at least, is how it seemed at first. The experience of nitrous oxide is momentarily revelatory, yet ultimately shallow. It is like hearing the opening phrase of a monumental symphony, except the same notes repeat again and again and again. Davy and his companions, including Coleridge, slowly confronted the fact that this new drug was not a pathway to enlightenment. It was just another intoxicant. The gas was the newest entry in a ledger that had been successively enlarged since the sixteenth century. Davy's announcement marked the globalization of a new psychoactive drug. It was one preceded by tobacco, laudanum, cannabis, gin, and countless others. It would soon be followed by morphine and cocaine.

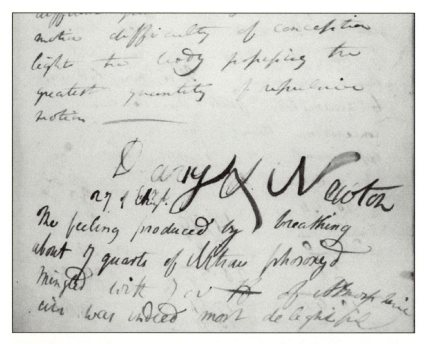

Figure 26. A page from Sir Humphry Davy's lab notebooks written under the influence of nitrous oxide, 1800. Royal Institution MS HD/13c. Courtesy of the Royal Institution, London, UK.

As we have seen, new ways of altering mental states spread around the globe in the seventeenth and eighteenth centuries. Previous chapters of this book have looked at these movements from the perspective of colonialism, commerce, spirituality, and science. This chapter tries to go inside the heads of consumers: what did it *feel like* to be a user of psychoactive drugs in the seventeenth and eighteenth centuries? From peyote in Mesoamerica and ayahuasca in Amazonia to nitrous oxide in Bristol, the euphoric, delirious, or simply *altered* subjective experience offered by novel intoxicants became part of the fabric of everyday life.

This shift was not restricted to any one country or social class. If the sixteenth and seventeenth centuries were the key periods in which new food crops, diseases, and domesticated animals became global forces, then the eighteenth century was the era in which novel mind-altering substances became widely available to the common person—not just to the denizens of London's Gin Lane but to untold millions in North and South America, sub-Saharan Africa, China, and Southeast Asia.[5] Like a new compound produced in a chemical reaction, intoxication itself was refigured by the joining together of concepts and methods of mental alteration from Africa, Asia, the Americas, and Europe.

Before going further, it will be helpful to clarify what I mean by "intoxication." The focus here is on substances that are often classified in the present day as narcotics or hallucinogens: drugs that significantly transform subjective mental states in a manner similar to (but, as we will see, sometimes very different from) drunkenness. At the time, grappling with how these transformations worked prompted new ideas and new questions. Did the devil create these experiences, or did gods, or something else altogether? Which types of altered mental states are compatible with socially acceptable behavior and "civilized" societies? Why are some forms of intoxication so prized that they become compulsions or addictions? Could this abuse be prevented by changing the nature of the substances themselves—and, if so, what did this say about the workings of the human brain?

And, floating above it all, the question of profit. Who benefited from the globalization of intoxication, and at what cost? Intoxication didn't just offer the promise of poetic revelation or freedom from worldly cares. It was worth money—lots of it.

For some time now, historians have recognized that a series of important changes in cultures of intoxication around the world took place during the eighteenth century. In the "native ground" of the North American interior, alcohol traded by French and British merchants fundamentally destabilized indigenous American social structures.[6] In colonial Angola, new, high-proof varieties of rum and *cachaça* altered West Central African religious and social life.[7] In China, the rise of opium smoking was "facilitated" by the earlier spread of New World tobacco at the hands of Portuguese merchants and other long-distance traders.[8] And in Iran, the water pipe, or hookah, opened new opportunities for blending opium, hashish, and other smokable psychoactive drugs.[9]

These were not isolated changes. They weren't even restricted to the realm of drugs: the decades bookending 1700 witnessed an increasingly global circulation of all sorts of "exotic" material goods, from maps and clothing and weaponry to medicines and foods.[10] It's a shift that we can see in paintings of the period, with their Canadian beaver hats, Chinese silks, and Amazonian animals.[11] Intoxicating substances, however, played a special role in this transformation in the world of goods: they were uniquely destabilizing to subjective mental states, and thus uniquely morally suspect.

The genre of *singerie* paintings, popular in the commercial centers of the Low Countries, toyed with these themes. In these paintings, we find monkeys drinking and smoking to excess. But their gluttony for novel intoxi-

Figure 27. David Teniers the Younger, *Monkey Trick* (c. 1670?). Courtesy of the Royal Museum of Fine Arts, Antwerp.

cants is matched by their greed for all sorts of other material signs of wealth, from fine clothing to tulips (Figure 27).

The singerie genre gives us a hint of how intoxicating substances fit into a larger panorama of social change. Mind-altering substances like tobacco, laudanum, and gin were simply one among a host of addictive and euphoria-inducing options available to consumers in the decades bookending 1700, from gambling and printed pornography to tulip-collecting and dueling. But the monkeys tell us a story that joins together these goods around the theme of intoxication and addiction. They are, in a sense, slaves: slaves to their desires, to their new material possessions. And it would not have been lost on early modern viewers that slaves and other colonial subjects made this material revolution possible.[12]

The singerie paintings introduce an important theme of this chapter. Intoxicants caused social instability insofar as they differed from prior acceptable norms of intoxication. In the context of Africa and Europe, for instance, alcoholic intoxication had a millennia-old tradition of use as a social aid, religious sacrament, and medical treatment. Although the introduction of alcoholic spirits to indigenous cultures of North America marked a qualitative shift in the available palette of mind-altering substances, this was not the case in Angola, where palm wine had a deep history. In European depictions of intoxication, the moral condemnation was not directed toward drunkenness itself—for habitual alcohol use was nearly universal in medieval and early modern Europe—but against the irrational devotion to "novelty," whether it came in the form of Virginia tobacco or Spanish wine.[13] By contrast, the effects of Mesoamerican entheogens were qualitatively different from alcoholic intoxication. There was no pre-trodden pathway to fit a drug like peyote into the European social order. Entheogens became "tools of the devil" rather than potential saleable commodities like chocolate or tobacco, which were ultimately able to overcome their original stigma in Europe.[14]

No less than the singerie apes, natural philosophers like Davy were also drawn toward novel intoxicants. Intoxication, for a relatively short time during the late seventeenth and the eighteenth centuries, became socially acceptable as an epistemic tool for natural philosophers, even if those intoxicants could not be broadly commodified. Hooke kept a careful drug diary that included regular use of opiates.[15] Other members of the Royal Society and its French, Italian, and Iberian counterparts did not hesitate to test narcotics on themselves, right up to the time of Friedrich Sertürner, the chemist responsible for isolating morphine, in 1804.

However, this era was relatively short lived, and self-limiting. A culture of self-experimentation made sense in a world in which natural philosophers sought to enlarge their sensory tools and mental understanding through any means necessary, effectively turning their own bodies into scientific instruments. The globalization of new varieties of intoxication became one of the enduring legacies of the so-called Age of Reason. At the same time, these same substances were denounced as causes of irrationality. One exception that proved the rule was the case of James Young Simpson, a Scottish physician. Simpson's reckless decision to test chloroform (a highly potent neurotoxin) as a potential anesthetic in 1847 led to fame in his lifetime but ignominy forever afterward. The chloroform clearly had intoxicating effects. Simpson was said to have tested it on himself, ultimately collapsing in an "unwanted hilarity" and fallen unconscious. Upon waking, it was later claimed, he remarked "This is far stronger and better than ether."[16] However, Simpson billed the drug not as an intoxicant but as a surgical anesthetic, and he downplayed both its poisonous properties and its psychoactive effects.

Simpson's use of chloroform pointed to one of the only possible avenues for the use of intoxicants in a nineteenth-century scientific setting: surgical anesthesia. The vast vistas of the mind unlocked by certain psychoactive drugs had to be reduced to a simple "on" or "off" switch for consciousness in order to make intoxication palatable to modern science and medicine.

Deep Histories of Intoxication

Here we will focus on specific instances when different understandings of intoxication met one another and the new cultural formations that resulted from these meetings. Intoxication was a potent driver of cultural change in the Old World, particularly Europe and South Asia. Their default mode of intoxication—the use of alcohol—proved to be a potent cultural barrier when it came to understanding alternatives. It was a frontier that proved difficult to cross: even after Europeans had moved into Mesoamerica, they appear to have found it difficult to inhabit the mental space that allowed them to see indigenous entheogens as anything other than sources of either drunkenness or witchcraft.

The strange story of an Indian sultan who used opium and cannabis candies to travel to Mexico in his sleep offers an example of these epistemological barriers. The account is from a European—Garcia da Orta, the

Portuguese Jewish apothecary whom we've met in previous chapters—and we have every reason to believe that da Orta's own cultural biases colored his retelling. The sultan Bahadur of Gujarat, da Orta wrote, explained to a Portuguese colonial administrator around 1535 that "when at night he wanted to go to Portugal or Brazil or Turkey or Arabia or Persia, he did not have to do anything more than eat a little cannabis [*bangue*]" rolled into an electuary along with sugar, nutmeg, mace, camphor, and opium.[17] But da Orta only told the story in brief. As he put it, the cannabis and opium electuary was "not one of our medicines, and we should spend no more time on it."

What did da Orta mean by this?

As a factual matter, opium and cannabis had been part of Western medicine since before there was a West. But there was a kernel of truth in da Orta's claim. Prior to Coleridge and Thomas de Quincey, Europeans typically did not conceptualize opium as a gateway to profoundly altered mental states, much less hallucinatory dreamscapes. Likewise, European accounts of cannabis almost entirely recommended topical use for such things as joint pain. Many early modern applications of the drug depended on modes of administration (like topical application on the skin) that did not allow the most biologically active opioid alkaloids and cannabinoids to cross the blood-brain barrier. Barring a few exceptions (Herodotus described Scythian warriors who threw hemp leaves and seeds on braziers and "howled with laughter" as they inhaled the smoke), I have found little recognition of the psychoactive properties of the smoke of cannabis in early modern European sources.[18]

This was, perhaps, partially because western Eurasian variants of the plant were much lower in psychoactive compounds like THC than those that were cultivated in South and Central Asia. Overall, it would seem, medieval and early modern European cultures enjoyed a far more limited relationship with altered mental states than did those of South Asia or Africa.[20] There was, of course, one important exception: alcohol. As we'll see, alcohol intoxication exerted a powerful influence over "epistemologies of intoxication" throughout Europe. This stood in contrast to Muslim and South Asian experiences with intoxication, which were less focused on only one substance. Few words for intoxication existed in European languages beyond those used to describe drunkenness. For instance, an Arabic or Farsi speaker might elect to describe Bahadur's dream using an archaic meaning of the word *kayf*, implying an opiate-derived high or pleasure, distinct from alcohol intoxication.[21] For Europeans, he was simply drunk.

Europeans did, in fact, possess a very well-developed notion of hallucinations, altered states, and transcendent experiences. However, these were almost entirely filtered through the expression of Christian religious devotion. Acolytes in the Society of Jesus, for instance, underwent intense spiritual trials that could induce deeply altered mental sates. Among early modern Catholic religious orders, claims of intense hallucinations were practically routine. St. Teresa de Ávila promoted a mystical form of "mental prayer" in which the rational mind gave itself over to the workings of the Holy Spirit. For Teresa, this included the vivid experience of an angel thrusting a flaming golden spear into her heart.[22] St. Martin de Porres, born to an African mother in Lima, Peru, in 1579, followed in the astral footsteps of the sultan Bahadur, "bilocating" from Lima to Mexico City in addition to Kyoto and Manila.[23] But these were the product of divine (or demonic) inspiration. To attribute such marvels to the ingestion of a drug (or even to *any* cause beyond the supernatural) was, for early modern Christians, unacceptable meddling in a domain that belonged to the divine.

Persian and South Asian medical traditions did not draw the same distinctions between the medical/material and the spiritual/immaterial, with mystics in both Sufi and Vedic traditions practicing forms of "divine intoxication" that often had a material basis in psychoactive substances.[24] The oldest Vedic scriptures, dating from about 1700 BCE, speak of a sacred drug called "sauma" or "soma" that was ritualistically consumed as part of the worship of the God Indra. In a series of digs in the late 1980s and early 1990s, the Soviet archaeologist Viktor Sarianidi uncovered evidence of ritualized drug use in a temple complex in Margiana, a site associated with the earliest Indo-Iranic migrations to the Indian subcontinent around 1900–1700 BCE.[25] Chemical analysis of deposits on stone mortars and pestles at the site showed traces of opium poppies, cannabis, and ephedra. These paleobotanical findings point to a series of encounters with intoxicating drugs stretching back four millennia in South Asia. From the Bronze Age to the present, intoxication in the Indian Ocean world has appeared in a multitude of guises but with one constant: the use of psychoactive substances in a spiritual context. This differed fundamentally from Christian traditions, which (with the important exception of Communion wine) tended to strictly demarcate medicinal or recreational use of intoxication substances from the immaterial intoxication of spiritual states.

The "South Asian complex" of diverse styles of intoxication spread widely. Cannabis, for instance, appears to have been brought into India during Vedic-era migrations, and carried out of it by merchants of the Indian Ocean world. A Portuguese missionary named João dos Santos, for instance, noted that the peoples of what he called "Ethiopia oriental" (Southern and Eastern Africa) used cannabis for its intoxicating effects. The local word that dos Santos identified with the drug, *bangue*, strongly suggests a transmission of cannabis culture from South Asia via the Indian Ocean trade, a movement backed by archaeological evidence.[26] Recalling his experiences of the late 1580s and the 1590s, dos Santos wrote that the southern African people he called the Cafres "dry the stalks and leaves [of *bangue*], and after they are well-dried they turn them into a powder, and this they eat . . . and so they grow very satisfied, and with comfortable stomachs." Dos Santos primarily discussed the plant as a tool for avoiding eating, but he noted that "if they eat much at a time, they become drunk in just the same way as if they had drunk a great deal of wine."[27] Fifty years later, the first governor of the Dutch colony at the Cape of Good Hope recorded a similar observation but identified the drug of choice among the so-called Cafres as *daccha*. This could refer either to cannabis (from the Khoikhoi term *dachab*) or to the psychoactive dagga plant (*Leonotis leonurus*). He described a "dry herb which the Hottentots chew and which makes them drunk," but which also resembled opium in its effects.[28] Dagga, cannabis, and calabar bean all figured in the divination and healing work of the *nganga*, and their work became subsumed under the Luso-African category of *feitiçaria*.

Europeans balked at any such "spiritualization" of intoxication derived from physical substances. But this wasn't the only difference between these two Old World drug complexes. Another distinction involved what I am calling the "normative model of intoxication." As we saw with the case of Bowrey in Machilipatnam, European traders were more than willing to partake in the use of novel intoxicants like *bangue*. But they lacked a substantive mental category for making sense of these and other new forms of intoxication: a substance was either "like wine" or "like opium." Perhaps if one were to present an Aztec with intoxicants that had been foreign to pre-Columbian Mesoamerica (such as gin, cannabis, and opium) they would have sorted them into categories based on the socially acceptable psychoactives available to their own culture; for example, this one is "like peyote," the other one "like tobacco."

When an intoxicant passes from one society into another, in other words, it must confront a mental model of intoxication predicated on past experience with other mind-altering drugs. If a drug is sufficiently similar to an existing variety of intoxicant, then it can be integrated; if it is too different in its effects, however, it runs the risk of being attacked as a poison.

Challenging the Normative Model of Intoxication

Historian David Courtwright, writing about the vast array of psychoactive substances in use in the pre-Columbian Americas, called it a "psychelic Eden."[29] But as he noted, most of these substances failed to become global commodities. With the notable exception of tobacco and chocolate, these drugs fell prey to the notion embedded in the word *intoxication* itself: *toxic*. When new psychoactives circulated during the era of the Columbian Exchange, their critics often resorted to labeling them poisons. King James of England, for instance, portrayed tobacco as a foreign invader that had poisoned the "body" of England itself. The king, as the "proper physitian" of that body, sought to heal the damage caused by this new toxin by fighting against the "stinking and unsavorie" habit of tobacco smoking.[30] Likewise, the Mughal emperor Jahangir's personal physician advised that the "foreign" drug be banned because he deemed it to be a poison.[31] In the case of drugs like tobacco, chocolate, and coffee, such calumnies failed to sink in. Although tobacco was initially thought of as a poison in both Europe and several other parts of the Old World (such as the Mughal court under Jahangir), within a single generation it had become naturalized from Iceland to India.

One reason for this change had to do with the differing psychoactive properties of the drugs in question. Tobacco and chocolate are relatively mild; other New World drugs, like peyote, can be massively destabilizing from both a psychological and a physical perspective. They were, perhaps, simply too experientially different from drunkenness to be integrated into a European model of acceptable mental and physical states. However, encounters with extreme forms of mental alteration ultimately led to changes in how intoxication was theorized by Europeans. The "normative" model, which referenced the most common intoxicant in a region to explain the effects, was no longer sufficient to differentiate between substances as diverse as tobacco, cannabis, and laudanum. It was not enough to say that they made one drunk. A new epistemology of intoxication was needed. Drinkers who, in centuries past, had only low-alcohol substances like beer or palm wine to drink now had high-proof spirits. Patients who may have once been prescribed ordinary opium could now select from a range of different opiate medicines with outlandish claims and attractive names.[32] The manufacture

and consumption of intoxication became enmeshed in an emerging capitalist order, one that demanded constant novelty. Intoxicants comprised an
under-recognized part of what historian Jan de Vries calls the "Industrious
Revolution," a steady increase in the buying power and "household economy" of European workers in the two centuries preceding the more famous
Industrial Revolution.[33]

The eighteenth century witnessed a new way of thinking about psychoactivity—not as a mysterious process or a supernatural power but as the
logical result of physical encounters occurring within the body. Inspired by
the new diversity of drugs available on a global stage, thinkers began to develop a more nuanced view of intoxication that depended on mechanistic or
"corpuscularian" principles.[34] Humoral reasoning had relied on a parallel
between the visible world of everyday chemical reactions and the invisible
realm of body and mind. But these new "mechanical" or corpuscularian
thinkers, such as Boyle and Sennert, took this a step further. They used elaborate, mechanistic theories of acids and alkalis, or sharp and soft particles,
to make judgments about the psychoactive effects of specific drugs. Aided

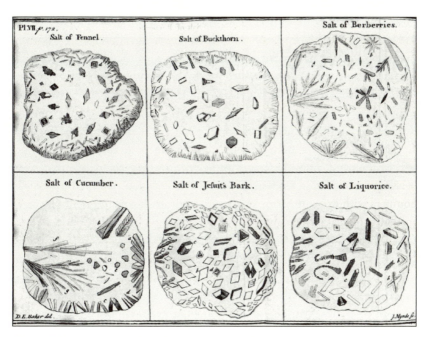

Figure 28. "Sharp" particles of substances, as depicted in Henry Baker, *Employ-
ment for the Microscope, in Two Parts* (London, 1753). Courtesy of the Wellcome
Library.

by the ability to observe drugs under a microscope (Figure 28), physicians were able to develop a new vocabulary for imagining why some drugs had negative effects on mind and body, yet proved to be compulsively reusable. Addiction and intoxication were now potentially knowable on a physical level, as a result of physical particles that blocked or otherwise altered the mechanical workings of the body. It was the fulfillment of Boyle's hope that "occult" qualities of drugs would one day be revealed by science.

The older humoral theory of early modern medicine drew a clear line between narcotic medicines—mind-altering drugs that were dominated by a single "quality"—and "compound medicines" in which the effects of an individual substance like opium had been carefully balanced against those of other ingredients. The "atomistic" approach to understanding intoxication as a material action of particles within the brain, which became more popular in the second half of the seventeenth century, made this distinction more ambiguous. It emphasized individual constituent particles, taken as "specifics," rather than the total combined effect of an apothecary's "compound." In 1604, the French atomist Joseph Duchesne conjectured that opium induced sleep because of "stinking" salts that "stupefy" and "astonish the brain" in the same manner as hemlock, the poison that killed Socrates.[35] Building on Duchesne, Neapolitan aristocrat-turned-apothecary Donzelli speculated that opium particles possessed a "soporific and stupefying quality," an essence hidden in the "vaporized spirits" of the substance.[36] Donzelli, too, believed that both opium's dangers and its benefits derived from what he called its *solfo narcotico, e stupefattivo*, the "narcotic and stupefying sulfur" that comprised its psychoactive essence.[37] By positing a mechanistic basis for intoxication and habituation, these concepts opened the door to a vision of altered states that made it theoretically possible to alter the action of specific particles in the brain.

The art of drugs, in part, consisted of skillfully refining and mixing these various intoxicating essences so that they wouldn't harm the body. Technologies of removing the intoxicating or poisonous "virtues" from drugs were proprietary trade secrets, but they became increasingly familiar to consumers with the rise of chemical medicine.[38] A transitional step in this process can be seen in *Luz da Medicina*, published in 1664 by the Portuguese court physician Francisco Morato Roma. Roma saw opiates not as poisons but as a category of drugs called "anodynes." However, anodynes could *become* poisons if improperly prepared, leading Roma to caution specifically against the use of "that type of anodynes that we call Narcotics." Unlike more harmless anodynes (Roma mentioned "a warm bath of water"), narcotic remedies "suffocate the spirits, provoke sleep," and "take away the senses." The specific narcotics Roma mentioned had all been known in the Mediterranean world since ancient times: opium, henbane, and "medicamentos opiados" from Greco-Roman-Arabic sources, like philonium and theriac. Although familiar, Roma warned, "these ought not to be applied without the greatest caution, in cases of extraordinary need." Given their intensely "frigid" humors, these "poisonous enemies of nature" were to be resorted to only when a patient's life was at risk.[39]

Half a century later, things had changed in Lisbon. The physician João Vigier advanced a very different theory of narcotics. In his *Thesouro Apollineo* (1714), an eclectic mix of Galenic and chemical remedies, Vigier defined narcotics simply as "all medicines which cause sleep," and he included not only traditional Mediterranean drugs like opium and mandrake but also substances from the New World and the Indies like tobacco.[40] The mind-altering effects of narcotics, Vigier believed, depended on their alteration of "os espiritos," the animal spirits. Drawing upon recent terminology from chemical medicine, Vigier theorized that narcotics contained "an abundance of volatile oils," "volatile salts," and "some terrestrial parts" that "impeded the action and filtration" of the animal spirits throughout the nerves and thus caused changes to the brain.[41]

This marked the beginning of a period when new varieties of nonalcoholic intoxication were experimented with publicly and were at least *somewhat* socially acceptable. It is easy to forget that, at one time, even tea and coffee were classified as narcotic or intoxicating drugs. In addition, tobacco, ambergris, and various spices were all at times thought of as intoxicating. Yet, to varying degrees, they had won public trust by 1700. Around that time, John Jones's *Mysteries of Opium Reveal'd* actually made the counterintuitive argument that opium intoxication was something to be celebrated because it lent itself to a life of productive labor. Jones praised opium's effects on the emotions, causing a "brisk, gay and good Humour. . . . Ovation of the Spirits . . . charm[ing] the Mind with Satisfaction, Acquiescence, Contentation, Equanmity, Etc."[42] Jones compared opium to wine. However, he also classified it more as a stimulant than as an intoxicant, since he believed that it causes "Expediteness in Dispatching and Managing of Business" especially when taken in the morning in the manner of a cup of tea. However, taking too much could lead to "Alienation of the Mind" and "Madness."[43] It seemed possible to some—for a time—that opium could be made to fit into the "normative" model of intoxication. This would change, however, later in the eighteenth century.

Entheogens, a New World Counterexample

The Americas stand apart from the drug cultures of Europe and South Asia. This was not necessarily a result of distance. Two of the most popular drugs of the era came from colonial Mexico: tobacco and chocolate.[44] But in many ways, these two substances were anomalous, perhaps because their mind-altering effects were relatively subtle. *Tabacum rusticum* has some mild hallucinogenic properties, but, for the most part, these two do not provoke reveries like the cannabis- and opium-soaked dreams of the sultan of Bahadur. They were much easier to adapt into other cultural modes precisely because they appeared within the context of diet and fashion, alongside coffee and tea. Although both chocolate and tobacco were initially medicalized and sold by apothecaries, it did not take long for them to move into the realm of leisure consumption.

The same could not be said for the entheogens of the New World. Because of both their inherent effects and their role in non-Christian religiosity, certain American intoxicants failed to become global commodities until the twentieth century. Yet they still circulated, if not in material form, then in written accounts, which frequently framed them in demonic terms. Poisons were not necessarily construed as demonic in origin by medieval and early modern European authorities. To a large extent, however, American entheogens were. Iberian missionaries frequently claimed that entheogens offered access to Satan, so they suppressed these particular forms of psychoactivity using methods and language familiar from witchcraft trials.

In a 1681 letter, Padre Juan Lorenzo Lucero, the Jesuit superior of a mission in the Portuguese Maranhão, described a man he called "the great wizard" (*el mayor hechicero*) among the Jivaro people of the western Amazon. This man lived in a special house where he conducted "continual invocations, orations and prayers consecrated to the Devil."[45] One of the most important tools of these "evil exercises," according to the Padre, was "drinking the juice of various herbs, whose natural effect is to intoxicate a man with such giddiness in the head that he falls to the floor."[46] This was a likely reference to the DMT-containing blend known as ayahuasca. A Jesuit missionary named Pablo Maroni, writing about the same region in 1737, reported that "in order to perform divination, some drink the juice of a white datura blossom with the figure of a bell, while others drink a vine vulgarly called ayahuasca."[47] Although Maroni acknowledged that ayahuasca was also used as a medicine ("they also use it for curing common infirmities, principally headaches"), he emphasized that the drug's main function was as a tool for "those who want to prophesize." For Maroni and his fellows, it was essentially equivalent to summoning the devil.

Maroni's account of ayahuasca users in the deep Amazon (which may be the first European mention of the drug by name) fixated on the state of sensory derangement that ayahuasca produced, which was said to involve "being deprived of the senses from mouth to bottom . . . for even two or three days." Maroni connected this loss of control over mind and body to the preternatural realm of demons. The Indians who believed in the "lies and fictions of the diviners" who used ayahuasca, Maroni believed, had fallen for "dreams that represent the Devil" and superstitions which led them to attribute "all deaths that commonly happen to the effects of some spell [hechizo]."[48] Writing later in the eighteenth century about events that occurred in the 1750s, another Jesuit, Padre Veigl, regarded as "beyond doubt superstitious" the drink "known as *Hayac hausca* among the Amazonian Indians." The drug "makes one utterly powerless," Veigl wrote, "sweeping one away into a prolonged reverie in which they dream wonderful dreams, which they do not seek for, seeing them in visions." Veigl's firsthand, subjective account of the effects offers a tantalizing hint that he had tried the drug himself. Regardless, Veigl still associated the hallucinogenic vine with "choreas diabolicas" (demonic dancing or shaking) and use in "maleficia" (sorcery).[49]

Something similar had played out before, during the Spanish conquest of Mexico. Then the drug in question was peyote (*Lophophora williamsii*), a Mexican cactus, which is a naturally occurring source of the powerful hallucinogenic alkaloid known as mescaline.

There is some evidence that peyote initially won admirers among the Catholic Church in post-conquest Mexico. For instance, Francisco de Losa, a curate at the cathedral of Mexico City, produced a compendium of writings on medicine and the apocalypse attributed to a hermit named Gregorio López (1542–96) that recommends the use of "peyote molido con pimento" for pains in the neck.[50] The initial interest in the plant, as this reference suggests, was as a potential medicine, not as a dangerous intoxicant. In the 1570s, Francisco Hernández identified two types of cactus that he called peyote.[51] Hernández's tone was neutral yet detached, referring both to the plants used for joint pain and to their divinatory properties. Although Hernández knew that peyote was psychoactive, he focused more on its practical role as a divinatory tool than on its intoxicating or potentially demonic properties: "The plant, when pounded, is said to a cure for pains of the joints. It is said to have miraculous properties ... those who devour it are able to divine and predict things. For instance, whether, on the following day, the enemy will make a rush at them, or whether it is a good idea to stay put, or whether someone has stolen from them some object or other, and other things of this type, which the Chichimeca believe is to be learned from this medicine."[52] Given their belief in demonic intercession in human life, it is notable that Sahagún and Hernández don't frame the intoxication produced by the drug in terms of demonic possession or witchcraft.

Several other Spanish chroniclers who wrote about peyote or psilocybin did make this connection, however. Toribio de Benavente Motolinía, one of the earliest Franciscan missionaries in New Spain, described the effects of hallucinogenic psilocybin mushrooms used by the Aztec and Chichimec as "a most cruel manner of inebriation" that allowed some Mexica he was observing to "see a thousand visions, especially snakes, and as they were all out of their senses, it seemed to them that worms were eating them alive, and thus half-raging they charged out of the house, desiring that someone might kill them. . . . These mushrooms are called in their language *Teonanacatl*, which can be translated as 'Meat of the Gods,' or rather of the devil which they worship."[53] As the Inquisition moved into New Spain, a number of trials involving charges of witchcraft or idolatry centered on the ritualized use of hallucinogenic substances like peyote and *ololiuqui* (the seeds of a type of morning glory that contain a compound known as LSA, a close cousin of LSD).[54] An image from the Codex Magliabechiano, created circa 1528 and reproduced here as Figure 29, has been identified by some ethnobotanists and historians as depicting the ritual consumption of psilocybin mushrooms alongside Mictlāntēcutli, the Aztec god of the underworld.[55] By 1620, the Inquisition in New Spain had explicitly banned the possession of peyote and "and any other [drugs] used for the same effects, under any name or appearance."[56] Throughout the colonial period, Holy Office officials in Mexico City continued to prosecute healers, often indigenous women, who were found to be in possession of the banned substance.[57] However, use of pre-Columbian hallucinogens continued even after this ban. In 1625, for instance, a Zapotec healer was convicted of idolatry by the Inquisition of New Spain due to his use of *ololiuqui*.[58]

Figure 29. Detail of an image that may depict *teonanácatl* (psilocybin mushrooms) in the Codex Magliabechiano, fol. 90, mid-sixteenth century, Biblioteca Nazionale Centrale, Florence, Italy. Image is from a 1904 reproduction of the original MS, now in the public domain, courtesy of Wikimedia Commons.

The Inquisition edict of 1620 that had banned the use of peyote had made a point of denying that the drug's effects stemmed from any "inherent quality" of the plant itself. Instead, the document argued that the "fantasies and hallucinations" (*fantasias y representaciones*) associated with the drug were due to "the intervention of the Devil, the true author of this abuse." Yet others who wrote about peyote disagreed. The Spanish chronicler Bernardino de Sahagún described *peiotl* used by the Chichimeca "in place of wine, in the same fashion as the evil mushrooms [*hongos malos*] which are called *nanacatl* and which also make one drunk like wine."[59] In another passage, Sahagún wrote that peyote was used "in parts of the north . . . to see frightful or laughable visions; during this time they are drunk for two or three days."[60] Lacking any cultural correlate to the hallucinogenic or empathogenic effects of tryptamine-based drugs like peyote and psilocybin mushrooms, Sahagún was unable to describe the mental state of the Chichimeca who imbibed in the drug in terms other than "drunk" [*borracho*]. However, he seemed to recognize the word's inadequacy, since he didn't imply that the *visiones* produced by the drug were a result of the state of drunkenness but simply another effect that accompanied them.

This would prove to be a crucial distinction. For it was these visions (and not the state of being *borracho*) that Inquisitors persecuted. By the early seventeenth century, the religious officials of New Spain had reached a conclusion that would later be shared by their brethren observing ayahuasca in the Amazon. The "evil mushrooms," hallucinogenic morning glory seeds, and divinatory cacti of Mesoamerica were, according to the Inquisitorial interpretation of 1620, little more than tricks of the devil. This view held that the supposed "virtues" of these drugs were not simply a byproduct of their inherent intoxicating properties. Instead, they were due to the specific and active intervention of the Devil. Even among Iberian elites, however, this interpretation took over a century to gain precedence. And among common folk, it continued to be widely ignored. Despite the best efforts of Inquisitors, persecution of indigenous and mestizo users of psychedelic substances continued throughout the eighteenth century.[61] These cases provide tantalizing hints of the persistence of a non-European model of entheogen usage which was structured as a dialogue between drug and consumer, not as a state of drunkenness or demonomania. For instance, in 1630 a mulatto woman named Petrona Babtista was subject to an Inquisition trial for her use of peyote in the province of Michoacán. The woman described her usage as a dialogue with the plant itself, not with the devil. "When I drank it in the dry season," she claimed, "the peyote would feel good and thank me."[62]

To sum up: debates over psychedelic substances in colonial New Spain hinged not just on *whether* a drug was intoxicating, but *how* it was intoxicating. The Inquisitorial edict of 1620 had clearly stated the view that the remarkable properties of the peyote and "peyote-like" drugs used by Mesoamericans were not inherent to the substance itself, but a due to demonic "intervention." However, medical commenters had not necessarily agreed: Francisco Hernández had instead portrayed the "prophecies" or "visions" granted by Mesoamerican entheogens as inherent to the plants themselves, and as only one "virtue" among a host of other more standard medicinal properties. It's important to note, as well, that missionary orders in the Iberian empire were by no means opposed to non-European medicines or even intoxicants as a general rule. Indeed, Iberian Jesuits were sometimes accused of being *too* willing to embrace exotic drugs, such as the snakestones from

Mombasa in East Africa that Jesuits in Rome held up as quasi-miraculous cures for poison.[63] At issue was not the existence of intoxicating effects, but the manner in which those effects manifested. Although some acceptable substances did have mind-altering properties, they typically did not provoke "visions" (and, hence, associations with demonic influence) in the manner of peyote, psilocybin, or ayahuasca. It was the profound and almost supernatural state of mental alteration engendered by these plants that tended to provoke objections.

This established a reoccurring pattern. Novel drugs that could not fit into normative frameworks of intoxication or medical use became socially unacceptable, following a period (sometimes years, sometimes decades) of experimentation. The decision among global consumers to accept New World drugs like tobacco or chocolate but reject peyote and psilocybin, however, depended on more than the biological effects of these different drugs. After all, opium could also produce intense and even hallucinatory experiences. Yet Europeans did not, at least initially, slot opium into the category of a demonic intoxicant. This is striking given that one of the most famous vernacular European texts on opium intoxication, Jones's *Mysteries of Opium*, offered a *positive* version of the demon possession motif. For Jones, opium intoxication felt like a kind of supernatural "possession" rather than a demon. He wrote of the effects of a moderate dose of laudanum "so inexpressibly fine and sweet . . . that [they] are very difficult for me to describe."[64] Jones ventured, "Tis as if a good Genius possessed, or informed a Man; therefore People do commonly call it a heavenly Condition."[65] Here "possession" figured, surprisingly, as a positive effect of a drug, not as a Satanic negative. As we'll see in the next chapter, opium increasingly figured as *foreign* in the eighteenth century, but it was never widely framed as *demonic*.

American entheogens may have simply been too epistemologically foreign to become global, at least at the hands of European go-betweens. This is a striking fact of the early modern drug trade. After all, psilocybin mushrooms and peyote cacti are now thought to offer some of the most compelling and powerful varieties of altered states known to science, along with clinically proven medical benefits in certain cases.[66] But as we've seen, globalizing a drug depended on its *cultural translatability*, which is perhaps just another way of saying its ability to be commodified, and not only on its inherent biological properties. The spell that enclosed entheogens in their New World bubble would not break until the second half of the twentieth century.

From Self-Experimentation to Racialized Subjects

We have seen how Garcia da Orta cast judgment on those who consumed cannabis and other "narcotic" drugs. Yet these claims were highly subjective: da Orta framed cannabis as a useless trifle, whereas Hooke argued that it was potentially useful in the treatment of madness. This difference of opinion does not mark any seismic shift in understandings of intoxication between the 1560s and the 1660s. Instead, it points to the eclecticism of beliefs about Indies drugs. These opinions were often based on idiosyncratic experiments that took place in tropical or colonial spaces. For instance, João Curvo Semedo based his beliefs about the "miraculous" properties of two Angolan antivenoms on the report of a "foreign surgeon" in Angola who performed what Semedo called an *experimenta* by testing the drugs on poisoned hens.[67] This practice mirrored Robert Boyle's "trial" of a bezoar by administering it to a poisoned dog in the same period but was notable for having taken place in Africa, not London.

Although such tropical experiments with poisons and animal trials were poorly documented, they were frequently referenced by authorities like Semedo and Lobo. The tropics became a laboratory in which competing epistemologies of intoxication played out. One popular view was that the blood inside the body (and wine and opium outside of it) underwent analogous chemical reactions such as fermentation and coagulation.[68] The heat of the tropical belt greatly increased this danger. A 1711 Portuguese guidebook to medicine in the tropics, *A Light for Surgeons at Sea*, likened the bodies of sailors on tropical voyages to the casks of wine they carried for trade with Africa, which acidified and spoiled in the heat.[69] The author, a surgeon on Portuguese slave ships, noted that he wrote from personal experience.

Natural philosophers drew on these firsthand reports of humans "fermenting" in the tropics to argue that intoxication itself was a kind of fermentation or coagulation inside the brain.

Intoxicating substances were like lemon juice in cream, coagulating the fluids within the brain and preventing rational thought. Richard Mead speculated that loss of reason, or delirium, was produced by particles "pressing the Orifices of the Nerves" and disturbing the flow of "the Liquor of the Nerves" through the brain.[70] Since Mead was writing about the intoxication produced by tarantula poison (drawing on reports from "an ingenious Gentleman who lived several Years in Barbary"), he argued that spider poisons produced "an extraordinary Fermentation" of the body's fluids.[71] The particles of the body coagulated into what Mead called "*Moleculae,* or small Clusters," and produced blockages in the brain that influenced emotional states and rational thought.[72] Francisco Suárez de Ribera, writing in 1730s Madrid, held a somewhat more positive but equally atomistic view of intoxicants. For Ribera, narcotics were "medicaments which dissipate awareness and provoke sleep" by "suppressing the motion of the animal spirits" through the nerves and "inducing torpor, calming pains [and] extinguishing heat."[73]

One upshot of these theories was that they evaded supernatural explanations for how psychoactivity worked. This mechanistic way of understanding psychoactivity coincided with a new, Enlightenment-era focus on "engineering" racialized bodies.[74] Both African bodies and tropical drugs were conceived of as uniquely suited to the rigors of plantation labor and were regarded as "transplantable" between equatorial regions. The drug trade, slavery, and imperial transplantation schemes were not only interconnected but also mutually constitutive of one another. This was nowhere more evident than in the portside slave markets of Bahia. The surgeon João Cardoso de Miranda had arrived at these markets in the first decade of the eighteenth century as a teenager, most likely having served as a barber-surgeon's apprentice on a slave ship.[75] Within a decade, he established himself as an unlicensed yet successful medical practitioner who moved fluidly between the slave markets and the mansions of wealthy merchants. Miranda himself was both a healer and a slave trader. He boasted that he was able to make enormous profits by purchasing sick slaves newly arrived from Angola and curing them with his own proprietary remedies.[76] Miranda's approach to health was unorthodox: he railed against the practice of bleeding, pointing out that it could not be administered "in Bahia, where most of the sick are slaves" because many Africans couldn't communicate the precise nature of their diseases to the physician. Yet Miranda observed that the slaves "do not die for lack of bleeding" and concluded that the lancet of European physicians usually did more harm than good.[77]

Miranda's writings on the diseases endemic to 1730s Bahia reflect the rise of so-called "tropical empiricism," a practice that depended on the analysis of the long-distance movements of peoples and diseases as well as on adapting to new climates and pharmacopoeias.[78] In his discussion of the treatment of the *Mal de Loanda* (disease of Luanda) which afflicted many slaves from Angola, Miranda wrote that "when I had reflected further on the cause of such a great illness, I found myself growing more and more confused." The cause could not be attributable to the specific humors of Africans because it was also caught by Luso-Brazilian crewman, nor was it due to the malign influence of the African climate because it continued to afflict them in Brazil. "I realized that it might be possible to utilize the same remedy for each one of the patients who appeared to suffer from various ailments," Miranda concluded.[79] He called his cures *"remedios específicos"*—specific remedies. The target? A concealed root cause of a particular disease—that disease's occult virtue, in other words—that manifested differently to the sensoria of different people in different places.

The rise of specifics (universal cures) created a new conception of human bodies as universal and functionally interchangeable.[80] This shift relied not only on theoretical debates in Europe but also on the observations of lesser-known figures in the colonies and on the life experiences of the enslaved people they bought, sold, and treated. These tropical practitioners and patients offered granular viewpoints on the epochal transformations of the Columbian Exchange in general and of the globalization of intoxication in particular.

One difference in these emerging theories of specifics was an emphasis on "habit." A Dutch book attributed to the notorious French sexologist Nicolas Venette described the use of "Narcotics" like cannabis and jimson weed (*Datura stramonium*) in the Indies, which "are objects of trade in the East Indies, like tobacco in the West." The author cautioned that "Europeans do not feel the same effects from the use of these narcotics as do the Asians and Africans." However, this was not because of some intrinsic physical property that differentiated Europeans from Asians and Africans. It was simply a product of habituation: "Habit makes these drugs produce different effects on those who use them, and we observe among us [Europeans] that they confer tranquility of soul, pleasure, and an itching of the body, in place of the sexual distractions that are described in other authors."[81]

Rather than understanding intoxication using older concepts of poisoning or occult virtues, medical professionals thus began to think of intoxication in racialized terms. Some bodies (like some commodities) were more prone to spoilage through fermentation or souring, leading not only to disease but also to a weakening of the rational faculties. However, these authors could not agree on whether "Northern" bodies and minds were *more* or *less* suited to resisting the corrupting effects of tropical travel and tropical drugs.

These differences of opinion were never adequately resolved. The lack of a

Figure 30. "Doctor Syntax and his wife making an experiment of pneumatics," undated colored aquatint by Thomas Rowlandson. Courtesy of the Wellcome Library.

clear theory of how intoxication worked—and how it might differentially affect human groups—ultimately made self-experimentation with intoxicants unacceptable for "men of science." Sir Humphry Davy's use of nitrous oxide was, in a sense, the final triumph of a declining practice, one that began in the previous century. By the closing decades of the eighteenth century, using an Indies drug with psychoactive properties in experimental trials had become socially unacceptable. Davy's "gaseous Oxyd," being a chemical product of scientific experimentation, belonged to a different category.

But even then, the public reception of nitrous oxide dashed Davy's hopes of the gas becoming a tool in the natural philosophical arsenal. Critics of the drug attacked it as antithetical to reason. The famed caricaturists James Gillray and Thomas Rowlandson both skewered Davy in print, ridiculing users of his gas as senseless fools (Figure 30). In the end, even a drug produced in European laboratories by European hands was still fatally corrupted, impure. Davy's sublime substance became, within a sadly short length of time, a recreational intoxicant which was growing increasingly unacceptable among supposedly "rational" folk. It had fallen from the heights of scientific progress to become a pastime of dubious drawing rooms and dances.

It had become, in short, a drug.

Psalmanazar and the Racialization of Intoxication

In May 1763, an inhabitant of London could have visited an impoverished corner of the East End and heard a strange tale. There was an old man who lived on Ironmonger's Row, recently deceased, who had been a favorite of the street urchins and the hack writers. No one knew his real name. They didn't even know what country he was from, just that he spoke with an accent that was difficult to place. His hair, once blond and shoulder-length, had long since turned gray. Decades earlier, he had embraced Christ as his personal savior and renounced his former sins—but he still depended on a nightly dose of laudanum. If the visitor came across Samuel Johnson in a tavern or on the street, he might have heard that this strange character was "the best Man he had ever known."[82] Others would remember him as a ridiculous fraud. All agreed that he had lied about being a Taiwanese cannibal prince, when he first arrived in London sixty years earlier—but the old man didn't like to talk about that. When asked whether he had ever broached the subject with his old friend, Dr. Johnson said "he was afraid to mention even China."[83]

What little we know about this strange man, who called himself Psalmanazar after an Assyrian emperor from the Old Testament, comes from a memoir he left behind in a drawer and asked to be published in the London papers after his death. Psalmanazar's *Memoirs of * * * *, commonly known by the Name of George Psalmanazar, a reputed native of Formosa* was published as a book in 1764. Today, it is occasionally cited by historians of fraud or by literary scholars intrigued by the question of whether it influenced Jean-Jacques Rousseau's *Confessions*, which he began writing soon after.[84]

One thing these accounts have missed is that Psalmanazar was perhaps the first person to publish a firsthand description of being an opiate addict. He wrote in his memoir that he felt compelled "to give some account of that vast quantity of laudanum I have been known to take for above these forty years . . . in order to undeceive such persons as may have conceived too favorable an opinion of that dangerous drug, from any thing they may have heard me say" in the past.[85] In order to convince the Londoners of 1704 that he was truly an Asian prince, Psalmanazar seems to have developed a series of unusual habits that would "perform" his exotic origins. He ate "raw flesh" covered in spices; slept in a chair; claimed to have eaten numerous babies; and, it seems, intentionally cultivated an opium addiction. In his memoir, Psalmanazar simply described these "extravagant ways" as part of his "vanity and senseless affectation of singularity."

Psalmanazar used exoticizing tropes such as cannibalism and excessive drug use in order to demonstrate his bona fides as a legitimate "Asian." His vision of Formosa was, above all, an exotic one. Several of his other claims, such as the Formosans' supposed proclivity for sacrificing thousands of male infants every year or their worship of hideous idols (Figure 31), appear to have been based in part on accounts of pre-Columbian Mesoamerica. It is possible that Psalmanazar's performative drug taking was also a kind of mélange of accounts from the East Indies (like da Orta's description of Bahadur) and Spanish accounts of ritual drug use among the Aztecs (like those of Sahagún). What we know for sure is that Psalmanazar seems to have regarded his opium use as a key part of his performance of foreignness. Psalmanazar wrote that he "pretend[ed]" to take a "vast excess" of the drug "by way of ostentation" during the period of his imposture.[86] In reality, the doses he was consuming were still so high as to put him at risk of overdose: his "dangerous draughts," as he put it, were potentially "fatal, to

Figure 31. "The Idol of the DEVIL," from George Psalmanazar, *An Historical and Geographical Description of Formosa* (London, 1704). Courtesy of the Huntington Library.

any man that had a less strong and happy constitution than I was blessed with."[87] Throughout Psalmanazar's narrative of barely concealed childhood abuse, imposture at a young age, and gradual descent into a penniless and disgraced young adulthood in London, we find the specter of this laudanum addiction. It was not all bad, however. For one thing, Psalmanazar's performance of exotic origins made him a "great favorite. . . with the fair sex." For another, Psalmanazar believed that he had developed a less intoxicating form of laudanum.

Psalmanazar's narrative is fascinating not just because it offers a "confession" of addiction but also because it includes a quasi-scientific recipe for how to *treat* opiate addiction. In his *Memoirs*, Psalmanazar described how he became troubled by his addiction and tried to develop a chemical method for "stripping the opium of all its pernicious qualities," including its addictiveness. He bought Jones's *Mysteries of Opium* and used Jones's theory of opium intoxication to derive a method that caused "the most vicious and narcotic parts [to be] scummed off" via the mixing of the juice of Seville oranges with alkalis:

> When I began to feel the inconvenient effects of it, which was not till a good number of years of using it, I thought it high time to lessen the usual dose (which was then about ten or twelve tea spoonfulls morning and night, and very often more) as fast as I conveniently could, and in about six months' time had reduced myself to half an ounce per day, somewhat weaker than the common Sydenham [an opiate]. I still continued decreasing; but such was my foolish vanity, that, to conceal my reduction, I added some other bitter tincture, especially that of *hierapicra*, or some other such corrective, among it, to appear as still taking my usual quantity.[88]

Psalmanazar relapsed during a cold Oxford winter, the severity of which, "forced me, though much against my will, to have recourse to [opium] again."[89]

Psalmanazar's case shows how early modern Europeans had begun to internalize a racialized performance of intoxication. Psalmanazar intentionally developed his habit in order to physically make himself into an Asian. Much like his consumption of raw meat and sitting in chairs to sleep, it was more than just for show. In addition to performing an exotic identity, it was a kind of practice intended to habituate himself. This reflected prevailing beliefs that regarded habit in what would come to be thought of as Lamarckian terms—that is, the way we eat and comport ourselves leads to permanent alterations. "[Opium] is a poison for those of us who are not accustomed to it, unless we are sufficiently healthy and robust as was Monsieur Charas [a famous doctor to the king of Spain] when he took twelve grains," Venette had written.[90]

Psalmanazar's opiate addiction offers a personal view of what would otherwise be a somewhat abstract story of cultural shifts and technological change. The work of the physician Thomas Sydenham and his colleagues in the 1660s and 1670s had set in motion a process of refining and isolating the psychoactive properties in raw opium latex that would ultimately lead to the discovery of one of the first alkaloids, morphine, in 1804.[91] But it also laid bare an emerging racial and class-based distinction in the social permissibility of intoxication.

Unknown Pleasures: Intoxication in the Public Sphere

In the early seventeenth century, intoxication became bound up with concerns about both madness and the adoption of new cultural practices. As King James put it—in words that call to mind the smoking monkeys of the singerie genre—imitation of tobacco smoking from "beyond the Seas" had made the English "like Apes, counterfeiting the manners of others, to our owne destruction." For James, the adoption of tobacco smoking in Europe was not simply an issue of public health. It was a spiritual crisis. Because he knew that tobacco was an element in indigenous American spirituality, James believed that Europeans who consumed it risked transforming not only their bodies but their minds and souls as well.

At the end of the eighteenth century, another technological innovation brought concerns about intoxication to the fore. The innovations of Lavoisier, Priestley, and the alkaloidal chemists facilitated the creation of novel psychoactive drugs. This was an entirely new form of technological drug creation, relying on the tools of the laboratory rather than the transmission of preexisting biota or knowledge. But this desire, too, was suffused with anxieties about unreason. Paradoxically, the practices of rigorous experimental science that led to the creation of substances like nitrous oxide also led to the *dissolution* of those methods in the grips of a drug that overrode both the reliability of the senses and the rational faculties. Davy's famous nitrous oxide experiments were not a radical break with the past; they were the capstone on two centuries of ambiguous scientific engagement with intoxication as both a tool and a goal. Turning one's own body into an experimental apparatus was a common objective of Enlightenment science. At the same time, however, self-experimentation with drugs conflicted with scientific decorum, risking addiction and the loss of objectivity.[92]

The rise of a globally connected community of savants and scientists (what some call the Republic of Letters) made possible the globalization of intoxication and its elevation as a scientific tool. But it also set strict limits upon it. Drugs that straddled the borderlands between unreason and creativity, like Davy's gas or Psalmanazar's opiates, were celebrated by some natural philosophers and enjoyed success as consumer products. But they were not sustainable as Enlightenment intellectual projects and thus could not be integrated into the "normative models" of intoxication that social elites deemed acceptable.

The emergence in the eighteenth century of a "public sphere" with a wide network of participants interested in drugs, medicine, and nature produced a confusion of theories. But these individuals had something in common: they were bringing new experiences of intoxication and psychoactivity into view. Davy used his nitrous oxide experiments to vault into the mainstream of public life in Britain. Psalmanazar used his opium addiction as a tool for a successful imposture and insisted, as a dying wish, that his account of opium addiction be printed in the papers. Catholic missionaries, reporting on the "demonic" drug use by Native Americans, published their vivid accounts. Eighteenth-century natural philosophers embraced intoxication as a powerful empirical tool and a potentially lucrative commercial asset. The goal was to exploit intoxicating substances as material for scientific experiments and engines of commercial profit. Initially, at least, drugs were not oppositional to the Age of Reason: they were a key part of it.

In the nineteenth century, global consumers gained access to dozens of new psychoactive substances: strychnine (1818), ether (1848), cannabis tincture (popularized as a medicine by William O'Shaughnessy in the 1840s), cocaine (1859), and, still later, novel products of chemical synthesis like heroin (1874) and amphetamine (1887). It became normal to prescribe branded drugs like Vin Mariani (red wine infused with cocaine) for "nervous fatigue," or cannabis, alcohol, and strychnine for headaches. These new intoxicants passed easily across the boundary dividing the medical and the recreational: before long, substances like ether, which began life as avant-garde medical treatments, had become party drugs. "High" and "low" cultures of drug use began to solidify in the nineteenth century, with legal regimes to match. From Thomas de Quincey on laudanum to William James on nitrous oxide, a vanguard of scientists and writers continued to tap into the new culture of globalized intoxication to which the eighteenth century had given birth.

It has been a common approach to attribute to Davy and to those who came after him a turn *against* Enlightenment science and its ideals and *toward* a Romantic yearning for sublimity and irrationality. But this ignores the fascination among so-called Enlightenment scientists with intoxication and mental alteration. Indeed, one aspect of the era of "Romantic science," perhaps, is the social stigma that began to gather around self-experimentation with drugs. Davy is a kind of Janus figure in this regard: in his early career facing backward, to an earlier era of quasi-alchemical questing after miracles and unhesitating self-experimentation, and in his later years beating back criticism that this quest was unscientific or unseemly. Indeed, Davy suffered significant reputational damage later in his career from his earlier nitrous oxide research, despite the fact that it had made his name as a young scientist.[93]

Self-experimentation with drugs may have gone somewhat underground, but it never really went away. In 1882, another young upstart, William James, published a positive account of nitrous oxide as a cognitive tool. "Medical school; divinity school, school! SCHOOL! Oh my God, oh God; oh God!" an intoxicated James had scribbled frantically in his notes, claiming that the drug's effects allowed him to finally comprehend Hegel.[94]

In the end, Davy and James and Freud and all of the scientific self-experimenters who came after them, leading right up to Timothy Leary and Alexander Shulgin (the Berkeley-trained chemist who popularized MDMA), didn't represent a fundamental break. They were the inheritors of a legacy of experimentation with mind-altering substances dating to the origins of modern science itself. The attempt to "purify" intoxicating drugs and strip them of their associations with non-European cultures resulted in the creation of far more dangerous artificial substances. It's an irony that in some ways can be seen as a template for the subsequent history of drugs and pharmacy—a history of missed opportunities and good intentions gone awry. In the next chapter we'll follow that path, digging deeper into the surprising history of the seductive drug that ensnared Psalmanazar and countless others.

CHAPTER 6

Three Ways of Looking at Opium

I must mention with gratitude the goodness of God Almighty, who has given opium to human beings for the relief of their miseries.

—THOMAS SYDENHAM, *OBSERVATIONES MEDICAE* (1683)

The workers in the warehouse have learned not to fear heights.

To look down, when standing at the highest levels, is to face death. The shelves seem to go up forever. Seven men standing at their full height, arms held upward to pass the spheres of the substance, one to the next, would reach only halfway to the top. Most keep their hair in tightly woven braids; a few wear turbans. The work has made them muscular. They spend their lives in this series of vast chambers. There is a geometric rigor here—a system of spheres, planes, and lines. The spheres are why this place exists. There are tens of thousands of them, each capable of killing more than a hundred people. The total contents of the chambers would likely be sufficient to poison each and every inhabit of Patna, the Indian city in which the workers live.[1] But these workers do not deal in poison. They deal in opium.

Did the laborers in this warehouse sample the drug itself? Certainly, opium's innocuous smell, a pleasant but cloying scent of flowers, would have been ever-present. And so, too, was the evidence of wealth. Vast wealth: the kind of wealth that builds cathedral-like warehouses, and moves empires to action.

The image of these anonymous laborers in an opium warehouse in northeast India was created in the 1850s. By this time, the global opium trade was old and comfortable. Its participants had famous names like Delano and Forbes. And although the opium trade would not become a true black market until well into the twentieth century, by the 1850s it was already a commerce of a substance that was (in some places and in some con-

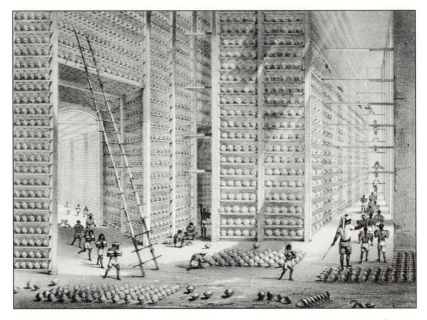

Figure 32. "The Stacking Room, Opium Factory at Patna India," lithograph after W. S. Sherwell, c. 1850. Courtesy of the Wellcome Library.

texts) an illegal drug. In 1799, a public edict of China's Jiaqing emperor had sought to ban imports of opium into Chinese territory.[2] "The use of opium originally prevailed only among vagrants, and disreputable persons," the edict lamented, "but it has since extended itself among the members and descendants of reputable families," as well as groups like students and even some "officers of government who, infatuated in their attachment to this drug, make an habitual use of it."[3] The edict was duly reported in British newspapers, but was effectively ignored by the European opium merchants of Canton (present-day Guangzhou).

Eleven years later, in 1810, the Jiaqing emperor bitterly condemned the drug once again. "Opium has a harm," a new edict proclaimed. "Opium is a poison, undermining our good customs and morality. Its use is prohibited by law. Now the commoner, Yang, dares to bring it into the Forbidden City. Indeed, he flouts the law! However, recently the purchasers, eaters, and consumers of opium have become numerous. Deceitful merchants buy and sell it to gain profit."[4] It was the beginning of a dance that we're still locked in—a dance between what is legal and what people want, between taboo and desire. And, in many times and places, it has been a dance between colonialism and sovereignty. Regardless of whether opium and the wars it inspired was the *direct* cause of the fall of the Qing dynasty, few would deny that the opium trade carried out by European merchants, and that trade's apotheosis in the First Opium War (1839-42), played a significant role in bringing imperial China to its knees.

The Jiaqing emperor, then, was correct. Opium did have a harm. And the ability to harm is also a form of power. To understand how the latex of a humble flower took on such an outsized importance in the nineteenth century, we need to go backward, to the world of the preceding centuries. For the most part, this was a world in which opium was both legal and widely available. By the seventeenth century, however, it was a world in which opium was becoming increasingly suspect. This chapter charts the history of that suspicion. It shows how the fears of non-Christian religiosity, racialized bodies, and foreign intoxication explored in earlier chapters coalesced around a single substance. It is a story that brings together the lives of anonymous workers in tropical warehouses and fields, the growing masses of those who would eventually be labeled "addicts," and the men of business who profited from both.

Papaver somniferum, the opium poppy, is one of the plants that has stood longest at the side of humans. It is surely one of our species' most ambiguous botanical allies. It has been a bringer of both death, and of relief. It is an ancient native of Europe, yet has become an enduring symbol of Orientalism. Today, opium continues to serve as the raw material for a host of copyrighted and hugely valuable pharmaceuticals, while also exemplifying a premodern culture of healing that has largely faded from the Earth.

How, then, should we see the drug that came to be known as opium? What can we say about this strange drug, simultaneously European and non-European, ancient and modern, beneficial and harmful? The first way of seeing opium is to see the plant within it—the simple flower, millions of years old, that humans began to domesticate around ten thousand years ago. For most of this history, opium was not a drug rolled up into a ball and smoked. We can't see the flowers in Figure 32, but their presence is everywhere felt within it. Opium is, after all, a natural product. But it's one that has been domesticated since before recorded history. Like the sacred psychedelics of Mesoamerica, it has a deep history of altering, and being altered by, *Homo sapiens*.

The second way of seeing opium is as a thing that is meant to be turned into smoke. A heady and intoxicating smoke that is expensive, oriental, exotic, yet also thought of in terms that are mechanical, capitalist, and experimental. A thing to be bought and sold, a thing to burn to test purity, a thing to be consumed to aid in the vast labor of a globalizing world.

The third way of seeing opium is as a raw material for industrialized pharmacy: the thing from which morphine is made. This is the phase that we, in many ways, take as the normative one today. Opium poppies are still grown in vast quantities by medical suppliers, but we have divorced this trade and this iteration of the drug from its own history. In the first century since morphine was invented, we also divorced synthetic opiates from the moralism that grew up around smokable opium. Only in the past decade or two, really, has that moralism and that fear returned, now clustering not around the figure of the Chinese laborer with his opium pipe but around the desperate American yearning after OxyContin or heroin.[5]

By focusing on these three freeze-frames of opium in specific times and places, I hope to clarify the changing role of that drug in recent history. I also hope that this approach may serve as an example of a type of historical analysis of drugs that allows for biological continuity across time—the morphine molecule doesn't change—while also respecting the enormous amount of variation in terms of how different cultures experience a given drug's effects. The morphine molecule exists outside of time and culture, but the opium ball most definitely does not. Too many drug histories assume that a drug is a fixed entity that circulates, unchanged, in different times and places. Others, however, sometimes make the opposite mistake, of neglecting present-day medical or scientific knowledge for fear of appearing presentist or culturally chauvinistic.

Like a photo burst of an object moving through air, these three views of opium serve to highlight both the discrete identities of the drug in different times and places, as well as the continuities between them. In doing so, this chapter walks the reader through the new theory of drugs and drug history that arises from this book—a theory that hopefully can be applied to different situations and that can have implications not only for early modern history but also for drug policy today and in the future.

"A Drug to Bring Forgetfulness of Every Ill"

In the beginning, there was just a flower. A beautiful example of its kind, brilliant red or pale pink, with delicate yellow stamens and serrated leaves. Just a flower, but an addictive one.

Addiction is a modern concept that cannot necessarily be applied, wholesale, to different times and places.[6] Cultural norms of drug use are ever changing, and they can vary widely. Indeed, they are changing as I write these words. As scholars of contemporary drug use have pointed out, the degree of addictiveness of many drugs has been intentionally overstated because of social and political biases and the profound effects of "set and setting."[7] Such biases are not set in stone. As cannabis legalization ramped up throughout the 2010s, societal norms regarding the habitual use of the drug changed rapidly.[8] However, I do not believe that addiction is entirely a cultural construct. It would be a mistake to pretend that some consumers of drugs like opium in the premodern world did not suffer under a kind of bondage very similar to that which we today call addiction.

The reason lies in a strange biological fact. Through an evolutionary process that remains mysterious, a certain species of poppy (*Papaver somniferum*) evolved to produce a molecule, morphine, that mimicked the dopamine-releasing properties of naturally occurring "endogenous morphines," or *endorphins*, within the human brain.[9] These endorphins are neurotransmitters that are released by the brain at moments of pain (as a counterbalancing mechanism) or emotional or physical pleasure, such as orgasm, laughter, or the "runner's high" after physical exercise. The latex of *Papaver somniferum* can consist of up to 20 percent morphine by weight, along with other alkaloid molecules like thebaine and codeine, which also happen to bind with mu-opioid receptors in the human brain.

It was, perhaps, a freak of chance that a certain type of flower began to produce molecules that corresponded to the chemical signatures of orgasm or laughter. But it was not by chance that this particular flower became an enormously successful crop. Simply put, humans like endorphins, and hence they liked morphine and the other narcotic alkaloids in the opium poppy. An evolutionary pas de deux ensued. This chapter thus takes the inherent addictiveness and mind-altering properties of opium as a basic starting point. The plant's appealing, mind-altering property was, after all, the reason why the opium poppy spread across Eurasia.

Or was it? *Papaver somniferum* is not just one of the world's most valuable drug crops—it is also a food crop, particularly important as a source of cooking oil. As we proceed through the deep history of opium, we need to be careful not to jump to conclusions about the uses to which the opium poppy has been put in different times and places. *Papaver somniferum* does not number among the "Neolithic package" of domesticated southwestern

Asian native crops, like emmer wheat and lentils, that led to the so-called Agricultural Revolution in the Late Neolithic period (c. 8000 BCE). But it has an ancient lineage. Surprisingly, given the plant's current range, opium poppies appear to have been native to western Europe.[10] Around seven thousand years ago, early farmers in an area stretching from present-day Spain to Germany began to transplant and domesticate the wild *Papaver somniferum*. Some of the earliest archaeological evidence comes from the Linear Beaker Culture, which ranged over modern Germany and eastern France in the 4500–3500 BCE period. At one such find, from a village dated to around 5000 BCE, two opium poppy seeds were recovered along with domesticated varietals of wheat and other food crops.[11] It is not clear whether opium poppies were being used as a drug at this early date, or even whether they were intentionally domesticated at all. One guess is that opium poppies initially made their way into human settlements a bit like dogs did: perhaps the flowers were margin-dwelling opportunists that moved in at the edges of farmland, taking advantage of the sheltered environments human agriculturalists had created for their wheat and barley crops. To this day, other species of poppy are notable agricultural weeds that thrive along the edges of wheat fields.[12]

By around 4000 BCE, the domesticated opium poppy occupied a range across the Western Mediterranean region.[13] Although it is difficult to prove that opium latex was being used recreationally or medicinally at this early date, recovered samples of *Papaver somniferum* have been shown to contain psychoactive alkaloids. Opium compounds were even found in human bones from one Late Neolithic site near present-day Barcelona.[14] Another find from a Neolithic tomb near Granada is particularly suggestive: opium poppy capsules were ritually buried alongside a body, carefully placed inside woven-grass containers.[15] Although there is robust evidence for the cultivation of opium poppies in present-day France, Spain, and Germany from about 4000 BCE onward, there is actually no evidence for the use of the opium poppy among the inhabitants of the Fertile Crescent in the same period. This European origin for opium will be important to keep in mind later in this chapter.

It is not until the Second Intermediate Period in Egypt—an era of massive social upheaval, economic transformation, and widespread population movements—that even tentative evidence for the use of opium appears in the archaeological record of the ancient Near East.[16] Opium residues also appear in Mycenaean Greek sites, and the drug definitively enters the tex-

tual record under the name *opion* in Greek medical writings of the fourth
and third centuries BCE. By the time of Dioscorides, writing in 77 CE, the
opium poppy was widely known throughout the Roman and Persian Empires as a botanical with a powerful "cooling power" that alleviated insom-
nia, lessened pain, and treated swellings.[17] The heads of the flower could be
boiled and drunk, or the latex of the pods could be collected and formed
into pills. The basic outlines of this description would persist until the seventeenth century, as Dioscorides became a foundational text in Islamic, medieval European, and early modern European medicine.

Innovations in the use of opium came primarily from medical practitioners from the Muslim world, particularly from Persian physicians like
Yūhannā ibn Māsawayh (777–857 CE) and Abū ibn Sīnā (980–1037 CE).[18]
The earliest medieval European references to the use of opium as a surgical
anesthetic reflect this influence. Starting around 1000 CE, medical manuscripts from Germany, Italy, and Sicily began referencing a narcotic *spongia
somnifera* (sleep-bearing sponge). The earliest mention of the preparation
comes from a German "antidotary" (list of recipes for antidotes) from the
tenth century, recommending a mixture of opium, mandrake, hemlock, and
henbane to induce a deep sleep prior to surgery.[19]

Although opium never left Europe, innovations in the use of the drug in
a medical and surgical context increasingly took place to the east, in Persia,
or in regions on the edge of the Christian world, like Salerno, in which medical practices mingling Jewish, Christian, and Muslim influenced flourished.
Perhaps this contribution from medieval Muslim physicians and apothecaries played an early role in making opium seem more foreign to Europeans.
But this does not seem to me to offer a sufficient explanation for why European perceptions of the drug transformed so radically in the sixteenth and
seventeenth centuries.

How Opium Became "Oriental"

The story told above would have greatly surprised seventeenth- or eighteenth-
century Europeans—and, perhaps, some people of the present day as well.
When opium is discussed in the popular press, it frequently accompanies
images of Afghan poppy fields surrounded by desolate mountains. As we've
seen, however, opium poppies turn out to have been domesticated in settings that look more like a landscape by Cézanne. Not only did the earliest
known efforts to domesticate *Papaver somniferum* take place in Europe, but

the plant was not widely known in regions east of the Aegean before traders from the west brought it there, thousands of years after its domestication. The assumptions of earlier scholars, who proceeded from Orientalist assumptions about opium's origins and characteristics, has blinded us to a simple and startling fact. Opium is not a "foreign" import from "the Orient."[20] It is a drug that is *from Europe*.[21]

In a world of practices like bloodletting and scarification, opium was (arguably) a relatively benign and, at times, a uniquely effective treatment.[22] It could be grown readily in European household gardens, it was solidly affirmed by the ancients, and it was relatively inexpensive. It was the only effective painkiller known in a time when surgeries frequently led to unbearable pain and often death. Moreover, in a world in which dysentery or diarrhea could be fatal, even side effects of the drug, like constipation, could potentially confer lifesaving benefits. So why wasn't opium embraced as an "indigenous" plant by Europeans? Answering the question of how opium became an "Indies" drug takes us down a winding path. It is one that includes the spread of African and Amerindian smoking technologies in the Old World in the sixteenth century, as well as the rise of medical alchemy in Europe.

Although *Papaver somniferum* was in wide use throughout the Mediterranean world by the time of the Roman Empire, sustained maritime links with the Indian Ocean in the seventeenth and eighteenth centuries expanded the scope of the opium trade and consumption.[23] In the early modern period, opium from Egypt and Persia won praise for its potency and became a prized variant of the drug. (Specific strains of *Papaver* can contain multiple times more opiate alkaloids—and thus merit a considerably higher value— than others.)[24] By the eighteenth century, opium had already become an archetypal "Indies drug" in European metropoles: an intoxicating, heady, and profoundly evocative substance that combined foreign origins with domestic availability. A body of exotic lore grew up around opium's reputed role as both an aphrodisiac and an aid to battle among the Turks and Persians. Giuseppe Donzelli of Naples repeated a commonly held belief when he wrote that opium was prized by "Turkish soldiers, who eat it especially when they are in times of danger at war, becoming almost drunken with it and thereby not noticing their danger."[25] The Dutch traveler Jan Huygen van Linschoten encountered opium in the Indian Ocean and fixated on its addictive properties and its purported aphrodisiac effects.[26] Linschoten, like many of his peers, regarded the effects of the preparations of *Papaver* used in the east to

be substantially different from the painkilling and sleep-inducing properties known to medieval and classical authors. For one thing, he believed that
users of the drug "dieth without faile" if they went four or five days without
consuming it. Thus, he wrote, "it is a kinde of poyson." However, Linschoten
also noted that opium was useful "for lecherie: for it maketh a man to hold
his seede long before he sheddeth it, which the Indian women much desire,
that they may shed their nature likewise with the man."[27]

The exoticization of opium sometimes arose from translation errors. For
instance, opium appears several times in the Boxer Codex, one of the oldest
surviving European texts from the Philippines. But it does so in disguise.
The manuscript, written around 1590, appears to be a Spanish translation
of a Portuguese original produced several years earlier. As a result, a passage on "the Javanese and Their Manner of Fighting" mentions that "they
also ingest a certain herb called *antion*, which gives them considerable vigor
and strength. It makes them lose their minds and sends them into a frenzy,
and in this state they set upon their enemies, shrieking *amoq, amoq!*"[28] The
phrasing "a certain herb called *antion*" implies unfamiliarity, and the herb's
use as a supplement for, literally, running amuck also serves to distance the
author from what seems at first glance to be an unfamiliar Javanese stimulant. But *antion* is nothing more than a transcription error made by the
Spanish translator: the original Portuguese author spoke of *anfião*, which in
turn is descended from Greek *opion*.[29] The Javanese were simply rehashing
the familiar trope of the warrior using opium (or wine) as a form of consum-
able courage. To a European reader of such narratives, however, the altered
names and unfamiliar cultural contexts could have served to distinguish
such "oriental" drugs from the humble poppy latex to be found in the local
apothecary shop or in farmers' fields.

Another potential factor in the conversion of opium from a familiar European medicament to an Indies drug was the changing relationship between opium and social class. In the Middle Ages, some of the most popular
preparations containing opium had been "alexipharmic" (anti-poison) remedies that involved dozens of compounded medicinal drugs and required
intensive labor. For instance, Venetian treacle (derived from *theriac*, a common word for opium in both Arabic and Farsi) required a maddeningly
complex process of creation whereby precisely measured amounts of more
than fifty herbs were combined with powdered flesh of poisonous snakes
and then blended with opium and oddities like roasted copper and Lemnian
earth.[30] The resulting decoction was hugely expensive, not only because of

the exotica it contained but also because of the exceptionally time-intensive nature of the work.

As opiates grew in popularity as drugs accessible to "middling sorts," so too did associations with racial and religious degeneration because of its addictive "virtues." One charge levied against the drug was that Europeans processed it differently, and hence phenomena such as opium's reputed aphrodisiac properties were not necessarily transferable. Jones, in his 1701 work *Mysteries of Opium*, had described these differing sexual effects as one of the key "paradoxes of opium." As the Brazilian unlicensed physician João Cardoso de Miranda put it, "the Moderns" had demonstrated that all agues and fevers were caused by "fermentations and acidic juices that are transmitted to the blood and perturb the body's natural economy."[31] This could lead to a "souring in the brain" and "blockage of the nerve fluid" that gave rise not only to fevers and scurvies but also to madness, melancholy, intoxication, and idiocy. At issue in debates about opium's differing effects was the question of how the "nerve fluids" within human brains reacted to geographical and climatic change. If opium's psychoactive effects relied upon a model of the brain that depended on phenomena like "fermentation" and "souring," then these effects also depended upon the climate in which it was taken and how the consumer's body was humorally constituted.

Another major impetus for the shifting social and cultural roles of opium in the early modern period came from technological changes. The adoption of opium, tobacco, cacao, and other novel crops through the trading entrepôts of the Indian Ocean and South China Sea accompanied a parallel experimentation with material culture and technology. In the case of tobacco, this experimentation gave rise to a huge variety of new pipe forms. As a vehicle for the delivery of psychoactive and addictive alkaloids, pipes were a radical new technology of drug consumption in regions like Europe and East Asia, which had no prior access to them, contributing to both a newfound recognition of psychoactivity and to new fears of foreign imports. Pipes were powerful sacramental objects in the pre-Columbian Americas, but they also played an important but less widely recognized role in premodern Africa, where (prior to the sixteenth century) tobacco was unknown but cannabis widely cultivated.

It is often assumed that these New World pipes were the progenitors of all Old World forms. However, this assumption seems likely to be false. Archaeologists have identified a particular set of pipe forms from the pre-Columbian Americas, which were then modified by European and African smokers in the late sixteenth and the seventeenth centuries.[32] Although tobacco did not reach the Old World until the post-Columbian era, some sub-Saharan cultures used a different type of pipe to smoke cannabis, with some surviving examples dating to the thirteenth century CE.[33] It is still unclear to what degree these African pipes influenced global cultures of smoking. But there does seem to be one specific debt owed to African pipes. In the sixteenth century, the famous type of water pipe known as the *hookah* or *nargilah* was first mentioned in historical sources, somewhat mysteriously finding its way to the courts of the Persian and Mughal emperors in a state that was already highly polished and materially sophisticated (Figure 33). This would seem to imply an earlier point of origin, but the trail runs cold surprisingly quickly. One historian of drugs in the early modern Middle East considers both a sixteenth-century Persian and North Indian origin, favoring the latter. Yet, in fact, the earliest evidence for water pipes seems to date to the cannabis-smoking technologies of East Africa.[34] While some early water pipes use coconuts native to South Asia, the very earliest documented vessels appear to have been based on the calabash, originally native to South Africa.[35]

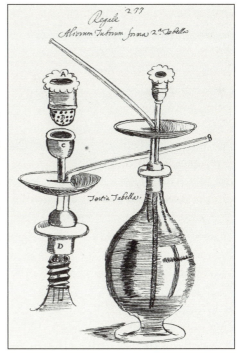

Figure 33. A Persian water pipe from the University of Pennsylvania MS Codex 122, *Viridarium regale*, late seventeenth-century Italian, based on an engraving in Johann Neander, *Tabacologia* (Leiden, 1622). Courtesy of Kislak Center for Rare Books and Manuscripts, University of Pennsylvania.

In short, the water pipe plausibly originated in East Africa. Although this technology seems to have been first used to smoke cannabis or dagga, it would seem that the spread of tobacco in the Indian Ocean by Portuguese traders in the early seventeenth century encouraged experimentation with new smokable drugs. One result of this process of globalization was the rise of opium smoking.

The modern opium pipe is a heated tube that warms but doesn't fully combust opium resin.[36] Although combusting opium is psychoactive, it loses many alkaloids as a result of the application of direct flame. Avoiding direct flame and high heat, as in a water pipe, makes the drug more bioavailable. Meanwhile, during the rise of the hookah in Africa, the Middle East, and South Asia, laudanum preparations taken orally were becoming increasingly popular in Europe. This led to a shift toward *nonsmokable* forms of opium in the West at precisely the time that novel technologies for *smoking* opium were spreading in Asia and Africa. Divergent trends of usage in the Indian Ocean world and Europe seem to have inadvertently had the effect of making the water pipe a popular tool for opium use in South Asia and the Middle East but little more than an exotic curiosity in Europe.[37]

Thus, our second way of looking at opium, as an exotic object, was shaped by the globalization of a new technology (the water pipe) and a new process (chemical medicine). Because opium smoking was seemingly first taken up in the trading worlds in the Indian Ocean region, *smoked* opium became thought of as fundamental, foreign, and degenerate. Ironically, the origins of smokable opium appear to be a product of the cross-pollinations among European traders (such as those of Goa and Ayutthaya) whose dual trade in both tobacco and opium seems to have driven the emergence of a smokable form of opium mixed with tobacco known as *madak* throughout maritime Southeast Asia.[38] The chemical transformations of opium in this period, though at times looked upon with suspicion, not only became popular but also gained a veneer of scientific novelty in the eighteenth century and were thus drawn back into the main line of the history of pharmacy. Meanwhile, so-called "crude" opium became a mysterious substance spirited from the lands of "the Turk" or "the Indies" into the shops of the West. It was when opium was reprocessed, chemically altered, and resold as a novel medicament under names like "laudanum" or "Sydenham's drops" that the drug became acceptably "modern" and disaggregated from its foreign associations.

European authors in the seventeenth and eighteenth centuries increasingly emphasized the special proclivity that Turks, Persians, and Indians had for the drug. François Lamure, a medical lecturer at Montpellier in 1746, for instance, taught his students that "among the Turks . . . sometimes they take as much as one ounce [of opium] to keep themselves agitated, and to refresh the blood to stay active in battle, like our soldiers use *eau de vie*."[39] So far, this was merely repetition of a common trope about opium being used as an aid for fighting (or sex) by the Turks. But the Montpellier professor then linked the effects of the drug to experimental observations about the material characteristics of human blood. "One has opened many days after [battle] the Cadavers [of the Turks], in which the blood has remained fluid for three days," he wrote. "Hence all the symptoms which laudanum produces stand as proof that it is not cold, as the ancients say."[40] Here, opium continued to be associated with the Turk, but it was mixed with a rhetoric of experimentation that drew upon dissection of Turkish cadavers on the battlefield and not just on older humoral reasoning. It is also significant that Lamure equated Turkish opium with European laudanum at this late date.

On the one hand, Lamure's was an up-to-date view of the matter, joining older humoral thinking with contemporary empiricism. On the other, it revealed the author's conservatism because he assumed that all opiates were alike. The author appears to have not considered whether the opium written about by Greco-Roman authors differed from the laudanum common in eighteenth-century Europe or from the specialized preparations sold in Istanbul, applying the same term "laudano" to it all.

The eighteenth century witnessed a fracturing of this unified view of the drug. It was a fracture that was driven by precisely the sort of language we've seen so far: associations of "crude" opium with Turkish warriors, Indian princes, and sexual exploits in the East. Meanwhile, opium-contained preparations like Sydenham's drops grew increasingly distant, both socially and epistemologically, from their crude or raw antecedents. They were sophisticated products of up-to-date technologies, safe for European bodies, and empirically verified. The contours of a larger transformation—the vilification of foreign *drugs* and the benediction of scientific *pharmaceuticals*—were being carved out.

How Morphine Became "Modern"

"Did we know the mechanical affections of the particles of Rhubarb, Hemlock, Opium and a Man, as a Watchmaker does those of a Watch," John

Locke had mused in 1690, "we should be able to tell before Hand that Rhubarb would purge, Hemlock kill, and Opium make a Man sleep."[41] The isolation of alkaloids like morphine and quinine during the Napoleonic era seemed to augur the realization of Locke's dream, offering a scientifically verifiable and testable method of studying and consuming drugs. For more than a century, stretching between Locke and Friedrich Sertürner, a number of innovations relating to the "purification" of opium led to the development of tinctures and isolates that seemed to alter the drug's fundamental properties.

With contemporary eyes, it appears that a significant percentage of early modern European medical preparations contained opiates and thus functioned as narcotics in the modern sense, regardless of how historical actors chose to classify them. But from an early modern European perspective, techniques of preparation could totally alter the characteristics of a drug and hence transform its ability to intoxicate, addict, or heal. The proliferation of new experimental methods and materials that followed the Columbian Exchange demanded a new attention to specific physical characteristics. It also led to great confusion over how to classify the various opiates. It was part of a process by which the origin of a drug became less important than the technology that had altered it. Just as quina was refigured into Jesuit's bark and "Agua da Inglaterra," opiates could be technologically refigured into substances that were not necessarily believed to share the same characteristics as raw opium. These chemical transformations reshaped opium's social role. In the end, they effectively split the drug in two: pristine white powder on the one hand and "raw" natural product on the other.

In the decades leading to the Opium Wars, European chemists were busy purifying and decontextualizing non-European imported drugs, attempting to strip them of addictive or poisonous properties—and divorcing them from associations with supposed indolence, lethargy, and "slavish" addictions of the non-Western world. Medical writings about narcotics frequently mentioned the dangers to patients who, as Lamure put it, "take too great a dose of laudanum . . . imprudently, when the doctor is not called." Patients who indulged in the drug could suffer a "phrenetic delirium," which stood as the flip side to the association of opium with sleep.[42] Francisco Suárez de Ribera warned that opium must not be prescribed to "infants, the elderly, and the debilitated"; to patients "with obese bodies"; or to those with melancholy or phlegmatic temperaments.[43] The question then became this: If the root cause of addiction was some kind of personalized process in the brain, then couldn't chemistry be used to "fix" the substances *before* they entered the brain?

In his *Atalaya da vida contra as hostilidades da morte,* João Curvo Semedo offered one solution.[44] He argued that the "smoke of opium" was harmful, but that the drug could be chemically transformed into a purified liquid form that "doesn't do harm."[45] By the middle decades of the eighteenth century, chemists were conducting experimental trials of theories like those of Semedo in an effort to determine how different types of opiates influenced the "sentiments" of the mind and how these effects could be modified. The French court physician François Boissier de Sauvages de Lacroix, writing in 1751, reported on his experiments to determine whether opium was responsible for "diminishing the viscosity" of fluids in the body. The question was not just how narcotics altered the "molecules" of the blood and humors but also what de Sauvages called "the nervous fluids" responsible for "the forces of movement and of feeling." Citing Newton, de Sauvages speculated that the behavior of this fluid in the brain capable of transmitting thought and feeling could be "analogous to electrical currents . . . and to the matter of light."[46]

These investigations of opium used experimental methods to attempt to transform the subjective mental and physical effects of drugs. De Sauvages's conclusions were not terribly surprising: his experimental results, he wrote, were "strongly opposed to the opinions of the ancients, proving that opium, far from coagulating the blood, renders it notably cooler." Not only this, but "stramonium juice, tincture of saffron, and other narcotics produce the same effect." Although more research was needed to determine "the reasons for why these [narcotics] calm pains and bring about sleep," it seemed clear to him that "they render certain molecules of the blood and the lymph fine enough to become caught in the orifices of the nervous tubes, and block for a time the secretion of the nervous fluid."[47] What was different here was not the conclusion or the terminology but the use of quantitative measures such as specific gravity and the attention paid to measuring characteristics such as acidity, temperature, weight, and volume. In addition, de Sauvages was subjecting opium *itself* to chemical manipulation: he based his opinion on experiments involving the mixing of opium with samples of human blood, lymphatic fluid, and serum, to which various amounts of salts were applied.[48] In short, psychoactive drugs were now being treated in much the same way as other chemicals: not as quasi-magical forces but as substances that followed observable physical laws, like Newtonian light beams. And if their effects were not caused by devils or supernatural forces but instead by quantifiable material characteristics, then these could also be precisely modified through chemical technologies.

The figure who did more than anyone to achieve this ambition was the German chemist Friedrich Sertürner, born in 1783. Sertürner's announcement, in 1805, that he had isolated a chemical from the "salt of opium" that he dubbed "Morphium" was a key moment in the history of medicine.[49] The isolation of "morphium," better known as morphine, marked the beginning of the "alkaloid era," a period of pharmaceutical innovation that led to the isolation of a host of psychoactive substances collectively known to chemists as alkaloids, including strychnine (1817), atropine (1819), caffeine (1819), and nicotine (1828). At first, Sertürner was frightened by what he discovered. Morphium, he warned, had "terrible effects." A miniscule quantity, far smaller than any comparable dose of opium, was able to kill a dog. Later, he conducted an experiment in which Sertürner himself (along with three young test subjects) overdosed on the new substance. After noticing that "the animal powers seemed to be raised" with a half grain of morphine, the amount was doubled and then tripled, leading to "a sense of stunning in the head" swiftly followed by acute stomach pain, vomiting, fainting, and "a kind of dozing reverie." For Sertürner, this was a frightening experience: "If we may judge from this rather disagreeable experiment," he concluded, "morphium, even in small doses, is a violent poison."[50] Sertürner's opinion later changed, however—especially after 1827, when the Merck family purchased the rights to his drug and began mass-producing it. He settled in the city of Hamelin, famous for the Pied Piper myth, and operated a pharmacy, the Rathaus Apotheke, which sold his new invention.[51]

As with many firsts in the history of science, however, the first isolated alkaloid was not as novel as it might at first seem. Sertürner himself did not use the term "alkaloid"; he simply described morphine as a "salt" of opium. In this, he was looking backward to a century and a half of previous work. The psychoactive properties of intoxicating drugs like opium were theorized by some seventeenth-century European thinkers in mechanical terms: blockages of tubes in the brain, fermentations of the blood, oily or acidic molecules, and the like. A 1708 review in *Philosophical Transactions* by the Oxford physician John Freind gives an apt summary of this mindset. All chemistry, it claimed, is a process of joining together or separating "bodies," the former through calcination, sublimation, and distillation, and the latter by fermentation, digestion, extraction, precipitation, and crystallization.

Freind denounced certain chemical manipulations of opium that "are made by the fumes of Sulphur, or by acid Liquors," because these can dangerously coagulate or thin the blood. But he encouraged experimenting with the precipitation of a chemical medicine with "Salts" that "attract" and "cohere with" particles in a drug and thus form new "Bodies."[52] The language was vague, but the implications clear. Even a century before Sertürner's break-through, narcotics like opium were thought to be capable of being chemi-cally transformed and given new properties and forms, just as lead could, theoretically, be turned into gold.

Yet if the underlying concept of a purified "salt of opium" was not new, the ability to mass-produce such a product was. The rise of morphine as a widespread consumer product in the 1830s and 1840s marked a decisive shift.[53] "Opium" had never been a single drug in a strict pharmacological sense: like many medicinal plants, *Papaver somniferum* contains a complex mix of psychoactive constituents (morphine, thebaine, codeine, papaver-ine) that vary in proportion according to different varietals and preparation styles. The isolation of morphine was the culmination of an Enlightenment project of isolating and defining the individual functional parts of complex systems. (De Sauvages, for instance, was a close friend of Linnaeus who studied opium as part of a larger attempt to create a rational "taxonomy" of diseases and drugs.) The steps by which orientalized opium became "mod-ern" morphine were thus the end points of a process of disassociation that began decades earlier.

As we saw in Chapter 2, some efforts had been made to disassociate drugs like opium from the non-European and subaltern groups associated with them. Now it was possible to *disassociate a drug from nature itself,* or at least to materially remove it from the world of botany and plants. A Neo-lithic flower had become a nondescript white powder: the product of a labo-ratory, not a plantation.

An Early Modern View of Addiction

Now we come to an important question. It is clear that opium began to shift from being a traditional, "indigenous" remedy of Europe to a foreign and an exotic drug during the span of time running from about 1600 to 1800. It is also clear that the isolation of morphine and the process of chemical experimentation leading to it was transformative: drug sellers could now move beyond the vagaries of patent remedy names and identify individual psychoactive molecules, like morphine, caffeine, and, later in the nineteenth century, cocaine.

But what were the larger effects of these two changes? The same period also witnessed the knitting together of legal codes, emerging bureaucracies, early forms of governmental propaganda, and a nascent sense of national identity.[54] One characteristic of emerging centralized states was the creation of durable legal regimes that regulated perceived social deviancy. Without a powerful state, there can be no such thing as an illegal drug: state power is required to *make* something illegal (as opposed to taboo or religiously heterodox or socially unacceptable for a host of other reasons). The reverse was also true: widespread medical acceptance of novel alkaloids like morphine meant that these compounds fell into the emerging legal category of "pharmaceuticals," a subset of drugs that were heavily regulated but not a priori associated with illegality or deviance. The "orientalization" of opium pushed the drug into the edges of society over the course of the eighteenth and nineteenth centuries, resulting in opium's societal marginalization and, finally, the drive to make the drug illegal in dozens of countries. But it was not simply the association of opium and other drugs with "Oriental" intoxication or indolence that contributed to making some drugs illicit. It was the mingling of these associations with something resembling a "modern" concept of addiction.

Addiction is a vast and frequently controversial topic. Reasonable people can (and do) disagree about everything from the meaning and scope of the word itself to the legal and political implications of treating addiction as a pathology. For present purposes, though, I hope the reader will be able to agree with me on two key points. The first is that addiction exists as a neurobiological reality in human beings: in other words, that it is possible for the human brain and body to become so habituated to an external stimulus (be it a substance or a behavior) that the cessation of that stimulus brings physical and/or mental pain and a strong desire to resume its use. The second point is that addiction is not *solely* based in biology; throughout history, the range of what humans consider to be damagingly habit forming is constantly shifting and deeply linked to cultural beliefs.[55]

I believe it is important for us to acknowledge that opiate alkaloids activate addictive tendencies in some individuals; however, it is also important for us to avoid allowing present-day cultural biases to pathologize or moralize about this behavior. When I write, then, of the emergence of a "modern" conception of addiction in the eighteenth century, I refer to a cultural model in which addiction has become codified as a pseudo-pathology associated with "low morals," with debased behavior, and, often, with racialized views of the human body.[56]

Different societies build different edifices of interpretation upon the biological bedrock of a drug's inherent addictiveness. In medieval Christian and Islamic medicine, narcotic drugs like opium were associated with the loss of reason and the impulse to sleep. These early accounts did not tend to fixate on the euphoric or addictive properties of narcotic drugs. Cognates of the Greek word "narkotikon" were in wide usage in the Middle Ages, but the word referred simply to numbness or unconsciousness. Words analogous to "addiction" or "habit-forming" are relatively modern in origin.[57] Instead, medieval and early modern accounts of drugs that we would now regard as addictive used metaphors of slavery, sleep, and the soul.

Opium was linked not only to sleep but also to "stealing," enslavement, or loss of freedom. This connection was apparent even in the oldest European references to opium's psychological effects. The tenth-century Bamberg antidotary, for instance, described a slumber induced by henbane, hemlock, mandrake, and opium that caused the patient "to fall asleep as if his spirit had been stolen."[58] It runs up through de Quincey (who described opium as a "yoke of misery") and other nineteenth-century authors.[59]

In short, premodern opium was a narcotic in a classical sense. It was not necessarily something to be frightened by, but it was something to be cautious of due to its dangerous ability to block the "spirits," its coldness, and its resulting sleep-inducing effects. It was not considered uniquely dangerous and was not thought to warrant prohibition. After all, early modern Europeans believed a great many things were poisons that blocked the animal spirits. Edward Topsell, writing in 1607, also identified *cats*—specifically, cat brains—as a dangerous substance to ingest, for almost the same reasons that Ambrose Paré and other doctors warned about opium. Because cat brains were of an extremely dry humor, Topsell believed that they "stoppeth the animal spirits, that they cannot pass into the ventricle, by reason whereof memory faileth." Topsell concluded gravely that "though we are constrained to nourish [cats] for the surpressing of small vermine: so with a wary and discreet eye we must avoid their harms."[60] The humoral characteristics of an opium overdose may have differed from the effects of eating cat brains (one was "too hot," the other "too cold"). But the effects and dangers were held to be much the same.

By the end of the early modern period, something fundamental had

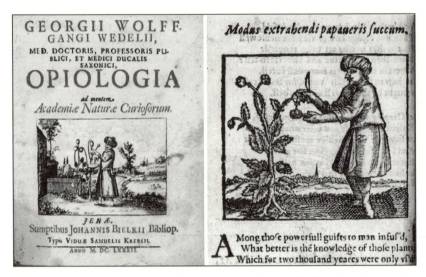

Figure 34. The title page from a 1682 German edition of Sala's *Opiologia* and a woodcut of a Turkish man harvesting opium, from the first English-language edition: Angelo Sala, *Opiologia, or, a Treatise concerning the Nature, properties, true preparation and safe use and Administration of Opium* (London: Nicholas Okes, 1618). Courtesy of the Wellcome Library.

changed. As the notion of what *exotic* meant comes into clearer focus in the seventeenth century, opium begins to take a place in the symbolic order alongside birds of paradise, parasols, pineapples, harems, man-eaters, and tobacco.[61] It was no coincidence that it also became increasingly bound up with new beliefs about addiction and addictive qualities among Europeans. The seeds of this shift are apparent in the decades bookending 1600, as authors like Garcia da Orta (*Colóquios*) and Angelo Sala (*Opiologia*) conflated opium and cannabis with fanciful tales of Turkish and Indian otherness.[62] At least initially, these condemnations did not depend on notions of addictiveness.

The argument in *Opiologia* and other works of the period was not that the drug was inherently addictive. It was that differences between Asian and European bodies meant that Europeans were better able to cope with its effects. The French physician Nicolas Venette wrote, for example, that he was convinced of the value of opium when it proved to be the only cure for a disease he suffered in 1688, "causing an excessive voluptuousness . . . and a perfect pleasure."[63] He speculated that *bangue* "is no other thing than the opium [*Amfiam*] of the Orientals" because, like opium, cannabis "inspires lovers to caress women and causes us to swoon into pleasant reveries."[64] However, these positive effects occurred "only if it is taken in a small quantity." If too much bangue or opium are taken at a time, Venette warned, "one becomes insensible" to such an extent that it was used by "Indian women" to "throw themselves, entirely insensible, into the fire" upon the death of their husband.[65]

In Venette's view, as in the view of others surveyed in this chapter, the value of bangue and opium were deeply shaped by the culture of the consumer: "Europeans do not feel the same effects from the use of these narcotics as do the Asians and Africans," he wrote. "Habit makes these drugs produce different effects on those who use them, and we observe among us [Europeans] that they confer tranquility of soul, pleasure, and an itching of the body, in place of the sexual distractions that are described in other authors."[66] The orientalization of opium had originally involved a presumption of racial difference between European opiate users and Asians who, as we see in Venette, were assumed to be more susceptible to its harmful virtues.

Opium also began to provoke a more troubling question: especially with more addictive preparations (like laudanum and smoked opium), Europeans began to see the enslavement of colonized peoples as a trait that drug use might provoke among *all* users, by stripping away the use of reason and the animal spirits. Sir Thomas Pope Blount, for instance, wrote that Persians' opium use "so weakens their Brains who take it continually, that they run the hazard of losing the use of their Reason, and the principal functions of their Understanding."[67] Habitual use of opium was increasingly thought to degenerate European bodies, strip away reason, and induce torpor. The emerging racist and Orientalist tropes of European attitudes toward inhabitants of the tropics slowly became refigured as symptoms of a new pathology: opiate dependence.

The Taming of Opium

This chapter began with a vast warehouse, a harbinger of what would ultimately be the most important step in the evolution of humanity's relationship with *Papaver somniferum*. From the late eighteenth century onward, opiates have served a dual role. On the one hand, smoked opium latex ("crude opium") emerged, as we have seen, as a symbol of "slavish" addiction and "Oriental" exoticism. But, on the other, a new vision of opium derivatives was in formation. First with laudanum, then with morphine and its cousin heroin, chemically derived opiates became celebrated as a paradigmatic creation of medical science. These modern by-products of opium benefited from a union of industrial-scale science and more efficacious mechanisms for targeting consumers, actuated by the rise of mass literacy, new advertising formats, and the increasing public profile of chemistry. With the rise of this third way of looking at an opium ball, the former two views began to appear not only "not modern" but also as uncivilized, inhumane, and, ultimately, illegal.

In his *Confessions of an English Opium Eater* (first published as an anonymous series in the *London Magazine* in 1821), de Quincey had recorded the view of three apothecaries in London that an "immense . . . number of amateur opium-eaters" existed in London at that time. He also relayed reports from cotton-manufacturers in Manchester, stating that "their work-people were rapidly getting into the practice of opium-eating; so much so, that on a Saturday afternoon the counters of the druggists were strewed with pills of one, two, or three grains, in preparation for the known demand of the evening." Although some might see this as a simple substitution, since the workers' wages "would not allow them to indulge in ale or spirits," de Quincey disagreed. Even if industrial workers' wages were to increase in the future, he wrote, the workers would never again "descend to the gross and mortal enjoyments of alcohol" once they had tasted "the fascinating powers of opium."[68]

Alcohol, of course, has been part of human societies for millennia and is unlikely to go anywhere. But de Quincey may have been onto something: opiates have, historically, had a close and tangled relationship with societies undergoing both industrialization and industrial decline.[69] We should be wary of drawing conclusions based on the writings of so unique and unreliable a figure as de Quincey. But there are other sources that corroborate his claim that industrial workers were becoming increasingly reliant on opiates in the early decades of the nineteenth century. "Immense quantities of white poppies are grown every year in England solely for the sake of the capsules," one report from 1859 claimed. "Could our crowded rooms wherein thousands earn their daily bread; could our factories, our mills, our suffocating dwellings, where the needle of the seamstress pursues its ceaseless flight, speak out, we should know better than we do now, where so vast a quantity of this poisonous but valuable drug is consumed."[70]

The author of these lines, in seeking to trace where opium "disappeared" to in England, allowed for the use of opium in "medicinal compounds" like morphine. This, to him, was acceptable. What was objectionable was the use of opium "in the crude state" by workers. There was a kind of symmetry here: the same English workers who were busily transforming the raw materials of the empire into modern English industrial goods were, themselves, reliant on a raw material from the empire. Raw opium was objectionable because it was *unimproved* opium—unimproved not only by the techniques of European medical science but also by a more nebulous cultural influence. A vague set of cultural signifiers (expensive cups and plates, fashionable gatherings, branded advertising in print) had allowed Mexican chocolate and Chinese tea to become acceptable to European consumers in the seventeenth century.[71] Narcotics like opium posed a special challenge because they unsettled the mind itself, shaking off the forces of reason and civility.

It was not preordained that opium would morph from being a socially acceptable cure to being a foreign fear in the early modern period. Some Europeans had argued that crude opium could be mastered. In 1682, John Chamberlayne explicitly drew on the examples of coffee, tea, tobacco, and chocolate to argue that Europeans should acculturate themselves to exotic or narcotic drugs, "taming" them in the process.[72] Even opium and hellebore, two of the most feared narcotics of the age, became seemingly harmless if the consumer's body was able to "naturalize" them. "A French Ambassador," Chamberlayne wrote, "was indispos'd, that he could never sleep; upon which he would often devour whole Ounces of Opium without being concern'd: and the Turks are often observ'd to swallow great Lumps of it, a tenth part of which would kill those that are not accustomed to Opiates . . . custom and conversation will make even the fiercest creatures familiar."[73] It is no coincidence that the language Chamberlayne used—"tame," "naturalize," "civil"—was identical to the rhetoric of European colonization. According to historian Peter Sahlins, French government officials and colonial leaders in the late seventeenth century adopted a "language of the animal world" that prized notions of tameness, envisioning French *artes* as transforming a barbarous nature into a rational and well-ordered imperial garden.[74] A similar, albeit temporally later, process is at work in Richard Drayton's influential study of the Royal Botanic Garden at Kew, whose proprietors envisioned their work as nothing less than the "Improvement" of the world.[75] In the New World, Africa, and Asia, these concerns with domestication and improvement translated into the notion that indigenous societies, like wild animals, required "taming" to become full members of the civil society of the believe that the same patterns—of coevolution with humans over a deep time scale, then a sudden change in usage due to globalization, and finally a split caused by scientific analysis, leading to an illegal "raw" version and a pharmaceutical "processed" one—are evident elsewhere. We can find it in everything from coca and cannabis to sarsaparilla, the now-banned carcinogenic compound in traditional root beer.[81]

However, there are also important differences among these substances. For one thing, not all drugs can be readily harvested on the industrial level required to produce vast spaces like the Patna warehouse. In the case of a compound like ayahuasca (based on the harvesting of wild plants and carefully guarded shamanic knowledge) commodification was nearly impossible. Opium was more prominent not just because it had a deep history of cultivation and use—after all, many now-forgotten or marginalized drugs did—but was because opium could move successfully through all three of the "views" studied here. It could be used in a traditional medical setting, consumed in alternative forms through new technologies, and ultimately turned into a cash crop grown on a massive industrial scale.

No single way of seeing opium ever became dominant enough to fully re-place those that preceded it. The different societal roles of opium are rarely erased; they are often overlaid. The result is a picture that is unmanageably complex. Confused, we lose our place. Without a clear point of origin, we simply take it for granted that the Chinese have "always" smoked opium or that Europeans "always" saw the drug as foreign. In fact, such statements are essentially the inverse of the truth.

Underneath the various personae that we apply to opium, there is the same assemblage of molecules: molecules that mirror endorphins inside the human brain, arising out of the strange alchemy of natural selection within a European wildflower, then joining humans as symbiotes in our species' takeover of the globe. From the earliest accounts of opium dependence in the premodern period up to the chronicles of journalist Sam Quinones in *Dreamland*, we see how the underlying biological features of a drug make themselves known in history.[82] But the *ways* that those biological realities are felt has varied wildly over time and place. Opium has been the vivifying weapon of warriors as well as the muse of dreaming junkies. It has been hailed as a panacea to be stocked in every apothecary shop and vilified as a societal scourge. It has been associated with men and women, with Europeans and Indians, with heterosexual and homosexual impulses, and with the demonic and the divine.

In short, we need to be careful, in drawing our three views of opium to a close, not to assume that these three views are all that is required. A hundred more could be written. The point is not to define the precise historical trajectory of this drug but to walk through a process of analysis. Indeed, by moving through these three ways of seeing an opium ball, this chapter also takes us through the larger arguments of the book.

Opium—in its three personae of flower, latex, and alkaloid—shows us how profoundly the route of administration and the technologies of preparation can change a drug's social function. This book has argued that fear of cultural difference stands at the core of the fear of drugs. Technology, by contrast, defines the *allure* of drugs: the dream of improving nature, altering the makeup of the human body and mind. Drugs are high tech. They are products of secret knowledge—often knowledge that has been deliberately effaced. And, as such, they appeal even as they frighten. Even one of the most ubiquitous medicinal crops in the Old World, a drug with its origins in Western Europe, could become foreign and frightening as a result of a change in the technologies used to prepare it. But at the same time as the opium smoker became a stock figure of the foreign for Europeans, another new technology (the chemical isolation of alkaloids) made morphine a paragon of Western scientific innovation.

We can extrapolate this story to other drug scares throughout history—and those still to come. A process of widespread adoption is initially shaped by a parallel process of exoticism or orientalism. This foreignness becomes tangled up with racial anxieties and with fears of commercial competition or bodily harm. The drug eventually splits into two halves: the licit (scientific, medicinal, legal, socially acceptable) and the illicit (barbarous, recreational, illegal, socially harmful). There is little functional pharmacological difference between OxyContin and heroin, but the social gap between the two is vast. Just as the opium pipe became, in Europe, an emblem of Oriental languor and slavish devotion, heroin in the United States has become a charged symbol, a totem of deviance. And, like morphine in the nineteenth century, prescription opiates became domesticated, familiar. Throughout the 1980s and 1990s, the pharmaceutical corporations producing opiate medications peddled them as valuable medicines without "serious medical side effects" that "should be used much more often."[83] Purdue Pharma gave away Oxy-Contin-branded fishing hats to physicians.[84]

These were appeals to familiarity and acceptability: this isn't a drug, it's a medicine. But beneath these appeals lies a deeper authority. It has two foundations: that of the medical expert and that of the corporation. Today, medical experts and corporations don't dirty their hands with black and sticky things like opium balls. That messy work has been pushed out of the frame, no longer in view. But without the earlier trade in drugs like opium—those vast, geometric halls, those workers in the rafters, that flower that becomes a drug which becomes a pharmaceutical—who can say where the corporation and the physician would be today?

Drug Pasts and Futures

Suppose an Apothecaries shop were furnish't with exquisite drugges, yet if the boxes want names for direction, or there want a Physitian to prescribe the medicine; it is to be feared, that in such a confusion, poison should be taken for cordials.

—GODFREY GOODMAN, 1616

Two well-dressed apothecaries stand before a wall of shelves stocked with drug jars bearing labels like *Modestie, Raison,* and *Memoire.* One is pouring a potion marked *Sagesse* (wisdom) into the opened mouth of a patient, who grips the pourer's arm uneasily. Below, court jesters wearing fool's caps tumble into a bedpan. To the right of these two—leaning in front of a distillation apparatus, a mortar and pestle, and a lengthy medical receipt pinned to the shelf—is a figure whose pose brings to mind a bread baker. But this is no baker sliding loaves of dough into a wood oven: it is an apothecary pushing a man on a long board into a distillation furnace. Above, the *phantasies* that had filled this foolish man's head emerge as the rarefied quintessences of distillation: horses, backgammon boards, armor, pantaloons, women, swords, theater masks, flowers, hunting dogs, and (somewhat unaccountably), a monkey brandishing a walking stick. An accompanying bit of doggerel assumes the voice of a mountebank, inviting all who read it to cure their foolish humors with the same unorthodox methods:

> *You, come here! Your head's constrained*
> *With fantasies, that make you pained:*
> *Of this sage Master, one can't deny*
> *That he will have your humours dry*
> *In no time flat, within his furnace—*

Great allegiance of many torments—
So too, he'll purge with healing potions
That can make the foolish cogent.

It is a hallucinatory and potentially nightmarish scene, but a popular one: at least seven variations of this image appeared in the first half of the seventeenth century, in four languages.[1] One German version offered an expanded caption in the voice of one Doctor Wurmbrandt (worm-burner), who implores, "Trust me to bring you back to your right mind" when you suffer from "wild imaginings as when . . . having become quite drunk . . . you are conscious of nothing, whether you are a man or woman."[2]

The cure is achieved not by phlebotomy (which Wurmbrandt professes to deplore) but by chemistry. A still worn over the head produces a kind of cognitive vapor that sublimates into the air and leaves the patient freed from psychological distress. It's a startlingly strange image. Yet it's also one that would have had an obvious metaphorical resonance for early modern Europeans versed in the notion of the human body as microcosm. After all,

Figure 35. "The doctor cures fantasy, and purges folly with drugs." Mattheus Greuter (Paris?, 1620). Courtesy of the Bibliothèque Nationale de France.

it was common to attribute psychoactivity to "vapors" that rose upward like steam. "A small dose taken by the mouth excites vapors that rise up to the brain, benignly troubling the imagination," was how the French physician Nicolas Venette had described the effects of opium in 1686.[3] Why not move from drugs that distill or refine the brain's vapors to practicing a kind of psychoactive chemistry directly on the human brain itself?

One goal of these prints was simply to poke fun at the rising fortunes of apothecaries and chemical physicians. But they also express fascination with the rise of new drugs that promised not only to cure diseases but, potentially, to augment the human mind and spirit. Robert Boyle's list of the desiderata he expected future natural philosophers to create included drugs to obviate the need for sleep and to cure the mad, and Hooke was already speculating around the same time that cannabis could "be of considerable Use for Lunaticks." These images reflect the dichotomies of drugs: between fear and fascination, familiar and exotic, physical and mental, and social and internal.

They also point to a division that has run throughout this work. The dual acts of the two physicians in these images—the purge of toxins from the guts, on the left, and the sublimation of the mind, on the right—seem to symbolize the emerging split between "scientific" drug use and everything else. In the early seventeenth century, the new chemical physicians were objects of ridicule. Yet the rationale for chemical medicine—its performance in an emerging Enlightenment framework, its royal patronage and expanding prestige—ultimately gave it a legitimacy that tropical drugs lacked. It was a harbinger of the divergences to come that, whereas the purgative drug administered in these images induces that most animalistic of all human functions, the distillation apparatus performs something sublime, immaterial, almost miraculous.

These images lead us back to the core question of this book: How did the early modern drug trade transform into the modern division between "licit" pharmaceuticals and "illicit" recreational drugs?

The preceding chapters have charted a shift away from the eclecticism of sixteenth-century drug use and toward a more limited, scientifically bounded approach to medical drugs. The seeds of the licit/illicit divide can be found in this process of separation, which was built on fears of counterfeiting and non-European spirituality. But other factors were also important, above all the rise of alkaloids in the nineteenth century. The isolation of morphine and quinine in the era of Napoleon arguably plays a role in the history of pharmacy that is analogous to Galileo's discovery of the moons of Jupiter in the field of astronomy. Both have become boundary-marking events in their respective fields. Although the Scientific Revolution is more famous, the alkaloid era of the early nineteenth century kickstarted a shift in global health, mass consumption, and legal norms that was similarly transformative.[4] The ability to isolate, manipulate, and mass produce pharmacologically active substances altered patterns of global trade, sociability, and healing. New drugs like quinine improved global life expectancy; new sources of psychoactivity changed how billions of people experienced the world and their place within it. The histories studied in this book gave birth to a modern society in which the use of psychoactive substances from caffeine to antidepressants and drugs to treat attention deficit hyperactivity disorder (ADHD) has become commonplace. But this process was by no means preordained. Things could have gone otherwise.

It was not clear in the seventeenth century whether certain substances would rise to the heavens or fall to earth. The growing precision of pharmacy was counterbalanced by the increasingly blurred boundaries between the recreational and the medical use of drugs. New varieties of intoxication (be they newly invented technological products like laughing gas, or newly globalized ones like cannabis) offered respites from lives of toil, as well as painful experiences of addiction. The contact zones between European colonies and indigenous societies were the laboratories in which the modern drug trade, and the modern concept of drugs, emerged.

In many parts of the globe, it was not until the eighteenth and nineteenth centuries that drugs moved from being expensive medicines to foundational elements of everyday life. In the three or four decades bookending 1800, the Chinese opium trade increased at a rapid rate; the cannabis culture of Jamaica began to coalesce around Indian and African laborers; morphine became a consumer product; and tobacco rolled in paper began, for the first time, to be called "cigarettes." Something that we could justifiably call a "modern era" of drug use was in the making, and many of the worldviews, practices, and customs surveyed in the preceding chapters were fading away.

The Modernity of Drugs

Any history of drugs, regardless of the time period it covers, must reckon with the human cost of drug laws in more recent history. By the latter half of the nineteenth century, the strands of thinking with and about drugs charted in this book had become bound together into a noose. As drugs became better defined, both scientifically and legally, they became increasingly important as an element of politics. The rise of centralized states that could assert effective legal control of drug use didn't just give rise to the modern era of drugs—it was, I believe, central to the development of modernity itself.[5] Scholars have argued that the colonialism of the late nineteenth century was defined by a shift toward an enforced, bourgeois moralism: a "violence of self-conscious and self-righteous transformation of social life."[6] Agents of empire increasingly sought to dominate colonized people's inner lives, to reshape their sense of themselves and their place in society in conformity to a system of moral purity. If this generalization is true, then we can see the rise of drug laws in the period between the mid-nineteenth century and World War I as the tip of the spear of a new and more intimate form of imperialism.

Drug use in the early modern world was often a kind of social performance: the courteous offer of a pipe or a teacup, the braggadocio of drunken warriors, the ritualistic intoxication of holy men and women, the aesthetic flourish of the water pipe or the snuff box. It was eclectic, disaggregated, decentralized, sometimes even anarchic; it was shaped by implicit assumptions, taboos, and beliefs rather than by formal regulations. As empires and states sought ever greater control over the bodies and minds of their subjects, drugs became a battleground for efforts to enforce new cultural, social, and economic norms. The act of regulating a substance also meant regulating the knowledge and social relations surrounding it. Drug laws, then and now, are almost always about something more than the drug itself.

The use of newly illegal substances grew more private, more individualized, over the course of the nineteenth and early twentieth centuries: a furtive, criminalized act of individual resistance to social convention, rather than a public expression of a social or spiritual order. The trajectory of illicit drugs stood in stark contrast to the trajectory of other drugs, like tobacco, that were both socially acceptable and open to corporate and governmental investment. In the 1940s and 1950s, the U.S. tobacco industry became a powerful tool for projecting postwar American power, aided by a symbiotic relationship between tobacco companies and U.S. federal government agencies.[7] Today, the nationalized tobacco industry in China accounts for between 7 and 10 percent of all government revenue.[8] In the decade preceding 1939, the German government encouraged widespread consumption of state-produced stimulants, such as methamphetamine, in a self-conscious effort to increase not only the economic production of the country (longer working hours with less sleep) but also its psychological state (chemically induced zeal and loosened inhibitions).[9] By asserting legal power over drugs and the drug trade, modernizing states didn't just expand their revenue base. They gained access to a more nebulous but no less important seat of power: the subjectivity of individual citizens and subjects.

The changing meaning and social functions of drugs in the nineteenth century also reflected a larger remapping of the natural sciences. Chemists, newly able to isolate the alkaloids within substances that had previously been the domain of botanists and collectors, began to conceptualize drugs not as holistic natural products (such as a leaf or a piece of bark) but as molecular entities (an alkaloid with a precise—and precisely describable—chemical structure). This "fixing" of drugs differentiated chemically described pharmaceuticals from those substances with actions that could not be scientifically explained. Whereas the purity of an alkaloid like quinine or morphine could be experimentally verified, the provenance and legitimacy of drugs like bangue rested on the reports of merchants, apothecaries, and cultivators. Likewise, chemically derived alkaloids tended to present visually as white powders, offering visible and material proof of their supposed purity.

By contrast, "Indies drugs" were highly variable on a sensory level, often presenting not as pure white powders but as noxious brews. The split between illicit drugs and licit pharmaceuticals thus rested not only on the discovery of alkaloids and of methods of empirical verification of drug purity and contents but on larger cultural and even aesthetic anxieties about the non-European worlds from which they hailed. If, as one historian has argued, the "consumer orientalism" of the seventeenth century had turned a novel substance like coffee into a global sensation by about 1700, a century later these exotic drugs emerged as the unsavory obverse of the pristine coins minted by chemists.[10]

Interestingly, in recent years this dichotomy has begun to invert. It is now *indigenous* botanicals that are prized by global medical consumers, while lab-made pharmaceuticals are becoming suspect. In the case of rhinoceros horn and other Chinese medicines, the binary never emerged: traditional medicines became "modern" commodities, seamlessly. Indeed, two of the oldest surviving multinational pharmaceutical companies turn out to be Merck, founded by a German apothecary in 1668, and Tong Ren Tang, founded in 1669. The latter (then, as now,) is a seller of traditional Chinese medicinal drugs. Twenty-first-century Western culture has lately nourished a facile cult of indigeneity that locates "authentic" or "natural" cures in "traditional" cultures of healing, especially those of so-called "Stone Age tribes" untouched by Western medicine. Yet, many such beliefs are themselves a legacy of colonial-era condescensions. In many respects, the drug trade nurtured by Western medicine shares the same historical roots as those labeled as "traditional." Both emerged out of the globalization and exploitation of the colonial era.

The Future of Drugs

This book has documented a wide array of substances. Some of them, like opium or cinchona, have well-documented pharmacological effects. Others, like the blood of a white hen, do not. My aim here has not been to perform a Whiggish autopsy on these cures, separating out those that "really worked" from those that were "merely" based on performativity, cultural expectations, or the host of other factors that present-day physicians would ascribe to the placebo effect. Any history of drugs in the premodern world needs to remain as nonjudgmental as possible about the substances it studies. At the same time, however, it is important to acknowledge that some drugs' historical trajectories were shaped by their pharmacological properties and not just by placebo effects or cultural imaginations. Understanding those histories requires us to address drugs' underlying biological characteristics while also considering the dazzling range of cultural interpretations that humans have overlaid onto these unchanging material factors.

The divergence between how different disciplines navigate this distinction between the biological and the cultural has led to frequent miscommunication. Social theorists have tended to view drugs as inherently addicting substances floating free from history or chronology.[11] For researchers in the natural sciences, by contrast, the term "drug" functions as an addictive substance that activates the reward system of the brain through the release of neurotransmitters like dopamine or serotonin, or as any type of pharmaceutical or natural product that exerts an empirically verifiable alteration in health.[12] When scholarship in the natural sciences and medical fields does deal with drugs as historically constructed subjects, it often does so in a way that recalls "just-so" stories. Recent scientific papers on everything from malaria to brain scans to pulmonary hypertension have offered potted histories of early modern drugs, but these short summaries of a drug's lineage tend to obscure the difficulty of tracing a drug as a coherent subject across time and space.[13] Although this scholarship rarely interacts with anthropological and literary studies of drug history, it shares with them an assumption that the globalization of drugs connects to the origins of modernity—in this case, of modern science and medicine.

The lack of communication and historical context in how these disciplines think about drugs is part of a larger failure of memory. Modern societies are like amnesiacs when it comes to drug policy, forever reinventing new moral panics, forever forgetting the lessons of the past. Unless we can remember the legacies of exploitation and misunderstanding that shape contemporary assumptions about the legal and social role of drugs, we will be doomed to repeat ourselves again and again.

Today, the illegal drug trade is one of the largest and most powerful industries on the planet, with illicit drug trafficking alone accounting for between $426 and $652 billion of economic activity in 2017, according to one estimate.[14] The pharmaceutical industry is even larger, accounting for more than $1 trillion in revenues in 2016 and on track to reach $1.4 trillion (2 percent of total global economic production, or "Gross World Product," by 2020).[15] And this purview excludes substances that we now classify as foods, like coffee beans, which number among the most widely traded commodities in the world. To these economic figures we can point to the role of drug violence in contemporary states, long-standing debates about the societal impacts of prescription amphetamine and opiate abuse, and the future promise of "nootropics" (smart drugs), which promise to increase cognition. We could also include the massive demographic effects of the suppression of diseases like malaria and the eradication of others like smallpox using the twentieth-century descendants of some of the early modern substances studied here.

At the same time, "research chemicals" that occupy a gray market have emerged as new global commodities. The most infamous such coverage surrounded "bath salts," a term that typically refers to MPDV, an amphetamine-like cathinone alkaloid synthesized from the traditional drug khat, which has long been hugely popular as a recreational stimulant in Yemen.[16] As this detail hints, many of the more recent drug scares actually have unexpected links to premodern drugs. Today, for instance, the sassafras tree is grown in large quantities as a cash crop in Southeast Asia. An unknown but significant proportion of this crop makes its way into covert factories that convert compounds in sassafras, known as safroles, into MDMA (ecstasy), and from these factories it is shipped to international hubs of the drug trade like London and Amsterdam. This quasi-alchemical process of transforming a tropical tree bark into a powerful psychoactive drug occurs mainly in Thailand, Malaysia, and Indonesia: the regions that East India Company ships once sailed to from the same British and Dutch imperial capitals.[17] It even seems possible that the crude versus sublime dichotomy studied in this book could reach an apotheosis with techniques like direct magnetic stimulation or BCI (brain-computer interfaces). These new forms of psychoactivity hold out the promise to effect a total separation between drug-like effects and the ingestion of a material, natural substance.

HAVING COMPLETED OUR travels, let us now return to the Miradouro do Adamastor in Lisbon, with its Museum of Pharmacy fronting a plaza of drug dealers. To reach this place, a walker in Lisbon can head south from the Rua do Poço dos Negros ("Street of the Burial Pit of the Blacks") and climb the Travessa do Judeu ("Alleyway of the Jews"). The two names have early modern origins, preserving forgotten histories. The *farmacias* nearby announce their wares with glowing green signs depicting a snake entwined around a palm tree—the special blazon of the Portuguese Order of Apothecaries, symbolizing the union of nature and knowledge. The signs bring to mind the old soldier Francisco de Buytrago and his Angolan tree of life. Yet they also point to the historical erasure of the apothecaries and of the more eclectic understanding of drugs that had flourished in the early modern world. The symbol on the signs is a nineteenth-century invention, and even the most traditionalist Lisbon pharmacies—I spotted more than one that still stocked ancient jars of moldering quina and opium—are just that: *farmacias* rather than early modern *boticas*.

Today, the multiple registers and functions of the early modern drug trade have become disaggregated. When I lived in Lisbon, there were the pharmacies and the drug dealers near Adamastor, but also the *ervanária* (herbalist) down the road from my apartment on the Rua do Poço dos Negros—who told me her family had been selling herbs in Lisbon for more than six generations—and the shops selling New Age remedies in the tourist promenades to the east. Not to mention the now-shuttered storefront up the hill in Bairro Alto, which Google Maps coyly classified as an "herb shop" but which was in fact a supplier of gray-market stimulants and hallucinogens packaged in Amsterdam and produced in China.

What will the future bring? A core argument of this book is that the conceptual and legal definitions of drugs have long been—and continue to be—in a state of constant change. Understanding the shifting definitions of drugs, and the imperial and indigenous histories of the drug trade and its discontents, has implications not only for scholarship but also for public policy. Portugal offered a model for the world to follow when it decriminalized all drugs in 2001. Drug laws today continue to disproportionately punish youthful and minority offenders. They lead to unnecessary police and border violence, contributing to inequalities that have persisted since colonial times.[18] However, advocates for drug legalization (as opposed to decriminalization) have failed to grapple with the deep historical entanglements of global commerce and drugs. Decriminalization would, I believe, be a substantial improvement over the legal regimes that currently exist in most countries. Full legalization, however, is far more ambiguous and, as yet, untested. Heroin, it's worth remembering, is a proprietary formula of Bayer Corporation (trademarked in 1895). Reopening the sale of such highly addictive substances to multinational corporations may not have the beneficent impacts that some hope for.

In the end, the history of drugs is a history of humans drawing artificial boundaries between substances that have always had, and will continue to have, a protean role in global cultures. Following the winding historical path of drugs leads us to the shifting barrier between the licit and the illicit drugs. But it also carries us through the history of the slave trade, the history of science, ecological change, and early modern globalization. Drug production helped fuel the rise of plantation economies, with their divisions of labor that foreshadowed the factory system and with their vicious violence enacted on enslaved bodies. The globalization of novel cures and intoxicants created new knowledge and new forms of sociability, as well as tremendous pain and conflict.

In the history of science, the globalization of non-Western drugs transformed understandings of both intoxication and addiction and helped spur the formation of new theories of consciousness. The effort to delineate mental processes impacted by intoxicants arguably led to a greater concern with subjectivity and the roots of thought itself. Going forward, it is possible that the scope of what we mean by "drug" will widen yet further and will offer new insights. It has become increasingly common to refer to the addictive activities in our digital lives, particularly the allure of social media, as "drug-like" or "intoxicating" in their effects. Looking forward, emerging technologies like virtual reality, direct brain stimulation, or mind-machine interfaces hold out the promise of drug-like effects on mental and physical states without the ingestion of any substance at all. Meanwhile, in the field of pharmacy, formerly illegal substances like MDMA and psilocybin are again being brought back into the fold of the medical.

As we stand on the brink of technological changes that will again transform the culture and commerce of drugs, it is difficult to guess what the future holds. Everywhere, older boundaries seem to be dissolving. But I will make one prediction: the medium and format of drug taking may change, but the impulses that lead humans to try to alter their physical and mental states will continue. Indeed, if history has taught us anything about drugs, it is that technological innovation and social change seem to *increase* this desire rather than to diminish it. The Age of Reason might have ended long ago. Perhaps the Age of Intoxication is just beginning.

Notes

Introduction

1 In 2001, Portugal became the first nation on earth to decriminalize recreational drugs for "personal use." See Specter, "Getting a Fix"; and Loo, van Beusekom, and Kahan, "Decriminalization of Drug Use in Portugal." On the history of Adamastor and its surrounding neighborhood, once part of an African-dominated area of Lisbon known as Mocambo (the Kimbundu word for "hideout"), see Sweet, "Hidden Histories of African Lisbon," 231. In 2013, and again in 2018, the space (which is also known as Miradouro de Santa Catarina) was temporarily closed to the public for remodeling and cleaning. At the time of the first closing, a city official in Lisbon explained to the *Público* newspaper that the miradouro had problems "with respect to the safety and conditions of the public space . . . owing to the presence of drug sellers." João Pedro Pincha, "Miradouro de Sta. Catarina fechado para obras o resto do Verão," *Público*, July 26, 2018. Accessed March 2, 2019. https://www.publico.pt/2018/07/26/local/noticia/miradouro-de-sta-catarina-fechado-para-obras-o-resto-do-verao-1839230.

2 Camões, *Lusíadas*, canto 5, stanza 39–40.

3 Ibid., canto 2, stanza 4. Translations are my own, but for an English version, see Camões, *The Lusiads*, trans. Landeg White.

4 For instance, Steven Pinker's best-selling book *Enlightenment Now* explicitly frames itself as championing "the thinkers of the Age of Reason" (10).

5 Throughout this book, I use the term "global" to describe connections or routes that spanned both the Western and Eastern hemispheres. Long-distance transport of drugs has an ancient history—witness, for instance, the pre-Columbian transmission of tobacco from its native growing range in the tropical Americas to a region spanning thousands of miles, from Canada to Patagonia. However, it was only in the sixteenth century that durable trade networks began to cross the formidable boundaries of the Atlantic and Pacific Oceans.

6 Croll, *Basilica Chymica*, 257. Oswald Croll's Latin recipe for what he called "tincture of mummy" begins: "Eligatur Cadaver hominis russi, integri, recentis sine macula, viginti quatuor annorum, suspensi, vel rotâ contriti, vel hastati." The word *russi* could mean either "red-haired" or "ruddy." Either way, it is perhaps the most oddly specific medical recipe of the entire era.

7   Klayman, "Qinghaosu (Artemisinin)"; Belgers et al., "Ibogaine and Addiction in the Animal Model, a Systematic Review and Meta-Analysis."

8   On the ancient evolutionary entanglement between drugs and humans, see Pollan, *The Botany of Desire*, 114–18.

9   Nesse and Berridge, "Psychoactive Drug Use in Evolutionary Perspective."

10 Shurkin, "Animals That Self-Medicate." Sick chimpanzees have been documented consuming antiparasitic leaves that have no value as foodstuffs, and some elephants appear to intentionally induce birth by consuming a specific medicinal tree from the *Boraginaceae* family.

11 Sherratt, "Cups That Cheered," in Waldren and Kennard, *Bell Beakers of the Western Mediterranean*, 81–114; Rojo-Guerra et al., "Beer and Bell Beakers."

12 Carod-Artal, "Hallucinogenic Drugs in Pre-Columbian Mesoamerican Cultures."

13 Nichols et al., "Psychedelics as Medicines"; Kraehenmann et al., "LSD Increases Primary Process Thinking via Serotonin 2A Receptor Activation."

14 Breen, "No Man Is an Island"; De Vries, "Limits of Globalization"; Hopkins, *Globalisation in World History*; Mccants, "Exotic Goods, Popular Consumption, and the Standard of Living."

15 Lamb, "Thousands Dead."

16 Carson and Anderson, "Bulletin: Prisoners in 2015," U.S. Department of Justice.

17 Illicit drug trafficking accounted for between $426 and $652 billion of economic activity in 2017, while the trade in legal pharmaceuticals generated more than $1 trillion in revenues in 2016. See May, "Transnational Crime and the Developing World," and an International Federation of Pharmaceutical Manufacturers and Associations report, "Pharmaceutical Industry and Global Health."

18 Moore and Mattison, "Adult Utilization of Psychiatric Drugs"; Han et al., "Prescription Opioid Use, Misuse, and Use Disorders in US Adults."

19 "Drug," definitions 1a and 1b, Oxford English Dictionary.

20 Freedman, *Out of the East*.

21 The category of drugs was created by Europeans; it did not necessarily have correlates in the languages and cultures of the Americas, Africa, or elsewhere. But although the term is a European one, the emergence of a global drug trade in the sixteenth and seventeenth centuries fundamentally altered many global societies, not just in "the West." Thus, this book is a study of the globalization not just of a group of substances but also of a set of ideas and terms that had localized points of origin but which have increasingly become viewed as universal by governments, consumers, and producers.

22 Arquivo Nacional da Torre do Tombo, Lisbon, Portugal, (hereafter ANTT) Cartas 876/16, "Carte de Manuel Botelho a D. João III sobre a colheita da pimento e outras drogas," Cochin, January 21, 1525, fol. 2r.

23 Two leading historians of medicine have argued that in early modern usage, "the word for 'spice' and the word for 'drug' were practically interchangeable." See Cook and Walker, "Circulation of Medicine in the Early Modern Atlantic World," 2.

NOTES TO PAGES 8–16

24 De Vos, "The Science of Spices"; Schiebinger, *Plants and Empire*; Schiebinger and Swan, *Colonial Botany*; Parrish, *American Curiosity*.

25 On the economics of the early modern drug trade, see Chakrabarti, *Materials and Medicine*; Dorner, "'No One Here Knows Half so Much of This Matter as Yourself'"; D. Walker, "Virginian Tobacco During the Reigns of the Early Stuarts"; Jenner and Wallis, *Medicine and the Market in England*; Wallis, "Consumption, Retailing, and Medicine in Early-Modern London"; Wallis, "Exotic Drugs and English Medicine"; and Zahedieh, *The Capital and the Colonies*.

26 Works that have been particularly helpful as guides in this regard include Boumediene, *La colonisation du savoir*; Campos, *Home Grown*; Courtwright, *Forces of Habit*; Curto, *Enslaving Spirits*; Goodman, Lovejoy, and Sherratt, *Consuming Habits*; Norton, *Sacred Gifts, Profane Pleasures*; Mancall, *Deadly Medicine*; Mancall, "Tales Tobacco Told"; and Schwartzkopf and Sampeck, *Substance and Seduction*.

27 Crosby, *Columbian Exchange*; Grove, *Green Imperialism*; Drayton, *Nature's Government*; Schiebinger and Swan, *Colonial Botany*.

28 On the overseas missions of the Jesuits and their overlap with Portuguese territorial claims, see Alden, *Making of an Enterprise*, ch. 4 and *passim*, and Brockey, *Journey to the East*, pp. 160–62, 197.

29 Russell-Wood, *Portuguese Empire*, 60.

30 Miller, *Way of Death*; Coates, *Convicts and Orphans*.

31 The "internal" slave trade that existed within the colonial Americas has recently begun to receive more attention, but we still know little about the role of indigenous American slaves in colonial Brazil. O'Malley, *Final Passages*; Klein, "Internal Slave Trade in Nineteenth-Century Brazil."

32 Brunsman, *The Evil Necessity*.

33 Coates, *Convicts and Orphans*.

34 On the entanglement between early modern empires and merchants, see Stern, *The Company-State*; Burnard and Garrigus, *The Plantation Machine*; and Beckert and Rockman, *Slavery's Capitalism*. See also Schiebinger, *Secret Cures of Slaves*; and Delbourgo, *Collecting the World*.

35 Berlu, *The Treasury of Drugs Unlock'd*; Pomet, *Histoire générale des drogues*; Semedo, *Atalaya da vida contra as hostilidades da morte*.

36 Moncrief, *The Poor Man's Physician*; Anonymous, *The Ladies' Dispensatory*.

Chapter 1

1 Stolz, Baten, and Reis, "Portuguese Living Standards, 1720–1980."

2 Arquivo Histórico Ultramarino, Lisbon [hereafter AHU], Pará, cx. 3, doc. 219. Francisco de Sá e Meneses to Dom Pedro II, Belem do Pará, December 30, 1683 ["Carta do governador . . . sobre o descobrimento que mandou fazer de drogas no sertão"]. On Lacerda, see also Biblioteca da Ajuda, Códice 51-V-43, "Ordem p.a por cap.m Andre Pinhr.o tirar alguns cavaleirotes das aldeas," Belém, November 15, 1682, ff. 24-24v; and Chambouleyron, "Prática dos Sertões na Amazônia Colonial."

3   Alkaloids are a class of naturally occurring compounds notable for their psycho-active properties. Some of the most famous include caffeine, nicotine, morphine, psilocybin, ephedrine, and quinine. The concept of alkaloids as a category of related drugs emerged in the 1820s, following the isolation of quinine from cinchona bark.

4   In reality, different species of the genus *Cinchona*, sometimes called "true" or Pe-ruvian quina by the Portuguese, grew in a band running through Spanish Peru and New Grenada. See Crawford, *Andean Wonder Drug*, 4. See also Crawford, "A 'Reasoned Proposal' Against 'Vain Science.'"

5   For Portuguese speakers today, the word *sertão* (backlands) evokes a specific eco-logical zone in northeastern Brazil: an arid scrubland between the coastal region and the *mato* (jungle). In its early modern usage, however, *sertão* was widely ap-plied to any unexplored or interior zone, including the Amazonian and Congolese rain forests.

6   The Estado do Maranhão was largely administratively distinct from the Estado do Brasil until 1774, when it was folded into the Brazilian colonial state. Long regarded as a backwater, today it remains a highly understudied segment of the Portuguese empire and of the Atlantic World more generally. A recent survey of the estado's environmental and cultural history can be found in Chambouleyron, *Povoamento Ocupação e Agricultura na Amazonia Colonial.*

7   AHU, Pará, cx. 3, doc. 219. See also AHU, Pará, cx. 6, doc. 697 (Rolo 9), April 13, 1684, Lisbon. "Sobre uma carta do governador do Maranhão, Francisca de Sá, dando conta de varios descobrimentos que tem mandado fazer, na fauna e na flora, como, dentre outras, arvore china, salsa parrilha e minas."

8   Lacerda may have been encountering speakers of the Gê language family, such as the Kayapó or Karajá peoples, who inhabited the region marked as "Provinca da Tacantins" in Figure 7. On the tangled history of the term "Tapuya," see Lowie, "The 'Tapuya,'" in *Handbook of South American Indians*, 553–56.

9   Crawford, *Andean Wonder Drug*, 7.

10 Ibid., 26. On the early history of malaria in the New World, see McNeill, *Mosquito Empires.*

11 All quotes from this paragraph are from AHU, Pará, cx. 3, doc. 219.

12 The Brazilian plants known as quina include *Deianira erubescens, Strychnos pseudoquina*, and *Remijia ferruginea*. The latter has been shown to have antima-larial activity, but none of these species of "quina-do-brasil" appears to contain quinine or related alkaloids. See Andrade-Neto et al., "Antimalarial Activity of Cinchona-like Plants"; and Somavilla et al., "Morpho-Anatomy and Chemical Profile of Native Species."

13 On this larger history of epistemological erasure, see Cañizares-Esguerra, "Ig-nored Global Scientific Revolutions."

14 Schiebinger, *Plants and Empire*; Safier, "Fruitless Botany"; Županov and Xavier, "Quest for Permanence in the Tropics."

15 Greenfield, *A Perfect Red*; Parsons, "Natural History of Colonial Science."

16 Crosby, *Columbian Exchange*; Diamond, *Guns, Germs, and Steel*; Mann, *1491.*

17 This is an extrapolation from evidence that Amazonia may have the highest amount of species diversity per hectare of any terrestrial ecosystem, as well as from ethnobotanical research. On the ethnobotany of psychoactive species in the Amazon, see Schultes, *The Healing Forest*. On biodiversity, see S. Joseph Wright, "Plant Diversity in Tropical Forests: A Review of Mechanisms of Species Coexistence." *Oecologia*. 130: 1–14 (October 12, 2001), doi:10.1007/s004420100809; and Hoorn et al., "Amazonia Through Time."

18 Or at least somewhere "east of the Andes"; see Clarkson et al., "Phylogenetic Relationships in Nicotiana."

19 This paragraph is a reconstruction based on geological data in Mapes, "Past and Present Provenance."

20 Denevan, *Cultivated Landscapes of Native Amazonia*; Heckenberger, Petersen, and Neves, "Village Size and Permanence in Amazonia"; Mann, 1491.

21 Mann, *1491*, 14.

22 See Dean, *With Broadax and Firebrand*; and Hemming, "Indians of Brazil," 119.

23 On debates over whether the concept of shamanism can be applied to radically different cultures (Central Asian, Amazonian, African), see Taussig, *Shamanism*; and Whitehead and Wright, *In Darkness and Secrecy*.

24 On the role of the shaman in the northwestern Amazon, see Goldman, Cubeo *Hehénewa Religious Thought*. Goldman notes that *payé* (which etymologically means "Thunderer") is in use as part of a lingua franca in the region.

25 Vidal and Whitehead, "Dark Shamans and the Shamanic State," 51.

26 Goldman, *Cubeo Hehénewa Religious Thought*, 370.

27 There is, admittedly, a risk in conflating observations from the 1930s and the 1630s. I do so here with the caveat that, because early modern accounts of Amazonian cosmologies and magical practices tend to dismiss them as simply "of the devil," capturing some sense of how Amazonian spiritual-medical practices would have functioned from a non-Eurocentric perspective requires the use of more recent sources. In citing Irving Goldman's fieldwork, I've tried to stay within the realm of broad generalities, which were transferrable across culture groups and time periods; for instance, the powerful dichotomy between healing and poisoning is evident in both seventeenth-century and twentieth-century accounts. For a nuanced discussion of how we might use such accounts to write deep histories of Amazonian cultures, see Safier, "Global Knowledge on the Move."

28 This is because the DMT contained in *Psychotria* is not orally bio-available without the presence of an MAO inhibitor, which partially blocks the action of monoamine neurotransmitters such as serotonin. This, in turn, helps to potentiate psychoactive alkaloids like DMT. See Dennis McKenna, "Monoamine Oxidase Inhibitors in Amazonian Hallucinogenic Plants: Ethnobotanical, Phytochemical, and Pharmacological Investigations" (PhD diss., University of British Columbia, 1984).

29 Vallard Atlas (Dieppe, c. 1547), gouache on vellum, HM 27, Huntington Library, San Marino, CA.

30 Correia, *Lendas da India*, 152. On sapanwood, see Hong-Chunk, "An Aspect of East Asian Maritime Trade."

31 Columbus, *Select Letters of Christopher Columbus*, 16. In the original Latin, Columbus had written of "reubarbarum et aliorum aromatum genera"—using the word *aromatum*, which could describe both spice and psychoactive drug.

32 Ramón Pané's "Relación acerca de las antigüedades de los indios" circulated as an unpublished manuscript and appears to have been written around 1498. On the book's history, see Janiga-Perkins, *Reading, Writing, and Translation in the Relación Acerca de Las Antigüedades de Los Indios*. A digital edition is available at https://es.wikisource.org/wiki/Relación_acerca_de_las_antigüedades_de_los_ indios.

33 Pané, "Relación," ch. XV, "De las observaciones de estos indios buhuitihu."

34 Saunders and Gray, "Zemís, Trees, and Symbolic Landscapes," 172.

35 Markey, "Stradano's Allegorical Invention of the Americas in Late Sixteenth-Century Florence."

36 For an overview of the debate over whether syphilis originated in the Americas and spread as part of the Columbian Exchange, see Mann, *1491*, "Appendix C: The Syphilis Exception," 406-8.

37 Malaria's transatlantic origins are charted in McNeill, *Mosquito Empires*, 53–54 and ch. 3; on the disease's connection to early treatments containing quina, see Crawford, *Andean Wonder Drug*, 26-34 and 47–53.

38 Nóbrega and Leite, *Cartas do Brasil e mais escritos*, 82.

39 On early Spanish efforts to overcome tobacco's "heathen" associations and make a case for its medical benefits, see Norton, *Sacred Gifts*, ch. 6.

40 De Souza, *O Pau-brasil na história nacional*, 70.

41 Sugar was one of the four substances lauded by the Jesuit João Giovanni Antônio Andreoni (writing under the pen name André João Antonil) in Antonil, *Cultura e opulência do Brasil*. On sugar's dual historical role as a food and drug, see Mintz, *Sweetness and Power*.

42 On the rise of the West Indies sugar trade at the expense of Brazil in the 1660s, see Schwartz, *Sugar Plantations*, 177-85.

43 Acuña, *Nuevo descubrimiento del gran rio de las Amazonas*. For a secondary source survey, see Smith, *Explorers of the Amazon*, and de Miranda, *Quando o Amazonas corria para o Pacífico*.

44 See Mora, "Early Inhabitants of the Amazonian Tropical Rain Forest," ch. 2.

45 Fernandes, *Organização social dos Tupinambá*, 29–44.

46 Schwartz, *Slaves, Peasants, and Rebels*, ch. 2; Schwartz, *Sugar Plantations*, ch. 3.

47 Manoel Calado, a Portuguese friar who visited the gardens, wrote that "the inhabitants of the land [in the sertão]" brought "strange animals which they found in the interior" to please Maurits's "appetite" for natural oddities and potentially lucrative new natural specimens. Local Indians, Calado wrote, "brought parrots, araras, jacis, canindes, jabotis, mutuns, Guinea fowl, ducks, swans, peacocks, turkeys, and chickens [in] great number, so many pigeons, that one couldn't count them, there they had tigers, the onqa, the suuarana, the tamandua, the bagio, the

quati, the saguim, the apetea, Cape Verde goats, Angolan sheep, the cutia, the paca, the anta, the wild pig, a great multitude of rabbits." Calado, *O Valeroso Lucideno*, 111–12

48 On the strained professional relations between Markgraf (also spelled Marcgrave) and Piso, see Boxer, *The Dutch in Brazil, 1624–1654*; and Whitehead, "The Biography of Georg Marcgraf (1610-1643/4)."

49 This interpretation is based on Brienen, *Visions of Savage Paradise*, 16.

50 Letter from Manuel Fernandes Cruz, Pernambuco, to King João IV, August 20, 1650, in Rau, da Silva, and Cadaval, *Os manuscritos do arquivo da casa de Cadaval*, 90.

51 Domingos Antunes Tomás, Biblioteca de Ajuda (Lisbon), codex 50-V-37, "Sobre o Maranhaõ e Parà e cativo dos Indios e forma de os haver cõ augmento do Estado," 3 November 1679, f. 394. For more details on this document see Chambouleyron, "Portuguese Colonization," 100. In the same period (1675) the Portuguese diplomat Duarte Ribeiro de Macedo was writing to the Portuguese Crown about the untapped commercial potential of "wild nutmeg" and "wild cloves" (*cravo*) from Amazonia. See Duarte Ribeiro de Macedo, "Discurso sobre a transplantação," ANTT, T/TT/MSBR/39.

52 João de Moura, BNP, cod. 585, "Descripção Historica, e Relação Politica, do grande Estado do Maranhão" (1684), fol. 24v. In addition to the Portuguese, he noted, "already in France we have seen a memorandum offered to the Cardinal Mazarin" regarding its conquest, "and another relation has been seen regarding the province in England, offered to the tyrant Caramuel [Cromwell] . . . regarding the ease with which they could occupy this land."

53 Pyrard, *Discours du voyage*, 281.

54 Ibid., 288.

55 Ibid.

56 Acuña, *Nuevo descubrimiento del gran rio de las Amazonas*, fol. 14r.

57 Ibid., 19v.

58 Ibid., fol. 20r.

59 Exceptions to this emphasis on French and British botanical bioprospectors include Cook, *Matters of Exchange*; Chambouleyron, *Povoamento Ocupação e Agricultura na Amazonia Colonial;* and Bleichmar, *Visible Empire.*

60 Kier et al., "A Global Assessment of Endemism and Species Richness."

61 Henry Lee, *The Vegetable Lamb of Tartary*, remains the most complete guide to early modern European beliefs about animals born from plants. On the search for early modern natural secrets as *venatio*, see Eamon, Science and the *Secrets of Nature*, ch. 8.

62 My thinking here is informed by recent studies in the human-animal boundary, which I believe can also be applied fruitfully to the historical relationships between humans and plants. See, for instance, Willerslev, "Not Animal, Not Not-Animal"; and Roger M. Carpenter, *The Renewed, the Destroyed, and the Remade*, 78-90.

63 For instance, in 1675 the French apothecary and chemist Nicolas Lémery speculated that "Metal Is the Effect of Fermentation" caused by heat from "the Sun, or

some subterraneous Fires." Lémery's vision of the formation of metals and minerals saw the earth itself as a body, its "vital force" composed of fires within the earth or heavens, and its "food" being earthly substances that this force digested and fermented." Quotes are from the English translation, Lémery, *A Course of Chymistry*, 51. On the alchemical, bodily and plant-based language of metals and mining, see Bigelow, "Mining Empire, Planting Empire."

64 De Orozco, *Directorio de beneficiadores*. "En q-e se comparan las betas o venas de metales con los arboles" and "Rasones q-e comprueban el tratado anterior," ff. 22v–24v. I would like to thank Allison Bigelow of the University of Virginia for bringing this document to my attention and sharing her transcription with me.

65 Vieira, *Cartas a Duarte Ribeiro de Macedo*, 211–12.

66 De Acosta, *Historia natural y moral de las Indias*, 222 ("plantas encubiertas en las entrañas de la tierra"). See also Bigelow, "Mining Empire," 212–13.

67 These examples were chosen at random from Berlu, *The Treasury of Drugs Unlock'd*.

68 "Quina is a bark from a tree called quina-quina which grows in the kingdom of Peru. . . . It is shaped like a cherry tree, the leaves round and tooth-like, the flower long and somewhat red, following a bark, or bean, which contains a flat 'almond,' white, and covered with thin hairs. . . . Quina ought to be compact, of a red color, and with a bitter taste. It cures intermittent fevers, reduced into powder and divided into two *oitavas*. It can also be infused into wine or other liquors." Vigier, *Pharmacopea Ulyssiponense*, "de Quina," n.p.

69 For instance, in a letter sent to the Capitão-mor of Ilha Grande de Joanes (an island now known as Marajó in the mouth of the Amazon, near Belém), Francisco de Sá relayed "orders from His Majesty to go and make discoveries in the *sertão*," but he also noted the presence of a *quilombo* of fifty-seven escaped slaves on the nearby Rio Guamá. Biblioteca da Ajuda, April 22, 1683, "Ordem para qual o Governador Francisco de Sá de Meneses, manda ao Capitão-mor da Ilha Grande de Joanes, em cumprimento de ordens recibidas de S.A., que va fazer descobrimento pelos sertões," 51-IX-31 f. 52.

70 On this short-lived trading company, see Chambouleyron, "Escravos Do Atlântico Equatorial."

71 Chambouleyron, "Cacao, Bark-Clove and Agriculture in the Portuguese Amazon," 4.

72 Chambouleyron, "Escravos Do Atlântico Equatorial," citing Biblioteca Publica de Evora, cod. CXV-2-16, fol. 11v.

73 AHU Pará, cx. 3, doc. 219, Francisco de Sá e Meneses to Dom Pedro II, Belém do Pará, December 30, 1683.

74 AHU Pará, cx. 3, doc. 219. "The surgeon assures me that this is better and more efficacious than before," de Sá wrote, "because with time it loses part of its effectiveness."

75 AHU Maranhão, cx. 6, doc. 697 ("Sobre uma carta do governador do Maranhão, Francisca de Sá, dando conta de varios descobrimentos que tem mandado fazer"). On *Cinchona huanuco*, see Pereira, *Elements of Materia Medica*, 981-82.

76 AHU Maranhão, cx. 6, doc. 697.

77 Mendo do Foios Pereira to the Duke of Cadaval (Nuno Alvares Pereira de Melo), Madrid, March 4, 1684, *Cartas Varias*, cod. 890 (K VII 17), fl. 84, reprinted in Rau, da Silva, and Cadaval, *Os manuscritos do arquivo da casa de Cadaval*, 272.

78 Carta do Mendo do Foios Pereira to the Duke of Cadaval, March 4, 1684, in *Cartas Varias*, 272.

79 Given the timing of this letter and the fact that a *consulta* (memorandum) offering an executive summary of de Sá's earlier report regarding quina and sarsaparilla was prepared for the Overseas Council in April 1684, we can surmise that Foios Perreira was here referring to the samples gathered by Lacerda and sent by de Sá to Lourenço de Almada. The timing also fits in terms of transatlantic shipping. According to Miller (*Way of Death*, 372), average shipping time from Maranhão to Lisbon was approximately 30 days. De Sá's letter would likely have reached the Overseas Council around February 1, 1684 (approximately thirty days after he postmarked it on December 30, 1683). De Sá's letter to his lieutenant Henrique Lopes da Gama regarding "drugs and other curiosities to send to D. Lourenço de Almada" is dated January 16, 1684. Allowing for a week or so for da Gama to send his samples of *drogas* to Belém, then another thirty days in transit to de Almada's palace in Lisbon, an investigation of the authenticity of these samples in Lisbon by March and April 1684 would make sense.

80 See the dedications in de Moura, *Syntagma chirurgico theorico-practico*; and Vigier, *Thesouro apollineo*.

81 In 1692–93, for instance, Mendo and the governor of Bahia corresponded regarding "the experience of a stranger regarding those sick with the contagion, and his anatomy of their corpses" as well as the possibility of transplanting cinnamon. Biblioteca da Ajuda, July 16, 1692, and July 18, 1693, 51-IX 30 f. 20.

82 Manuel Beckman, "Reprezentaço a S.M." (original in Biblioteca da Ajuda, reprinted in Maria Liberman, *O levante do Maranhã* (São Paulo, 1983), 73. On Beckman's Revolt and its historical context, see Lúcia Helena Costigan, "New Christians in the Periphery of the Iberian Empires," in Bauer and Mazzotti, *Creole Subjects in the Colonial Americas*, 259–64.

83 AHU, Pará, cx. 3, doc. 279, Artur de Sá to the Overseas Council, November 30, 1689.

84 Biblioteca Municipal de São Paulo, Codice Costa Matoso, fol. 506. The complete imports of the duke are recorded in Appendix VI of Boxer, *Golden Age of Brazil*, 353.

85 AHU, Icon M. 005 E, d. 90, letter from Capitao General da Capitania da Bahia, D. Fernando José de Portugal, 1st Conde de Aguiar, to Secretario do Estado da Marinha e Ultramar, Rodrigo de Sousa Coutinho, December 5, 1800.

86 AHU, Icon M. 005 E, d. 90-91. ("Uma arvore que se imaginava ser a quinera, mas . . . os boticarios mais experientes discordavem.")

87 Art historian Elizabeth Athens has argued that Baroque aesthetics played an important role in shaping how European engravers and artists depicted New World nature in this period. Elizabeth Athens, "Scientific Ornamentation: William Bar-

tram's Visual Rhetoric," paper presented at the Traces of Early America Conference at the McNeil Center for Early American Studies, September 27, 2013.

88 On the difficulty of translating between European assumptions of tropical nature and the situation on the ground, see Safier, "Tenacious Travels of the Torrid Zone."

89 Neri, *The Insect and the Image*, xiii.

90 AHU Pará, cx. 3, doc. 219.

91 On confusions about names, see Drayton, "Synchronic Palimpsests," 38-39.

92 See, for example, Schiebinger, *Plants and Empire*, 226–32.

93 Barrera-Osorio, *Experiencing Nature;* see also Furtado, "Tropical Empiricism," in Delbourgo et al., *Science and Empire*, 136-37.

94 Bleichmar, *Visible Empire*, 138. It is important to note a key difference between the cases examined here and Bleichmar's 1780s naturalists, however: the century that stood between them. In the 1680s, the "chemical analyses and medical trials" that Bleichmar refers to were still in a highly nascent and undeveloped form. Indeed, only a handful of savants in Europe (figures straddling the worlds of chemistry and medicine, like Robert Boyle, Pierre Pomet, and João Curvo Semedo) were capable of assaying the chemical makeup of tropical drugs in the manner that would become relatively common by the end of the eighteenth century.

95 On metropolitan European concerns with the replicability and reliability of colonial knowledge, see Cañizares-Esguerra, *How to Write the History of the New World*, 15-17; Daston, "Empire of Observation" in Daston and Lunbeck, *Histories of Scientific Observation*; and Schaffer, "Newton on the Beach."

96 On misunderstandings, see MacGaffey, "Dialogues of the Deaf," in Schwartz, ed., *Implicit Understandings*; and Sweet, "Mutual Misunderstandings."

97 Nappi, "Bolatu's Pharmacy Theriac in Early Modern China."

98 Van Leeuwenhoek, "Microscopical Observations of the Peruvian Bark," in Hutton and Pearson, *The Philosophical Transactions of the Royal Society of London*, 372.

99 Adapted from Alston, *Lectures on the Materia Medica*, 2: 10.

Chapter 2

1 ANTT, Inquisição de Coimbra, Processos, No. 352.

2 Ibid., fol. 82.

3 Ibid., fol. 109.

4 Biblioteca Nacional de Portugal (hereafter, BNP), Cod. 2259. José [Jozeph] Coelho, *Pharmaca que fes sendo boticario no anno de mil e seis sento e sesenta e outo* (1668). Maria Coelho may have also had some kinship with the Marrano apothecary Manuel Rodrigues Coelho, whose *Farmacopéia Tubalense* (Lisbon, 1735) was replete with Indies drugs. In her Inquisition file, Maria Coelho was associated with another female apothecary named Francisca Rodrigues, resident in Lisbon in the 1660s. On Manuel Rodrigues Coelho see Marques, "As 'Medicinas' indígenas."

5 Pelling and White's *Medical Conflicts in Early Modern London* exemplifies this skepticism toward early modern physicians' centrality, in effect relegating "offi-

cial" guild physicians to the sidelines and arguing that apothecaries, surgeons, empirics, quacks, midwives, and female healers were the more important purveyors of medical care in early modern times owing to their greater accessibility and affordability.

6 Cook, *Decline of the Old Medical Regime*; Leong and Pennell, "Recipe Collections and the Currency of Medical Knowledge," 133–52.

7 See Wallis, "Exotic Drugs and English Medicine," 20–46, which uses probate inventories of apothecaries and London tariff records to quantify drug imports in the seventeenth century. Imports of medicines from the New World and the East Indies, such as opium, ipecacuanha, sarsaparilla, guaiacum, bezoar stones, cinchona, coffee, cocoa, and tea enjoyed particular popularity, confirming the Restoration-era shift toward nontraditional remedies hinted at through the early research of Harold Cook. For other recent quantitative studies, see Dorner, "'No One Here Knows Half so Much of This Matter as Yourself'"; and Wallis and Pirohakul, "Medical Revolutions?"

8 The book history of seventeenth-century drug manuals can be incredibly complex, as will appear from an incomplete bibliography of the example mentioned here. François Monginot's treatise on quina bark and fevers, originally published in English in 1681 as Anonymous [François Monginot], *New Mystery in Physick Discovered*, was an altered translation of a work by the French physician Nicolas de Blegny, which appeared under a wide array of titles and author names. The original source was apparently de Blegny, *Zodiacus medico-gallicus*, which then appeared in French as de Blegny, *La Découverte de l'admirable Remède Anglois*, and again in two different versions in 1682 (*La Remède Anglois pour la guérison des fièvres* [Brussels: E. H. Fricx, 1682] and *La connaissance certaine et la prompte et facile guérison des fièvres, avec des particularitez curieuses et utiles sur le remède anglois* [Paris: V. A. Padeloup, 1682]). Meanwhile, an English translation had appeared in 1681 (A New Mystery in Physick Discovered) and, in an altered form, in 1682 as Talbor, The English Remedy.

9 Pomet, *Histoire Générale des drogues*, i.

10 Pomet's shop "á la Barbe d'or" appears to have lasted for a very long time. In a Napoleonic War–era soldier's newspaper, "essence of sarsaparilla" was advertised as being sold by one Fourquet out of "29, rue des Lombards, maison de la Barbe d'Or" (*Le Moniteur de l'Armée*, November 11, 1802, 4). In 1899, a Parisian antiquarian wrote that "one found on the Rue des Lombards a certain number of antique pharmaceutical signs, such as the Silver Pestle, the Beard of Gold, etc." (see Collet, "Vieilles Enseignes de Paris," 22). Pomet's sign would continue to be noted by tourists to Paris until as late as 1925, as noted in a 1925 issue of *Chemist & Druggist*, 102:563.

11 Pomet, *Histoire Générale des drogues*, i.

12 For an inspiring recent example of archival research that does manage to gain insights into subaltern healers, see Gómez, *The Experiential Caribbean*.

13 On apothecary shops as sites of exotic display, see Parrish, "Marketing Nature."

14 As Elaine Leong and Jennifer Evans have argued, female drug consumers played a

prominent role in the early modern medical marketplace, both as buyers of apoth-
ecary-made drugs and as buyers of raw materials for their own "kitchen physick."
See Leong, "'Herbals She Peruseth'"; and Evans, *Aphrodisiacs, Fertility and Medicine in Early Modern England*, 44–45.

15 Wallis, "Consumption, Retailing and Medicine." Throughout this chapter, I use
the term "apothecary shop" rather than "pharmacy," reflecting a distinction
somewhat analogous to Lawrence Principe's differentiation between "chymistry"
and "chemistry." Although apothecary shops evolved directly into pharmacies,
it is a mistake to collapse the two terms. The terms *boutique* and *bodega* both
derive from the late medieval term for apothecary shop in the Romance languages
(botica). In Latin an *apotheca* was a general storehouse or shop, originally derived from the Greek word for barn or warehouse, ἀποθήκη, literally "place where
things are put away." The *apothecarius* was originally any type of shopkeeper, and
apothecary/apothicaire/boticario apparently did not develop distinct associations
with *materia medica* until around the fourteenth century. See Aulesa, "Defining
'Apothecary' in the Medieval Crown of Aragon."

16 Walker, Doctors, *Folk Medicine and the Inquisition*, ch. 6.

17 This likely referred to North African birth, perhaps in Tangier, but is still unclear.
See Acosta, *Tractado de las drogas y medicinas de las Indias orientales*, 3.

18 Soyer, *Persecution of the Jews and Muslims of Portugal*, 293; Walker, "Role and
Practices of the Curandeiro and Saludador."

19 Cook, *Decline of the Old Medical Regime*, ch. 1.

20 Andrade, "Garcia de Orta and Amato Lusitano's Views on *Materia Medica*."

21 Da Orta, *Colóquios dos simples e drogas*, title page. Hereafter I cite from the 1891
edition of da Orta to allow for easier reference.

22 Da Orta, *Coloquios dos simples e drogas da India* (1891 [1563]), 19.

23 Loureiro, "Enter the Milanese Lapidary."

24 On the interconnections between Clusius and da Orta, see Cagle, "Cultures of
Inquiry, Myths of Empire."

25 On da Orta's posthumous reputation, see da Costa, "Identity and the Construction of Memory," and on racialized efforts to "purify" Portuguese medicine, see
Walker, *Doctors, Folk Medicine and the Inquisition*.

26 Smith, *Gabriel Harvey's Marginalia*, 158. The quote is from Harvey's marginalia
on the title page of a book called *In Iudaeorum Medicastrorum Calumnias* from
1570.

27 Cecyll and Dimock, "Conspiracy of Dr. Lopez."

28 Milton, *Paradise Lost*, 50.

29 Furetière, *Dictionaire Universel*, "Drogue," (n.p.).

30 Furetière, *Dictionaire Universel*.

31 Johnson, *Dictionary of the English Language*.

32 Furetière, *Dictionaire Universel*, "Qui pro quo," (n.p.). The entry adds: "Hence the
proverb: God guard us from the *qui pro quo* of the Apothecary and the *et cetera* of
the Notary."

33 On the prosecution of Portuguese apothecaries who failed to establish their social

bona fides, see Walker, *Doctors, Folk Medicine and the Inquisition*, and on the Inquisition trials of African healers in Portugal, see Sweet, *Domingos Álvares*.

34 Economists see the health-care industry, then and now, as a prime example of the importance of "asymmetric information." See Arrow, "Uncertainty and the Welfare Economics of Medical Care"; and Wallis, "Consumption, Retailing, and Medicine" 26–27.

35 On elite women as medical professionals, see Harkness, "Managing an Experimental Household"; and Rankin, *Panaceia's Daughters*.

36 Wendy Wall sees these female-authored receipts as part of a "sharable . . . experimental culture" that existed alongside, and informed, the empiricism of early scientific bodies like the Royal Society. See Wall, *Recipes for Thought*, 231.

37 Anonymous [W. M.], *Queens Closet Opened*, 25, 149-50. This book was typical of its era in terms of its inclusion of both medical and culinary recipes, or "receipts." These were divided into three headings: "The Pearl of Practise" described medical remedies, "A Queen's Delight" was devoted to candies, and "The Compleat Cook" included general cookery recipes. Similar manuals circulated in manuscript, such as Penn Van Pelt, MS Cod. 388, "Account book and recipe book," 1699–1703, and MS Cod. 626, "Hopestill Brett, Her Booke," 1678.

38 Fouquet, *Recueil de receptes choisies*.

39 Ibid., 126.

40 Ibid., 219.

41 Shirley, *The Accomplished Ladies Rich Closet of Rarities*. On "the closet" as a private and female space, see Stewart, "The Early Modern Closet Discovered."

42 Altough officially licensed female apothecaries were quite rare in the seventeenth century, many women managing households developed a high degree of ability and expertise in pharmacy; see Rankin, *Panaceia's Daughters*, 181–85 and Pelling and White, *Medical Conflicts*, 195.

43 Wallis, "Consumption, Retailing, and Medicine," 28.

44 ANTT, Inquisição de Lisboa, Processos, No. 11767, José Francisco Pereira (1731). Pereira's Inquisition file notes that he had previously spent time in Brazil, and it's possible that the hybrid form of Luso-African healing he practiced was developed there, perhaps in Bahia. On the role of African healers in colonial Brazilian society, see Sweet, *Domingos Álvares*, ch. 6, and on Brazilian apothecaries see Marques, "Natureza em boiões."

45 Pereira's case is among the most well-studied instances of early modern African medicinal practice in a non-African context. It is summarized in Harding, *A Refuge in Thunder*, 25–26, and in Lahon, "Inquisição, Pacto Com o Demônio e 'Magia' Africana"; also see Sweet, "Slaves, Convicts, and Exiles." Pereira had been successful enough to hire an assistant, José Francisco Pedroso, and before being arrested he had conducted a lively trade in protective bolsas containing *pedras de corisco* ("lightning stones," usually meteorites but sometimes also Neolithic flint tools akin to the "thunderstones" of early modern Northern European magical lore), as well as sulfur, bones, and herbs.

46 Breen, "Semedo's Sixteen Secrets," 353. For example, a manuscript medical text

created in Mexico City in 1771 (Wellcome Americana MS 23) contained over fifty recipes drawn from a Spanish translation and digest of Semedo's works.

47 Semedo, "De Varios Simplices," 1.

48 Ibid., 11.

49 On the phenomenon of physicians joining the Inquisition for social protection, see Walker, *Doctors, Folk Medicine and the Inquisition*, and on Inquisition punishments of African healers, see Walker, "Slaves, Free Blacks and the Inquisition in Early Modern Portugal."

50 Grehan, "Smoking and 'Early Modern' Sociability"; Romaniello, "Customs and Consumption," 184.

51 Azevedo, *Repertorio de todas las pragmaticas y capitulos de Cortes*, 78.

52 Montoro et al., *Ordinaciones de la imperial ciudad de Zaragoza*, 151.

53 Moyle, *Present Ill State*, 27.

54 Ibid., 27–28.

55 One representative example is Coelho's sketch of a flower growing out of a guitar tuning peg above an entry on the medical virtues of violet syrup, a visual pun on the close resemblance between violet (*viola*) and guitar (*violão*) in early modern Portuguese. BNP, Cod. 2259, *Pharmaca de Jozeph Coelho*, fol. 76r; for more images, see Breen, "Pharmaca of Jozeph Coelho."

56 Biblioteca Nacional de Portugal (hereafter, BNP), Cod. 2259. José [Jozeph] Coelho, *Pharmaca*, "de Simplisibus," fol. 13r-22v. Nearly half of the drugs sold by the Coelhos, according to one list recorded in José Coelho's notebook, appear to have originated in the East Indies or the Americas.

57 On the influence of Mesue (ibn Māsawayh) on early modern European pharmacy, see De Vos, "The 'Prince of Medicine.'"

58 BNP, Cod. 2259. José [Jozeph] Coelho, *Pharmaca*, "de Simplisibus," fol. 13r-22v.

59 In this, Jozeph Coelho was imitating a century of precedent: the Venetian physician Nicolò Massa, for instance, had argued in a treatise on syphilis, *Liber de morbo gallico* (Venice, 1532), that had lauded the virtues of guaiacum but speculated that it was related to Mediterranean species and defended its use by referencing medieval authorities like Avicenna. See Parrish, "Marketing Nature," 52–57.

60 One factor that may have brought things to a head was increasing demand for novel drugs and techniques on the part of consumers themselves; see Siena, "The 'Foul Disease' and Privacy."

61 Sweet, "Hidden Histories of African Lisbon," 236–37.

62 ANTT, Livros dos Feitos Findos, Livro 85, "Carregações de Productos de Botica de Manuel Ferreira de Castro," Lisbon, 1738-1750s.

63 ANTT LFF 85, Livro de Carregações, "Carregação que estando este prezente an.o de 1738 o para a Cidade de Bahia," 1738.

64 Archivum Romanum Societatis Iesu [ARSI], Rome, Opp. Nn. 17, "Collecção de varias receitas," Rome, 1764.

65 All quotes in this paragraph are from João Curvo Semedo, "Memorial de varios simples Que da India Oriental, da America, & de outras partes do mundo vem

ao nosso Reyno," 1, an undated treatise bound with the 1727 edition of Semedo's *Polyanthea medicinal.*

66 On this concept, see Cooper, *Inventing the Indigenous*, ch. 1.

66 Goodman, *Fall of Man, Or the Corruption of Nature*, 83. On Dutch efforts to popularize tea among seventeenth-century European consumers, see Cook, *Matters of Exchange*, 293–300.

68 Goodman, *Fall of Man, Or the Corruption of Nature*, 98–99.

69 On bodily and humoral corruption from the Indies climate, see Cañizares-Esguerra, "New World, New Stars."

70 Goodman, *Fall of Man, Or the Corruption of Nature*, 99.

71 James I, *Counterblaste to Tobacco*, 3.

72 Da Orta, *Coloquios dos simples e drogas da India*, 26r.

73 Ibid., 26r.

74 Cowan, *Social Life of Coffee*, 40. Cowan notes that many British medical authorities differentiated coffee from narcotics like opium, attacking its effects on sociability rather than on the body itself. However, anxieties about the effects of coffee on European bodies were also potent. As late as 1733, a Portuguese physician debated whether *caffé* was a "stupefacient," citing no less an authority than Francis Bacon. Abreu, *Historiología Médica*, 422.

75 Donzelli, *Teatro Farmaceutico*, 390.

76 Barham, *Hortus Americanus*, 2. Published after his death, Barham's book was based on notes taken in Jamaica during the 1740s.

77 Pitt, *Craft and Frauds of Physick Expos'd*, 37.

78 Cook, "Markets and Cultures."

79 Vigier, *Pharmacopea Ulyssiponense*, "Prologo," n.p. "para a saude dos enfermos esta quotidianamente pedindo por repetidas receitas."

80 João Vigier, "Tratado das virtudes e descrições de diversas plantas e partes de animais do Brasil e das mais partes da América ou Índia Ocidental, de algumas do Oriente descobertas no último século, tiradas de Guilherme Piso, Monardes, Clusio, Acosta e de outros e ainda a História das plantas da Europa e das mais usadas que vêm da Ásia, da África e da América," in *Pharmacopea Ulyssiponense*, 391-402.

81 Tepaske, "Regulation of Medical Practitioners," 61, citing remedies in Palacios, *Palestra Farmacéutica*, which went into multiple editions throughout the first half of the eighteenth century in Spain.

82 Semedo, "De Varios Simplices."

83 Berlu, *The Treasury of Drugs Unlock'd*. The book was popular, appearing in a second edition in 1724, a third in 1733 (both printed for Samuel Clarke), and a fourth in 1738 (printed for S. Ballard).

84 This list is derived from William Salmon, *Polygraphice*; Talbor, *The English Remedy*; and Semedo, *Polyanthea medicinal*, 811.

85 On knowledge disruption as a factor in early modern globalization, see Breen, "No Man Is an Island."

86 The infamous recipe for Coca-Cola, which has never been trademarked because

doing so would require the company to reveal its secret ingredients and thus open itself up to competition, is an example of an early modern-style proprietary formula surviving into the present day. On Coca-Cola's parallels with the wider history of drugs, see Gootenberg, "Secret Ingredients."

87 AHU, cx., 11, doc. 34, November 22, 1674, Francisco Tavares de Athayde to the Conselho; AHU, cx. 9, doc. 151, April 4, 1669 Provedor da Fazenda Lourenço de Andrade de Colaço to the Conselho.

Chapter 3

1 Early modern European drugs were conceived of as tools not only for curing diseases but also for influencing the external world, for instance through "sympathetic magic" imbued in a substance or an object. Christopher Bayly's concept of "charismatic goods" that retained their perceived powers across cultural contexts is useful in this context. As he has argued, substances like tobacco were not just medicines or recreational intoxicants but were substances conceived of as having innate powers that could influence both the consumer and the larger natural or social order. Thus they transferred value across long distances while also retaining specific cultural meanings. Bayly, *Birth of the Modern World*, 44–45.

2 On the history of "fetisheers" in the Atlantic world, see Sansi, "Feitiço e Fetiche No Atlântico Moderno"; Parés and Sansi, *Sorcery in the Black Atlantic*.

3 Although the modern conception of science had not fully formed at this period, I believe that the term is still useful in an early modern context, for reasons similar to those expressed in Harkness, *The Jewel House*, "A Note About Science."

4 This description and the quotations in the following paragraphs are gathered from AHU, Conselho Ultramarino Angola, cx. 13, doc. 51, February 7, 1688. See also cx. 13, doc. 88, for further documentation related to Caconda (which is sometimes spelled Kakonda).

5 On the Jaga of Caconda and his previous battles with Portuguese forces in the central highlands of Angola in 1685, see Thornton, *Warfare in Atlantic Africa*, 112, and on Caconda the region, see Candido, *African Slaving Port*, 73–75 and 245-48. *Jaga* as a title reflects early Portuguese use of the term as an ethnonym. Mariana Candido argues it was a "Portuguese creation" to "refer to nameless enemies, whose political and social structure was foreign to the Portuguese" (Candido, *African Slaving Port*, 59-60). Kakonda was a contested interior region with occasional control over the slave trade in Benguela. See Miller, "Requiem for the 'Jaga,'" and Beatrix Heintze, "Extraordinary Journey of the Jaga Through the Centuries." On the larger context of warfare and the slave trade in seventeenth-century Angola, see Ferreira, *Cross-Cultural Exchange*.

6 AHU, Conselho Ultramarino Angola, cx. 13, doc. 51, February 7, 1688.

7 On the rule of Queen Njinga, see Heywood, *Njinga of Angola*.

8 Torres, *Memórias contendo a biographia*, 211.

9 AHU, Conselho Ultramarino Angola, cx. 13, doc. 51, February 7, 1688.

10 For usage of *conjurar* as "to exorcize" or "to banish evil spirits," see de la Concepción, *Practica de Conjurar*.

11 De Menezes, *Henriqueida*, 279.

12 See also AHU, cx. 14, doc. 89, February 15, 1692, the minutes of the Luanda council regarding a campaign against another jaga named Dembo Ambuila. According to the document, it is "necessary and needed ... to fight for the respect of the Catholic Church," because of Dembo Ambuila's *maleficios*, a word that could mean either "misdeeds" or "sorceries."

13 *Nganga* was a West Central African term for practitioners of possession, sacrifice, healing, and/or cursing; early modern Europeans typically called them *feitiçeiros*, fetisheers, or sorcerers (*sorcières*). Ferreira, *Cross-Cultural Exchange*, translates *ganga* as "religious leader" (18). John Thornton describes the *nganga* as "a medium to the Other World," noting that the label was also used to describe Catholic priests (Thornton, *Kongolese Saint Anthony*, 54).

14 See Sweet, "Mutual Misunderstandings"; Sweet, "Slaves, Convicts, and Exiles"; and Sweet, *Domingos Álvares*. See also Calainho, "Jambacousses e Gangazambes," 141-76. For comparative perspectives on African magical practices in the West Indies, see Handler, "Slave Medicine and Obeah."

15 On the perceived magical powers of the eucharist and associated objects (such as the medieval use of communion wafers as protective amulets in horse stables), see Kieckhefer, *Magic in the Middle Ages*, 80; and Duffy, *Stripping of the Altars*, 276–77.

16 This was part of a larger blending of cultures in early modern Africa that included Portuguese *filhos da terra* (African-born whites), mixed-race local elites, and itinerant merchants (*pombeiros*), many of them women and some semi-autonomous slaves, who amassed substantial fortunes trading in enslaved captives to be shipped to the Brazilian plantations along with novel goods like cachaça, tobacco, European and Indian textiles, and guns. See Candido, *African Slaving Port*, 14, as well as Thornton, *Africa and Africans in the Making of the Atlantic World*, and Ipsen, *Daughters of the Trade*.

17 This etymology is explored in a pair of interesting articles by William Pietz; see Pietz, "Problem of the Fetish, I" and "Problem of the Fetish, II."

18 In this regard, this chapter builds on work by the geographers Judith Carney and Richard Voeks, who have shown how the patterns of the slave trade influenced Atlantic world ecological changes (Voeks, *Sacred Leaves of Candomblé*; Carney, *In the Shadow of Slavery*).

19 Pyrard, *Voyage*, 218–19.

20 On European fears of the health effects of tropical climates, see Cañizares-Esguerra, "New World, New Stars"; and Cagle, *Assembling the Tropics*, ch. 1.

21 Cañizares-Esguerra, "New World, New Stars."

22 Breen, "Flip Side of the Pharmacopeia."

23 Anonymous ["R. B."], *English Acquisitions in Guinea*, 46–47.

24 Ibid., 35.

25 Ibid., 38.

26 AHU Angola, cx. 11, doc. 100, March 26, 1678.

27 Ibid. Maria Portuondo (*Secret Science*, 93) argues that *experimenta* of this kind

might viably be translated as "experiments" full stop. Following Peter Dear's definition of a scientific experiment as "involving a specific question about nature which the experimental outcome is designed to answer," we could, for instance, classify this 1678 dispatch as reporting on *experimenta* with horses as fitting the bill. The *experimenta*, which I tend to translate as "trial" or "test," did indeed seek to answer a specific question about tropical nature (Do European animal and human bodies succumb more quickly to tropical diseases?). See Dear, *Discipline and Experience*, 11–31.

28 Zucchelli, *Relazioni del viaggio*, 91.

29 Lobo, *Itinerário*, 3. Nicolas Villault, a French traveler along the West African coast in the 1660s, similarly blamed "nipping Winds and Rains" for making "those parts so subject to worms." Villault, *Relation of the Coasts of Africk Called Guinee*, 212.

30 Villault, *Relation of the Coasts of Africk Called Guinee*, 208. Villault's account also offered a description of an African medical technique to remove the rain-bred worms: "If they perceive them advancing, they may hasten their journey, and pull them out little by little, if they find any stop or reluctance in the Worm, they must let them alone (least they break them) and tye a haire or a piece of silk about them . . . for they are of so venemous a quality, there is no way to preserve the person against its virulence but by cutting off the part" (Villault, *Relation of the Coasts of Africk Called Guinee*, 214–15).

31 Bosman, *New and Accurate Description of the Coast of Guinea*, 205.

32 See, for instance, AHU Angola, cx. 10, doc. 125, July 6, 1673, in which Balthezar van Dunen "makes petition to the Council, resident of Angola, where he has lived for thirty-three years with satisfaction and service for your Highness. He thinks himself to be old in age, with many ailments, and he believes there are no remedies for his illness in Angola, for lack of doctors. In respect of which, he desires to leave Angola with his household and family, and work on his health . . . he asks to go to Brazil with all of his family and goods."

33 AHU, Angola, cx. 8, doc. 37, August 13, 1664, "Petition of Daniel de la Sena, cirurgião Frances." AHU Angola, cx. 8, doc. 32, August 11, 1664, petition of surgeon Pedro da Silva for "purgas para a botica."

34 AHU Angola, cx. 9, doc. 62 October 20, 1666.

35 AHU, cx. 9, doc. 25, April 10, 1666.

36 "Drogas da terra" may refer to a range of substances, including minerals like gold or silver as well as *materia medica*.

37 AHU Angola, cx. 9, doc. 62, October 20, 1666. The *libongo* was a Portuguese-minted coin used in Angola, roughly equivalent to fifty réis.

38 AHU, cx. 14, doc. 89, February 15, 1692, a list of expenses, which includes ten arrobas of sugar, hatchets and sickles, two barrels of biscuits, vinegar, and 60$000 for the surgeon's wage. For comparison, the total cost of the sugar was 16$000.

39 AHU, Angola, cx. 12, doc. 122, February 10, 1684, petition from Francisco de Bivar Mascarenhas, captain of the infantry in Luanda, that "the ailments that he suffers require a change of climate, and of going away from the Kingdom to cure himself."

40 AHU, Angola, cx. 13, doc. 72, February 10, 1688.

41 Brown, *Reaper's Garden*.

42 Lobo, *Itinerário*, 4.

43 Ibid., 6.

44 Ibid., 41.

45 AHU, Angola, cx. 9, doc. 33, "Certificate of Luiz Goncalves de Andrade, surgeon-mor;" De Miranda, *Relação cirurgica, e medica*, 112.

46 Rome, *Relation brieve et fidelle du succez de la mission des Freres mineurs capucins*, 166-67. Fra Girolamo Merolla, an Italian missionary, likewise writes of an "enslaved surgeon" (*schiavo chirurgo*) treating mixed-race individuals in the Congo. Merolla, *Breve, e succinta relatione del viaggio*, 95.

47 Dampier, *New Voyage Round the World*, 91. Dampier also noted that African healers in Jamaica used "*Hyacinth, Alkermes* or *Clarie* [claret wine]" in their practice (91). Alkermes was an Arabic remedy that included raw silk, while hyacinth was a mixture of precious gems and metals (primarily zircon), and "clarie" was likely an alternate spelling of claret.

48 Merolla, *Breve e succinta relazione*, 99. As Cécile Fromont writes, iron and iron-working had a widespread connection to the supernatural and power over "invisible forces" in the Kongo and neighboring regions. See Fromont, *Art of Conversion*, 44.

49 Giovanni Antonio Cavazzi de Montecucculo, "Missione evangelica nel Regno de Congo" (circa 1665-68), Araldi Manuscripts, Modena, Italy, bk. 1, ch. 8, fol. 75. All quotes are from the online edition of Cavazzi's manuscript, trans. and ed. John Thornton: www.bu.edu/afam/faculty/john-thornton/cavazzi-missione-evangelica-2/book-1-chapter-8. On Cavazzi's preoccupation with what he saw as the demonic inspiration of Kongo rituals, see Fromont, *Art of Conversion*, 78-79.

50 Antonil, *Cultura e opulencia do Brasil*, 24.

51 Ibid., 28.

52 Atkins, *Voyage to Guinea, Brasil and the West-Indies*, 79.

53 Ibid., 79–80.

54 Pietz, "Problem of the Fetish, II"; and Sansi, "Sorcery and Fetishism in the Modern Atlantic."

55 Vasconcellos, *Vida do P. Joam d'Almeida*, 124.

56 Ibid., 124–25.

57 On the contents of *bolsas de mandinga*, see Santos, "Bolsas de mandinga no espaço atlântico."

58 Franco, *Imagem da virtude*, 734–45.

59 Ibid., 735.

60 Ibid., 612.

61 Lacerda e Almeida, *Lands of Cazembe*, 45.

62 ANTT, Inquisiçao de Lisboa proc. 2097; Calainho, "Metrópole das Mandingas."

63 Curto, *Enslaving Spirits*.

64 Schneider, *Dictionary of African Borrowings*, 62.

65 AHU Angola, cx. 11, doc. 107, June 10, 1678. This document is in very bad condi-

tion and is heavily water damaged. These quotes are fragments from a much larger block of text, some of which is indecipherable.

66 AHU, Angola, cx. 13, doc. 36, January 29, 1687.

67 Ibid., doc. 97, February 23, 1689.

68 Ibid., October 20, 1689.

69 Ibid., February 5, 1689.

70 AHU Angola, cx. 15, doc. 37, November 12, 1694. The physicians were A. Perez Lima and Andre de Silva.

71 See Miller, *Way of Death*, 296; and Curto, *Enslaving Spirits*, ch. 2.

72 Merolla, *Breve, e succinta relatione del viaggio*, 89–90. Mixing evangelizing with the distribution of spirits and tobacco reflected the practices of missionaries in the North American interior during the same period, who used brandy in ritual gift exchanges that took advantage of the perception that alcohol intoxication could confer spiritual power. Mancall, *Deadly Medicine*, 75.

73 Villault, *Relation of the Coasts of Africk Called Guinee*, 200. For the original, see Villault, *Relation des costs d'Afriques*.

74 Rome, *Fondation de la Mission des Capucins*, 122.

75 Curto, *Enslaving Spirits*, 36.

76 Although some have argued that the transatlantic transmission of Mesoamerican tobacco in the sixteenth century marked the introduction of the pipe to the Old World, archaeological evidence demonstrates the presence of sub-Saharan cannabis pipes from the thirteenth and fourteenth centuries CE. For instance, ceramic pipes excavated in Ethiopia have been carbon-dated to about 1320 and found to contain traces of cannabis residue (Toit, "Man and Cannabis in Africa,"19). In Zambia, pipe fragments have been found at an even earlier date of about 1200 CE: Philips, "African Smoking and Pipes," 310.

77 Jones, *German Sources*, 63, citing Samuel Brun's *Schiffarten* (1624).

78 De Cadornega, *História geral das guerras angolanas*.

79 On Cavazzi's manuscript and the complicated book history of Cavazzi's account when variants of it reached print, see Heywood, *Njinga of Angola*, 291–93 and Thornton, "New Light."

80 Although Njinga's pipe in Cavazzi's manuscript does not match their description of the Barbados pipe exactly, it does display the acute angle and fitting for a plant reed noted in the Barbados specimen. Handler and Norman, "From West Africa to Barbados."

81 Mancall, *Deadly Medicine*, 75.

82 Ibid., 75–76.

83 Akyeampong, *Drink, Power, and Cultural Change*, 4.

84 I borrow this term from Gordon, "Rituals of Rapture to Dependence."

85 Curto, *Enslaving Spirits*, 199.

86 On "Atlantic creoles," see Heywood, "Portuguese into African." On the anthropology and neuroscience of altered states of consciousness, see E. Cohen, *The Mind Possessed*; McNamara, *Neuroscience of Religious Experience*; and Bourguignon, *Possession*.

87 BNP, F.R. 437, cod. 13114, Francisco de Buytrago, "Arvore da Vida e Thesouro descuberto." The manuscript was apparently written in Lisbon in 1731, but it describes events in Angola in the 1710s and 1720s: Buytrago describes it as the work of "Sargento Mor Francisco de Buytrago, knight of the Order of Christ, in the space of twenty years in this kingdom." An internal reference to Buytrago's writings "seeing print" suggests that he intended to publish the manuscript; one suspects that, if Buytrago indeed pursued this plan, he was rebuffed by Inquisition censors. The provenance of the manuscript is highly obscure; as far as I can tell, it has only been described in print once, in passing. See Monteiro, "A Escrita da História," 80.

88 As Buytrago put it in an introductory note "to the pious reader," "I have divided this book into two tracts. The first is about the bark or tree of life and its great virtues. The second is about the extremely singular things which exist in the Kingdoms of Angola, Congo and other provinces, and of their singular virtues, and other very curious things." BNL, Buytrago, "Arvore da Vida," fol. 4v.

89 BNL, Buytrago, "Arvore da Vida," fol. 5v.

90 Ibid., fol. 5v-6r.

91 See Sweet, *Recreating Africa*; and Gómez, *The Experiential Caribbean* for two complementary articulations of the case for an "Africanized" Iberian Atlantic world.

92 Freedman, *Out of the East*.

93 Arrais, *Arbor vitae*. Arrais's original work, published in Lisbon in 1650, was titled *Novae Philosophiae et Medicinae de Qualitatibus occultis* (The New Philosophy and Medicine of Occult Qualities).

94 Arrais, *Arbor vitae*, 52.

95 Ibid., 51, 74. Arrais writes later of "*Opium* and other Stupefying Medicines," suggesting that this was the particular "Narcotick" he had in mind for his comparison (93).

96 BNL, Buytrago, "Arvore da Vida," fol. 7r.

97 The Italian Congo missionaries Cavazzi and Merolla described a bark with mingled healing and poisonous virtues, which they called "Ncassa" and claimed was used in ritual ordeals. See Cavazzi, *Istorica descrizione de' tre' regni*, 90–91; and Merolla, *Breve, e succinta relatione del viaggio*, 100.

98 Cavazzi, Istorica descrizione de' tre' regni, 91.

99 BNL, Buytrago, "Arvore da Vida," fol. 7r-7v.

100 The most likely candidate would be Cavazzi's "Missione Evangelica," also known as the Araldi manuscript, which is a narrative of Cavazzi's experiences as a missionary in Congo and Angola; the second volume of the manuscript is dated 1666. In Cavazzi's published account *Istorica descrizione*, based on the manuscript, Cavazzi described a bark he called *ncassa* as noted above.

101 BNL, Buytrago, "Arvore da Vida," fol. 8r.

102 Ibid., fol. 9r-9v.

103 For *nkasa* as a vernacular name for suaveolens in the Congo, see Neuwinger, *African Ethnobotany*, 302. Credit for identification of Buytrago's *emcassa* with *Eryth-*

rophleum suaveolens goes to Chelsea Berry ("Poisoned Relations" and private correspondence).

104 Both Merolla and Cavazzi mention ncassa as a medicinal drug used in "ordeals," but they attribute it to *feiticeiros* and not to Christian-oriented healers.

105 De Moura, *Syntagma chirurgico theorico-practico*, 541.

106 Eamon, *Science and the Secrets of Nature*, 189.

107 ANTT, Inquisição de Lisboa, Processo no. 597.

108 Sweet, *Domingos Álvares*, 62. The Inquisition trial of Miguel Ferreira Pestana, an "indio" arrested in Espirito Sancto in 1737 who "consorted with negros" and created healing *bolsas*, offers an intriguing suggestion that African healing practices were beginning to be adopted by indigenous Brazilians as well. ANTT, Inquisição de Lisboa, Processo no. 6982.

109 Wadsworth, "Charlatan in the Backlands," 75.

110 ANTT, Inquisição de Lisboa, Processo no. 3693, "Informação of Father Francisco Ferreira, Rodellas, January 18, 1740" fol. 19. See also Sweet, *Recreating Africa*, 183.

111 Amulets protecting against bullets played an important role in African spiritual healing up to the twentieth century. On transfers of African epistemologies of healing to colonial America, including through amulets, see Gómez, *Experiential Caribbean*, 139–42.

112 Atkins, *A Voyage to Guinea, Brasil, and the West Indies*, 94–95.

113 Sweet, *Domingos Álvares*, 133-38. On Afro-Brazilian healing practices, see Marquese, *Feitores do corpo*.

114 Den Bersselaar, "Negotiating Beer and Gin Advertisements," 403–4.

115 Semedo, "Memorial de Varios Simples," 30. On Semedo's connections to African *feiticaria* see Nogueira, *Entre Cirurgiões, Tambores, e Ervas*, ch. 2.

116 Ibid., 29. Semedo added that a "a foreign Surgeon named Monsieur Estruque . . . gave it to two chickens who had poison in their stomachs, enough to kill them, and giving one of them Minhaminha mixed with water and giving to the other the Pao Cobra with a mind to test which of these roots had more virtue against poison, he observed that both chickens escaped death."

117 Sansi, "Feitiço e Fetiche No Atlântico Moderno," 124.

118 Cañizares-Esguerra, *Puritan Conquistadors*, ch. 4.

119 Heywood and Thornton, *Central Africans, Atlantic Creoles*, ch. 4.

120 For more on this absence of African drugs in the early modern drug trade, see Breen, "Flip Side of the Pharmacopeia."

121 On the understudied field of poison history, see Gibbs, "Poisonous Properties, Bodies, and Forms."

Chapter 4

Epigraph: British Library, Sloane MS 4020, undated (c. 1700).

1 On Macedo's biography, see de Faria, "Duarte Ribeiro de Macedo"; and Neto e Cova, "O Pensamento Politico de Duarte Ribeiro de Macedo," which reprints original documents.

2 On Macedo's proposals, see Cagle, *Assembling the Tropics*, 255-60.

3 ANTT, Duarte Ribeiro de Macedo, "Discurso sobre a Transplantação das Plantas de Especiarias da Asia para a América," T/TT/MSBR/39. Transcriptions here were made from the manuscript at the ANTT, the text of which was later reproduced in a slightly altered form in Macedo, *Obras Ineditas*, 103–33. An unusual amount of uncertainty surrounds the dating of this letter because of a number of transcription errors: the document is misdated to 1633 in the ANTT's catalog and is misdated to 1782 in the printed transcription produced in 1817. The final page of the second section of the original manuscript reads: "Paris, 15th of March, 1675"; however, fol. 6v of the same section mentions that "after I had written these pages I found in the *Jornal de Scavans* of July 3, 1675 an extract from the *Jornal du Inglaterra* [*Philosophical Transactions*] where is discussed a discovery of the Royal Society regarding the cinnamon tree."

4 Macedo, "Satisfação Politica a Maximas Erradas" (1660?), reprinted in *Obras Ineditas*, 240.

5 Macedo, *Obras Ineditas*, 240.

6 Macedo, "Se he facil no Reino a introducação das Artes" (undated treatise), collected in *Obras Ineditas*, 40-41. On debates over the role of *techne* and *artes* in colonization, see Chaplin, *Subject Matter*, 40–43.

7 ANTT, Macedo, "Discurso," T/TT/MSBR/39, fol. 2v-3r.

8 On Vieira and his time in Rome, see Cohen, *The Fire of Tongues*.

9 António Vieira in Rome to Duarte Ribeiro de Macedo in Paris, January 23, 1675, in Vieira, *Cartas selectas*, 94.

10 Vieira to Macedo, January 23, 1675, in *Cartas selectas*, 94. Vieira had been interested in the commercial potential of *drogas* from the Maranhão and Angola since his youth. His early writings about the threat of the Dutch in Brazil and the Éstado da India hinged on their seizure of the drug trade. See, for instance, BNP Cod. 9259, "Obras várias de Padre Antonio Vieira," fol. 9v-11v (dated 1644). This and other manuscripts are partially transcribed in *Obras Varis do Padre António Vieira* (Lisbon, 1856).

11 Macedo, "Discurso," ANTT, T/TT/MSBR/39, fol. 3r.

12 Henning, "Montagu, Hon. Edward (c. 1636-65)," in *The History of Parliament: The House of Commons 1660-1690*, ed. B. D. Henning (London, 1983). Ralph Montagu (whose father was a baron) would ultimately be elevated to the position of 1st Duke of Montagu in 1705. Before this time, he had already amassed a considerable fortune, in part because of his infamous 1692 marriage to the eccentric heiress Elizabeth Monck. Montagu supposedly dressed as the Kangxi emperor of China in order to placate her desire to marry into royalty.

13 Locke served for a time as the personal physician to Montagu's wife: see John Locke to Dr. Mapletoft, Paris, December 4, 1677, in De Beer, *Correspondence of John Locke*.

14 Macedo, "Discurso," ANTT, T/TT/MSBR/39, fol. 5r. Macedo was referring here to the French translation of Sprat's book published as *L'Histoire de la Société Royal de Londres* (Geneva, 1669).

15 On continuity between early modern alchemy and chemistry, see Newman and Principe, *Alchemy Tried in the Fire.*

16 On the tangled history of peer review, see Moxham and Fyfe, "Royal Society," and on Robert Hooke's observation of cells, see Chapman, *England's Leonardo*, 63–64.

17 On Iberian empiricism, see Cañizares-Esguerra, *Nature, Empire, and Nation*; Barrera-Osorio, *Experiencing Nature*; and Portuondo, *Secret Science.*

18 The close ties between the Portuguese drug trade and the Inquisition are documented in Walker, *Doctors, Folk Medicine and the Inquisition.*

19 Bowrey, *Geographical Account of Countries*, 68.

20 Ibid., 80.

21 Ibid., 80–81.

22 Daston, "Empire of Observation," 90–91. In his later life, Bowrey became an ardent scholar of Asian languages, compiling the earliest Malay dictionary and even meeting with the famed "false Formosan" and Royal Society interlocutor George Psalmanazar to quiz him about the languages of Taiwan (see Breen, "No Man Is an Island," 402).

23 Another factor may have been the rise of so-called Muslim-captivity narratives on theater stages, which dramatized the kidnapping and forced conversion of Britons by North African pirates.

24 Bowrey, *Geographical Account of Countries*, 75. Petro de Loveyro numbered among what Bowrey elsewhere describes as the "Portingals" who "beare arms in the Honourable English East India Company's Service as private Centinels" (Bowrey, *Geographical Account of Countries*, 4). Loveyro seems to have adapted to the rising British presence in India quite early; already by 1663 he figured in a letter from an East India Company merchant at Balasor as the "experienced Pilott Pedro de Lavera" and he appears again as an agent in the East India Company's "private trade" in a 1678 letter, ferrying an illicit shipment of goods to the Maldives at the behest of an English merchant. See Richard Carnac Temple's footnote in Bowrey, *Geographical Account of Countries*, 75, citing a letter from Shem Bridges to Captain Charles Wilde, October 13, 1663, and Vincent and Read to Edwards at Balasor, January 29, 1678.

25 Freedman, *Out of the East*, ch. 3.

26 On experimental practices of natural history and medicine in the sixteenth-century Iberian Atlantic, see Barrera-Osorio, *Experiencing Nature*, ch. 3. On the complex nature of da Orta's empirical investigation of drugs, see Cagle, *Assembling the Tropics*, pp. 122–23 and 159–64.

27 Hernández, *Quatro libros de la naturaleza.*

28 Lorraine Daston and others have written on the impact of these "preternatural" phenomena on the trajectory of the history of science; see Daston, "Marvelous Facts and Miraculous Evidence in Early Modern Europe."

29 For instance, see Vigier's notes on "drogas modernas" above, 60–61.

30 Knox, *Historical Relation of the Island Ceylon*, 154.

31 Tuesday, November 5, 1689, and Thursday, November 7, 1689, entries in the diary

of Robert Hooke, reproduced in R. T. Gunther, ed. *Early Science in Oxford*, Vol. 10 (Oxford: Clarendon Press, 1935), 163.

32 If the "patient" truly was Hooke, then this may be the oldest example of a formula that has become common in reporting of illicit drug experiences: the attribution of an experience to a "friend" or, in the lingo of the Internet, "SWIM" (Someone Who Isn't Me).

33 Robert Hooke, "An Account of the Plant, call'd Bangue, Before the Royal Society, Dec 18. 1689," reprinted in Hooke, *Philosophical Experiments*, 209.

34 More precisely, Hooke speculated, it could "be of considerable Use for Lunaticks." Hooke, "Account of . . . Bangue," *Philosophical Experiments*, 210. Although European pharmacists and apothecaries had long used *Cannabis sativa*, the Western sibling of *indica* ("Indian hemp"), it was usually used in external treatments as a poultice, not taken internally, and evidently not widely used in a purely recreational context.

35 Shapin, "The Invisible Technician."

36 Bacon, *Sylva Sylvarum*, 210.

37 All quotes in this paragraph are from Bacon, *Operia Omnia*, Cent. X, 203.

38 It's unclear to what extent many of these physicians, such as Daniel Sennert, were working directly under the influence of Paracelsus or were simply responding to the same questions that absorbed him. On Paracelsan medicine and Sennert, see Joel A. Klein, *Chymical Life in Early Modern Europe* (forthcoming book manuscript).

39 Sennert, *Thirteen Books of Natural Philosophy*, 431, a translation of Sennert's 1632 *Epitome naturalis scientiae*.

40 Sennert, *Thirteen Books of Natural Philosophy*, 435, 439.

41 In addition to the evidence from primary sources, a recent chemical analysis of a surviving *mumia* jar has verified that it does indeed contain human remains along with minerals and plant materials consistent with an Egyptian origin; see Scholz-Böttcher et al., "An 18th Century Medication."

42 On empirical medicine in the early modern Iberian colonies, see Osorio, "Knowledge and Empiricism," in *Science in the Spanish and Portuguese Empires*; and Júnia Furtado, "Tropical Empiricism."

43 Semedo, "Memorial de Varios Simplices," 3.

44 Amaro, "A famosa pedra cordial."

45 The East India Company surgeon John Fryer claimed that the Jesuit pharmacy in Goa made an annual income of 50,000 xerafins on the sale of the stones. Fryer, *New Account of East-India and Persia*, 149.

46 Berlu, *The Treasury of Drugs Unlock'd*, 67.

47 Ovington, *A Voyage to Surat*, 155–56. The anonymous pamphlet *Fair play for one's life* (London: M. Wotton, 1708), attributed simply to "a gentleman of quality of North Britain," complained that the "Goa stone" was in high demand among groups ranging from physicians to "Sea Surgeons" and street hawkers of drugs "pedlar'd about from House to House" (5).

48 Griffith, *Observations made upon the Brasillian root, called ipepocoanha.*

49 Sloane, "On the Use of Ipecacuanha," 69.

50 Boyle, "Hydrostatics applied to the materia medica" (1690) in Boyle, *Philosophical Works*, 328.

51 Ibid., 329.

52 Royal Society Archives (RSA), MS 189, f. 16 (Robert Boyle's notes for his hydrostatics research, undated [1684?]).

53 Archives of the Royal Society, Boyle Papers, 8, fol. 20. On Boyle's desiderata, see Keller, "The New World of Sciences"; and Roos, "Perchance to Dream."

54 For an example of a binary opposition between the "rationalism" of the Royal Society and the concept of occult virtues, see Hall, "Boyle's Method of Work."

55 Though usually associated with Aristotle, this doctrine also owed a debt to Galen, who wrote about magical amulets and drugs that operated according to "unnameable properties," which were observable by the senses but could not be explained. See Copenhaver, "A Tale of Two Fishes," 380–81.

56 On the role of the microscope and other optical instruments in this changing notion of the occult, see Wilson, "Visual Surface and Visual Symbol."

57 One early eighteenth-century scientific author directly related Boyle's research into the "hidden Property" latent in drugs to quina: "Specific Medicines, are such as have a peculiar Vertue against some Disease; as the QuinQuina, or Cortex Peruviana, hath to cure Intermitting Fever . . . [they] have a Virtue to cure, by some hidden Property, this or that particular Disease. That there are such Medicines as these, in the latter and most proper sense of the Word, Mr. Boyle makes very probable" (Harris, *Lexicon Technium*, n.p.).

58 Robert Boyle, "The Notion of Specific Remedies Prov'd agreeable to Mechanical Philosophy: with the advantages of simple Medicines consider'd; and their Use recommended," in Boyle, *Philosophical Works*, 3: 546.

59 Boyle, "The Notion of Specific Remedies," in Boyle, *Philosophical Works* 3:548, 550–51, 575.

60 Hedrick, "Romancing the Salve,"161–85. In his *Suspicions about some hidden qualities of the air* (1674), Boyle noted in his preface that he considered using the phrase "Occult Qualities of air" in the title and speculated about the "peculiar Textures" that undergirded the workings of "what we call Sympathies and Antipathies." On Boyle's speculation about occult qualities, see Mary Floyd-Wilson, *Occult Knowledge, Science, and Gender*, 135.

61 Santo António, *Pharmacopea Lusitana*, "Prologo," 1.

62 Semedo, *Polyanthea Medicinal* (1704 edition), 117, 255, 529, 611, 617–18, and 606–21.

63 Abreu, *Historiologica Medica*, 422; Luis Caetano de Lima, "Epitome Willisiana" (1728), Biblioteca Nacional de Portugal, Manuscritos Reservados, cod. 2050-52.

64 Oldenburg to Thomas Hill, August 30, 1671, with enclosure for an unknown Jesuit in Brazil, in Hall and Hall, *The Correspondence of Henry Oldenburg*, viii, 236, 244. For the original document, see RSA Cl.P/19/73, "Enquiries about Brazil recommended to Thomas Hill." Gascoigne, "The Royal Society, Natural History and the

Peoples of the New World(s)" offers a brief discussion of this letter (545). Thomas Hill was a Lisbon-based merchant of whom little is known, aside from the fact that he was a music lover and friend of Samuel Pepys. He probably voyaged to Brazil on a trade mission, perhaps as a wine merchant. An earlier set of five questions for "Guiana and Brasil" had appeared in *Philosophical Transactions* vol. 2, no. 23 (March 1666): 422.

65 Robert Southwell to Robert Boyle, Florence, October 10, 1660, in *Works of the Honourable Robert Boyle* 6:297.

66 Southwell to Boyle, October 10, 1660, 298.

67 Robert Southwell to Robert Boyle, Rome, March 30, 1661, in *Works of the Honourable Robert Boyle* 6:299.

68 RSA, Journal Book of the Royal Society, vol 3, April 25, 1667, 70. A letter at the National Archives (S.P. 89/8 fol. 41) dated February 4, 1667, from Sir Robert Southwell to Lord Arlington commends Sir Peter Wych for his work as a special envoy, "whose behavior has given great and general satisfaction."

69 Lobo's longer narrative of his east African travels has a complex history. Lobo's original Portuguese has been lost, so the narrative survives in its French translation, published by Joachim le Grand as *Relation historique d'Abyssinie* (Paris, 1728). A young Samuel Johnson found the book interesting enough to translate into English, which (as Boswell tells it) he performed while he "lay in bed with the book . . . and dictated." Johnson's "epitome" of the French text was published as *A Voyage to Abyssinia* (London, 1735). However, *another* version of Lobo's travels, seemingly written by Lobo himself in Portuguese and much longer than le Grand's translation, was discovered by Manuel Gonçalves da Costa in 1947 and was published as *Itinerario e Outros Escritos Inéditos* (Porto: Livraria Civilização, 1971). Both Johnson and le Grand added extensive commentary to Lobo's original text (see Gold, "Voyages of Jerónimo Lobo").

70 RSA, Journal Book of the Royal Society 3:1666–68, February 28, 1666, fol. 67.

71 Oldenburg to Boyle, London, April 14, 1668, in *Works of the Honourable Robert Boyle*, 282. The boxes are also mentioned in da Costa, *Itinerário e outros escritos inéditos*, 666.

72 For Grisley's list of plants, see Birch, *History of the Royal Society* 2:372–73, and the original manuscript in the Royal Society Archives, Cl. P. 10 doc. 11, May 20, 1669. See also Grisley's *Desengano para a medicina* and *Viridiarum Lusitanum*. Grisley's written catalog, which survives in the Royal Society archives, was an elaboration on exotica not contained in his two printed works, both of which went into numerous editions throughout the seventeenth century.

73 Grew, *Musaeum Regalis Societatis*, 385.

74 Semedo, "Memorial de varios simplices," 11. Semedo called it *engala*, "an animal in Angola with the corpulence of a swine," whose teeth, when powdered, had "the greatest virtue in abating malignant fevers, even better than that of the true Bezoar stone" (especially when mixed with poppy water). One of the only other contemporary references to *engala* I have been able to find is in a Latin catalog of Kircher's cabinet of curiosities, which calls it "a most valid remedy against venoms

from the jungles of Angola . . . purchased from African hunters and in Italy and Portugal sold by merchants"; see Francisco Maria Ruspolo, *Musæum Kircherianum* (Rome: Georgii Plachi, 1709), 277. Olfert Dapper, a Dutch physician active in the later seventeenth century, described the *emgala* as "an animal like the wild boar" whose horns were an "antidote much used by the Portuguese." Dapper, *Description de l'Afrique*, 347.

75 Riley, "The Club at the Temple Coffee House," 96.

76 Grisley's petitions are from 1652 and 1657: ANTT, Registo Geral de Mercês, Mercês da Torre do Tombo, liv. 19, f. 402v–403, and ANTT RGM, 325208.

77 RSA, Journal Book of the Royal Society, vol. 3, August 10, 1668; and RSA, Classified Papers X (Botany), 1660-1740, Cl. P. 10, doc. 9, "Discurso das Palmeiras." Zupanov and Xavier ("Quest for Permanence in the Tropics," 536) observe that a contemporary hand has added a note on this manuscript "to send [Lobo] some spectacles and perspective glasses." They interpret this as a sign that the Royal Society intended to gift Lobo with eyeglasses for degenerating eyesight, which is possible given his age, but considering the context and the reference to "perspective glasses" as well as spectacles, I suspect this is in reference to a request of Lobo for materials for optical experiments, perhaps to construct a microscope. Hooke's *Micrographia*, after all, had come out just three years before and one suspects that Lobo would have been eager to take advantage of his new connections to the institution with which Hooke was affiliated.

78 Lobo, *Short Relation of the River Nile*.

79 Ibid., ii.

80 Odell, *Lore of the Unicorn*, 290.

81 On premodern European understandings of race, see Bartlett, "Medieval and Modern Concepts of Race and Ethnicity."

82 Dampier, *New Voyage Around the World*, 1:407.

83 Hacke, *Collection of Original Voyages*, 43. John Fletcher's plays *The Sea Voyage* and *The Island Princess, or the Generous Portuguese* also contain references to Portuguese as intermediate figures between Europeans and "natives."

84 For instance, Henry Barham claimed that ambergris made "[a man] as merry as if he had drank a great quantity of wine." Barham, *Hortus Americanus*, 2. Published after his death, Barham's book was based on notes taken in Jamaica during the 1740s.

85 Dampier, *New Voyage Around the World*, 72.

86 Tennent, *Physical Enquiries*, 29.

87 On the role of credit and trust in the global drug trade, see Harold Cook, *Matters of Exchange*.

88 Indeed, it is possible that it was Dr. Mendes who treated Catarina's "soar throat" upon her first arrival in England 1662, the illness that, according to one popular version of events, introduced the English court to tea. Mendes is a little-studied figure, appearing almost exclusively in the scholarship of the Portuguese historian of pharmacy José Pedro Sousa-Dias, especially his "A 'Água de Inglaterra' no Portugal das Luzes."

89　Harvey, *Conclave of Physicians*, 106. On Harvey's decidedly unorthodox rhetorical strategy, see Payne, *With Words and Knives*, 30–32.

90　*Diary of John Evelyn* 2:334, November 29, 1694. Although the apothecary was, he wrote, "reputed a Papist," Talbor was, in Evelyn's opinion, "in truth a very honest good Christian."

91　Surprisingly little is known about Robert Talbor (or Talbot). See Siegel and Poynter, "Robert Talbor, Charles II, and Cinchona," 82–85, for a short overview with a transcription of a fascinating primary source.

92　Sousa-Dias, "Jacob de Castro Sarmento."

93　Semedo, *Observaçoens Medicas Doutrinaes*, 440, 513, 582.

94　Semedo, *Polyanthea Medicinal*, 587.

95　Mendes's children are actually better known in Anglophone scholarship than he is because they became wealthy jewel merchants who played an important role in eighteenth-century London's Sephardic community. M. Woolf, "Foreign Trade of London Jews"; Gaster, *History of the Ancient Synagogue*, 96–98.

96　João Curvo Semedo, "Manifesto que o doutor Joam Curvo Semmedo, Medico, morador em Lisboa, faz aos amantes da saude" (Lisbon, 1708?), a pamphlet bound with Semedo, *Observaçoens Medicas Doutrinaes*.

97　The only confirmation of Pedro II's gift I have been able to find is a passing, uncited mention in a Portuguese medical lecture from the 1930s, so even this claim is somewhat suspect; see de Caires, "Esbôço Histórico da Medicina," 57.

98　See, for instance, Hamlin, *More Than Hot*; Barnett, *Book of Gin*; and Henry Hobhouse's unaccountably racist chapter on *cinchona* in *Seeds of Change*.

99　For more details on the preparation of *Água de Inglaterra* see Sousa-Dias, *Água de Inglaterra*, 112.

100 Contemporary flyleaf annotation in a copy of Leclerc's *Histoire de la Médecine* (Paris, 1702), transcribed in Siegel and Poynter, "Robert Talbor, Charles II, and Cinchona."

101 Talbor, Πυρετολογία, *a Rational Account of the Cause and Cure of Agues*.

102 Blegny, *La Découverte de l'admirable remède*, and Monginot, *De la guérison des fièvres*. The book history of the various treatises purporting to reveal Talbor's secret is maddeningly complex, although it is nearly universally claimed that Talbor's remedy was published posthumously, the first editions of the two books cited here actually appeared a year *prior* to his death in 1681. This error may, perhaps, have occurred because both books went into multiple editions after 1681 and these later printings are more commonly held by libraries.

103 Sousa-Dias, "Jacob de Castro Sarmento"; Sousa-Dias, *Água de Inglaterra*.

104 As Patrick Wallis has argued, late seventeenth-century advertisements for proprietary drugs and medicines were among the first instances of "true" branding—in the sense that they advertised commercially sold products in mass-market periodicals.

105 In 1936, Augusto d'Esaguy speculated (dubiously) that the remedy was "the most widely prescribed drug of its time" ("Agua de Inglaterra," 404-8). However, beyond the work of José Pedro Sousa-Dias, the drug has attracted scant scholarly

attention. See *Medicina Lusitana, soccorro delphico, a os clamores da naturesa humana* by Francisco da Fonseca Henriques, 1731, for more than twenty mentions of quina quina and "Agoa da Inglaterra."

106 See Alexander von Humboldt (trans. John Black), *A Political Essay on the Kingdom of New Spain* (London, 1811), 354. On Humboldt's knowledge of quina, see Karl S. Zimmerer, "Humboldt's Nodes and Modes of Interdisciplinary Environmental Science in the Andean World," *Geographical Review* 96(3) (July 2006): 348–49.

107 As John E. Lesch notes, the 1810s and 1820s were periods of frenetic activity in the realm of pharmaceutical chemistry. Lesch, "Conceptual Change in an Empirical Science."

108 Bernardino António Gomes's original casebooks from Brazil (1798-1808) still survive and represent an untapped resource in the history of medicine. To my knowledge, they have yet to be studied. The casebooks, which are owned by the University of Coimbra's Faculdade de Ciências e Tecnologia, have recently been digitized here: https://digitalis-dsp.uc.pt/html/10316.2/10545/globalItems.html.

109 Gomes, "An Essay upon Cinchonin," 420-31 (a translation of a report Gomes circulated with the Academia de Ciencias in Lisbon), and Gomes, *Ensaio sobre o cinchonino*. Bernardino Gomes, a naval surgeon who had treated fever patients in 1790s Brazil, performed parallel chemical analyses of both "true" quina (*Cinchona officianalis*) and quina do Brasil (*Portlandia hexandria*), creating extracts of their barks and subjecting them to chemical reactions like "precipitate with potassa" and oxygenation. Pierre Joseph Pelletier and Joseph Bienaimé Caventou are usually credited with the isolation of quinine, but in fact they merely published a more detailed and easily replicable version of the extraction process described by Gomes.

110 See Simões et al., "Scientific Revolution in Eighteenth-Century Portugal"; de Carvalho, *Portugal nas Philosophical Transactions*.

Chapter 5

Epigraph: Packer and Pratt, *Collected Letters of Robert Southey*, July 12, 1799.

1 Parfit, *Reasons and Persons*.

2 Tononi and Koch, "Consciousness: Here, There and Everywhere?"

3 On the role of nitrous oxide in Davy's initial fame, see Golinski, *The Experimental Self*, ch. 1.

4 For specific details of Davy's nitrous oxide experiments, see Davy, *Researches, Chemical and Philosophical, Chiefly Concerning Nitrous Oxide*; Jay, *Emperors of Dreams*, ch. 1; and Golinski, *Experimental Self*, 19–33.

5 For a novel attempt to reconsider the history of this period from the perspective of psychotropic substances, see Smail, *Deep History and the Brain*, ch. 5.

6 Mancall, *Deadly Medicine*.

7 Curto, *Enslaving Spirits*, ch. 1 and 2.

8 Benedict, *Golden Silk Smoke,* 6–7, 45–48.

9 Rudi Mathee, *Pursuit of Pleasure*, 124–27.

10 Schmidt, *Inventing Exoticism*.

11 For a fascinating overview of the global array of products in a specific early modern painting, see Brook, *Vermeer's Hat*.

12 On the larger context for singerie, see Robbins, *Elephant Slaves and Pampered Parrots*.

13 On alcohol's deep presence in early modern European culture, see Bennett, *Ale, Beer, and Brewsters*.

14 Norton, *Sacred Gifts, Profane Pleasures*.

15 See, for instance, Hooke's entry for October 1, 1672: "I took spirit of urine and laudanum with milk for three preceding nights. Slept pretty well" (Hooke, *Diary of Robert Hooke*).

16 Simpson, "How Chloroform Was Discovered," 207.

17 Da Orta disapproved of opium and, seemingly, all other mind-altering substances that he encountered in India. He included cautionary tales like that of the "Portuguese buffon" he knew in Balaghat whose consumption of an electuary made out of sugar, cannabis, and opium resulted in little beyond "sadness and great nausea." Da Orta, *Colloquios dos simples e drogas*, 27r.

18 Herodotus, *The Histories* 4:73, 75.

19 Likewise, it is one of the puzzles of drug history that opium appears not to have been widely used as a surgical anesthetic before the eighteenth century. There are a handful of exceptions, however: see Prioreschi, "Medieval Anesthesia—the *Spongia somnifera*."

20 Hillig and Mahlberg. "A Chemotaxonomic Analysis of Cannabinoid Variation."

21 Guest, "On the Elements of Language," 243.

22 Teresa of Ávila, *Life of Saint Teresa*, ch. 29.

23 Cussen, *Life and Afterlife of Fray Martin de Porres*, 122.

24 Matthee, *Pursuit of Pleasure*, 293–300.

25 Sarianidi, "New Discoveries at Ancient Gonur."

26 Toit, "Man and Cannabis in Africa."

27 Dos Santos, *Ethiopia Oriental* (Lisbon, 1609), 20v.

28 Van Riebeeck, *Journal*, June 2, 1658.

29 Courtwright, *Forces of Habit*, 56.

30 James I, *Counterblaste to Tobacco*, 1–2.

31 Jahangir, *The Jahangirnama*, 217.

32 On quack sellers of opium and opiates in early modern cities, see Emma Spary, "All the World's a Stage: Opium and the Domestication of Otherness in France around 1700," working paper, presented at the Intoxicants and Empire conference, April 22, 2017.

33 De Vries, *The Industrious Revolution*.

34 On corpuscularian thought and its relation to iatrochemistry, see Klein, "Corporeal Elements and Principles."

35 Opium, he argued, contained "a certain oily and sulphurous part" that produced "deadly passions and pains, by reason whereof men are constrained to use the imperfect Laudanum of Empirics, against the deadly hunger of such medicines." Joseph Duchesne *The Practice of Chymicall and Hermeticall Physicke*, trans. Thomas

Tymme (London: T. Creede, 1605), ch. 4, a partial translation of Duchesne, *Ad veritatem hermeticae medicinae ex Hippocratis veterumque decretis ac therapeusi* (Paris: Abraham Sagrain, 1604).

36 Donzelli, *Teatro Farmaceutico*, 341.

37 Ibid., 382.

38 Ragland, "Chymistry and Taste in the Seventeenth Century."

39 Roma, *Luz da Medicina, pratica racional.*

40 Vigier, *Thesouro apollineo*, 300–302.

41 Ibid., 300.

42 Jones, *Mysteries of Opium*, 22.

43 Ibid., 29–32. A sudden "leaving off the Use of Opium, after a long and lavish Use" leads to "intolerable Distress, Anxieties, and Depressions of Spirits" and a compulsive desire to return to taking it unless Wine is "use[d] . . . very plentifully, and often, as a substitute for Opium."

44 Norton, *Sacred Gifts.*

45 Letter from Padre Juan Lorenzo Lucero, S.J., to the Duque de la Palata, Viceroy of Peru, received November 20, 1681, and transcribed and printed in the "Noticias Auténticas del Famoso Río Marañon," *Boletín de la Real Sociedad Geográfica*, vol. 33 (Madrid, 1892), 26–27.

46 Padre Lucero to the Duque de la Palata, 27.

47 Pablo Maroni, "Diario de la entrada que hizo el P. Pablo Maroni de Ia C. d. J. por el rio coriño ó Pastaza . . . el año 1737," in *Boletín de la Real Sociedad Geografica*, vols. 26–27 (1889), 54. Ayahuasca is actually a combination of at least two organisms: the *Banisteriopsis caapi* vine and a secondary plant that contains the hallucinogenic alkaloid dimethyltryptamine (DMT). The caapi vine functions as a monoamine oxidase inhibitor (MAOI), making the DMT in many other Amazonian plants orally active and inducing a powerfully altered state of consciousness. Recently, ayahuasca has become popular as an alternative remedy in the West, often billed as a more "natural" or "holistic" alternative to psychedelics like LSD or MDMA.

48 Pablo Maroni, "Diario de la entrada que hizo el P. Pablo Maroni de Ia C. d. J. por el rio coriño ó Pastaza . . . el año 1737," in *Boletín de la Real Sociedad Geografica*, vols. 26–27 (1889), p. 55, and Christoph Gottlied von Murr, "Provinciae Maynensis in America Meridionali, ad annum usque 1768," *Journal zur Kunstgeschichte und zur allgemeinen Litteratur.*

49 Christoph Gottlied von Murr, "Provinciae Maynensis in America Meridionali, ad annum usque 1768," *Journal zur Kunstgeschichte und zur allgemeinen Litteratur*, 55.

50 Losa, *Vida del Siervo de Dios Gregorio Lopez*, 367. This is the fourth edition of a book that originally appeared posthumously in a printed edition in 1673, and appears to have been adapted from a work that now exists in two manuscript variants. The first is held by the Biblioteca Nacional in Madrid, while the second, held by the Vatican, appears to be a copy of the former made in the 1590s. Rafael Chabrán and Simon Varey speculate that elements of Lopez's medical writings derive

from the work of Francisco Hernández. See Varey and Chabrán, eds., *The Mexican Treasury*, 7.

51   Varey and Chabrán, *Mexican Treasury*, 125.

52   Hernández, Caput XXV, "De Peyotl Zacatensi, seu radice molli"; Hernández, in *De Historia Plantarum Novae Hispaniae* 3:71.

53   Motolinia, *Historia de los Indios de Nueva España*, printed in Icazbalceta, *Collection de documentes*, 23. The phrase "meat of the gods" appears to be based on a mistranslation.

54   For an overview of Inquisition trials involving the use of peyote and *ololiuhqui*, see Tavárez, *Invisible War*, 93-96.

55   Nesvig, "Sandcastles of the Mind." The mycologist Gastón Gúzman conjectured that the greenish tint applied to the mushrooms at the bottom of Figure 29 may have been intended to depict the telltale "blue bruising" associated with psychedelic mushroom species, particularly *P. cyanescens*. See Gúzman, "Nuevas observaciones taxonómicas."

56   Archivo General de la Nacíon (AGN), Mexico City, Inquisición, vol. 289, exp. 12, edict contra "el uso de la Yerba o Raiz llamada Peyote," signed by Pedro Nabarre de Ysla, June 9, 1620. For a transcription see Goggin, "Peyote and the Mexican Inquisition," and for further discussion see Sarabia, "Culture of Peyote."

57   For examples of the continued use of peyote by female healers after the 1620 edict see Sarabia, "Culture of Peyote" and Quezada Ramírez, "Prácticas terapéuticas."

58   AGN, Inquisiçion, tomo 510, exp. 133, as cited in Richard E. Greenleaf, "The Mexican Inquisition and the Indians: sources for the Ethnohistorian," *The Americas* 34, no. 3 (1978): 315-44.

59   Sahagún, *Historia general*, lib. X, cap. XXIX, 2. *Nanacatl* or *teonanacatl* refers to the Aztec hallucinogenic mushrooms of genus *Psilocybin*. Gastón Guzmán, "Hallucinogenic mushrooms in Mexico: An overview," *Economic Botany* 62, no. 3 (2008): 404-12.

60   Sahagún, *Historia general de las Cosas de Nueva España*, lib. XI, cap. VII.

61   Tavárez, *Invisible War*, 93-96.

62   AGN, Inquisición, tomo 340, exp. 28. Babtista also used the plant as a medicine ("for her health," according to the testimony of her niece) and as a practical tool ("to see who had been stealing things"). See the discussion of her case in Sarabia, "Culture of Peyote," 32-34. Relatedly, Martin Nesvig explores how, among the Huichol peoples of western Mexico, peyote was thought of as an entity to be "hunted" like deer. See Nesvig, "Peyote, Ever Virgin," 181.

63   Baldwin, "The Snakestone Experiments."

64   Jones, *Mysteries of Opium*, 20.

65   Ibid., 20 and 84.

66   Mithoefer et al., "Novel Psychopharmacological Therapies for Psychiatric Disorders."

67   Semedo, "Memorial de Varios Simples," 29; Boyle, *Medicina hydrostatica*, 329.

68   A representative recipe from Donzelli called for a "fermentation of opium" mixed with aloe, cinnamon, and brandy. Donzelli, *Teatro Farmaceutico*, 384.

69 Abreu, *Luz de Cirurgioens*, 16–17.

70 Mead, *Mechanical Account of Poisons*, 38.

71 Ibid., 32.

72 Ibid., 39.

73 De Ribera, *Quinta essentia medica theorico-practica*, 449.

74 Nelson, "Making Men."

75 João Cardoso de Miranda, *Relação cirurgica, e medica* (Lisbon: Officina de Manoel Soares, 1741). On barbeiros in colonial Bahia, see Mariza de Carvalho Soares, "African Barbeiros in Brazilian Slave Ports," in Jorge Cañizares-Esguerra, Matt D. Childs, and James Sidbury, eds., *The Black Urban Atlantic in the Age of the Slave Trade* (Philadelphia: University of Pennsylvania Press, 2013); and Júnia Ferreira Furtado, "Barbeiros, cirurgiões e médicos na Minas colonial," in *Revista do Arquivo Público Mineiro* (2005), 89–105, which devotes a brief discussion to Cardoso de Miranda.

76 "I can with very little trouble earn upward of fifty thousand cruzados each year with this cure, not counting what I earn from buying slaves at a price of six to twelve thousand réis; which after a few months by the grace of God alone are freed of their diseases and cured. These I sell for a just price, as I did the three which I bought from João Francisco de Carvalho, who lives on this beach in [Bahia]. I cured in his house a group [of slaves], having already given him the remedy with which to destroy this illness . . . and he offered to sell me the said three slaves for a price of six thousand réis each; and curing them all, I sold them for one hundred and fifty thousand réis." Cardoso de Miranda, *Relação cirurgica, e medica*, 9–10.

77 Cardoso de Miranda, *Relação cirurgica, e medica*, 13.

78 Furtado, "Tropical Empiricism."

79 On local knowledge in the Atlantic world, see Kathleen S. Murphy, "Translating the Vernacular: Indigenous and African Knowledge in the Eighteenth-Century British Atlantic," *Atlantic Studies* 8, no. 1 (2011): 29–48; and Neil Safier, "Global Knowledge on the Move," 134–35.

80 Cook, "Markets and Cultures."

81 Nicolas Venette, *La génération de l'homme, ou, Tableau de l'amour conjugal* (1687; Paris, 1778), 290.

82 Hester Thrale, *Anecdotes of the Late Samuel Johnson* (London, 1786).

83 John Hawkins, ed. *The Works of Samuel Johnson* (London, 1787), 206.

84 Breen, "No Man Is an Island."

85 Psalmanazar, *Memoirs*, 48.

86 Ibid., 48–49.

87 Ibid., 49.

88 Ibid., 50.

89 Ibid., 52.

90 Venette, *Generation de l'Homme*, 282.

91 On Sydenham's investigations of laudanum see Kramer, "Opium Rampant."

92 On self-experimentation, see Golinski, *The Experimental Self*, ch. 1.

93 Golinski, *The Experimental Self*, 40.

94 William James, "Subjective Effects of Nitrous Oxide," *Mind*, vol. 7 (1882). James mentioned that he was inspired to take the drug after reading a pamphlet called "The anesthetic revelation" in 1874, and he published a review of the work in the *Atlantic* in the same year (William James, "The Anaesthetic Revelation and the Gist of Philosophy," *Atlantic* (November 1874). Thus it seems likely that James's experiments with nitrous oxide began when he was relatively young, thirty-two years old.

Chapter 6

1 This is an estimate based on the estimated LD50 for opium detailed in Everett and Gabra, "Pharmacology of Medieval Sedatives."

2 On the early history of opium in China see Yangwen, *Social Life of Opium*, 11–12, and on the lead-up to the First Opium War during the reigns of the Jiaqing and Daoguang emperors see Yangwen, *Social Life of Opium*, 68–97 and Lovell, *Opium War*, ch. 2.

3 A translation of the edict appeared under the heading "Public Edict, addressed by the Hoppo, or Receiver-General, of the Customs, at Canton, for the Information of the Merchants appointed to trade with foreign Nations" in *The Annual Register . . . for the Year 1801*, 374–75.

4 Fu, *Documentary Chronicle of Sino-Western Relations*, 380.

5 For a superb recent journalistic account of OxyContin as a social and cultural phenomenon in the United States, see Quinones, *Dreamland*.

6 For an account of the history of addiction in modern times, see Courtwright, *Age of Addiction*.

7 Hart and Krauss, "Human Drug Addiction Is More Than Faulty Decision-Making."

8 On the twentieth-century history of cannabis's reception in North America, see Campos, *Home Grown*.

9 Hagen et al., "Ecology and Neurobiology of Toxin Avoidance."

10 Salavert, "Agricultural Dispersals in Mediterranean and Temperate Europe."

11 Chevalier and Bosquet, "Integrating Archaeological Data."

12 Salavert, "Le pavot (*Papaver somniferum*) à la fin du 6e millénaire."

13 Zapata et al., "Early Neolithic Agriculture in the Iberian Peninsula."

14 Juan-Tresserras and Villalba, "Consumo de la adormidera."

15 Unfortunately, an enormous amount of misinformation has spread surrounding the earliest appearances of opium in written sources. Hundreds of books have claimed that Sumerian cuneiform texts referred to opium as the "joy plant" [*hul gil*], despite the fact that this was proven to be false in the 1970s. See Breen, "Opium or Cucumber?" (https://resobscura.blogspot.com/2018/08/opium-or-cucumber-debunking-myth-about.html); and Krikorian, "Were the Opium Poppy and Opium Known in the Ancient Near East?"

16 This evidence comes from a circa 1600–1450 BCE jug containing opium residue

that originated in Cyprus. Koschel, "Opium Alkaloids in a Cypriote Base Ring I Vessel." However, this evidence has recently been contested; see Bunimovitz and Lederman, "Opium or Oil?"

17 Al-Ghazali, for instance, used the mysterious "cooling power" of opium to make an argument for God's supernatural powers. Al-Ghazali, *Deliverance from Error*, originally written around 1110 CE, trans. Richard J. McCarthy (American University of Beirut, 1980), sec. 142.

18 These two figures, also known as Mesue and Avicenna, became foundational authorities for early modern apothecaries. See de Vos, "Prince of Medicine."

19 Prioreschi, "Medieval Anesthesia—The *Spongia somnifera*." This text, as well as other antidotaries making use of opium, such as those from the School of Salerno, was strongly influenced by the works of the Persian physicians Muhammad ibn Zakariyyā al-Rāzī and Ali ibn al-ʿAbbas al-Majusi.

20 This assumption that opium is from "the East" has proven to be remarkably persistent. It strongly shaped Victorian accounts of the drug. As an example, see an anonymous account of opium smokers in 1868 London which describes the drug as "invested with a weird and fantastic interest (for which its Oriental origin is doubtless in some degree accountable)," cited as an epigram in Milligan, *Pleasures and Pains*. As Milligan argues, these types of accounts contributed to an Orientalist discourse around not only opiates, but a wide array of drugs in the twentieth century (*Pleasures and Pains*, 8–10).

21 Breen, "Opium or Cucumber?" Through early twentieth-century scholars, a Victorian-era account of opium preparation in India somehow became interpolated with a supposedly "Sumerian" account of opium. This error was later shown in Krikorian, "Were the Opium Poppy and Opium Known in the Ancient Near East?" but by that time (1975) the confusion had spread widely.

22 In seeking to avoid "presentism," historians of medicine have arguably thrown the baby out with the bathwater and abandoned an important dimension of historical analysis: subjective effects. Writing a history of drugs that ignores the degree to which some substances are subjectively felt to be more pleasant or biologically active than others amounts to wearing a kind of historiographic blinders.

23 By 1785, the East India Company was purchasing "1,830 chests of Bahar opium" per year, along with another 1,000 chests of Bengal opium. "Proceedings of the Governor General and Council of Bengal, relative to the Contract into which Messrs. Young and Heatley, for the provision of Opium," in Thomas Morton, ed. *Appendix to the India Courier Extraordinary: Proceedings of Parliament Relating to W. Hastings*, vol. 6 (London, 1787), 128.

24 Lahiri et al., "Genetic Variability and Diversity in Indian Germplasm of Opium Poppy."

25 Donzelli, *Teatro Farmaceutico*, 341.

26 Linschoten, *Voyage*, 113.

27 Ibid., 113–4.

28 Souza, *The Boxer Codex*, 434.

29 Ibid., 434.

30   Griffin, "Venetian Treacle and the Foundation of Medicines Regulation." To this day, opium is called *teriac* in Farsi.

31   Cardoso de Miranda, *Relação cirurgica, e medica*, 111–12. He described these "Moderns" as the Paracelsans van Helmont and Ettmuler and "the Cartesians [Francisco] Sylvius, [Thomas] Willis, Martin Martines, and others."

32   Monroe and Mallios, "Seventeenth-century colonial cottage industry."

33   Van Der Merwe, "Cannabis Smoking in 13th-14th Century Ethiopia," 77–80.

34   Ibid., 78.

35   Van der Merwe and Nikolaas, "Antiquity of the Smoking Habit in Africa," 147–50.

36   Rudi Mathee, *Persuit of Pleasure*, 126–32.

37   See Benedict, *Golden Silk Smoke*, chs. 1 and 2. This is striking because, as with cannabis, ingesting opium orally is a much slower and less effective route of administration than smoking it.

38   Benedict, *Golden Silk Smoke*, 6 and 27.

39   Wellcome Library MS 8789, François Lamure, *Traité de Matiere Medical*, May 1746, fol. 194.

40   Ibid., fol. 193.

41   Locke, *Essay Concerning Human Understanding*, 318.

42   Wellcome Library MS 8789, fol. 194.

43   Ribera, *Quinta essentia medica theorico-practica*, 449.

44   Semedo, *Atalaya da vida contra as hostilidades da morte*.

45   Ibid., 683.

46   "Ce fluide est l'organe des forces mouvantes & du sentiment; plusieurs expériences électriques portent à penser qu'il est analogue au fluide même électrique (ainsi que d'autres l'ont pensé) ou à la matiere de la lumiere, comme le croit Nevton." (De Sauvages, *Dissertation sur les medicamens*, 36–37). This type of abstract speculation about molecules, blockages, and "nervous fluids" was not new, although the electrical and Newtonian gloss that de Sauvages applied to it was novel.

47   De Sauvages, *Dissertation sur les medicamens*, 38.

48   Ibid., 41.

49   Sertürner, "Darstellung Der Reinen Mohnsaure (Opiumsaure)."

50   *The London Medical Repository and Review* (November 1817), 437.

51   At least two pharmacy historians have suggested that, given his frequent use of the drug, Sertürner himself may have been a morphine addict, although there seems to be no proof for the assertion. Schmitz, "Friedrich Wilhelm Sertürner and the Discovery of Morphine." Klockgether-Radke, "F. W. Sertürner and the discovery of morphine: 200 years of pain therapy with opioids." However, historical diagnoses are best avoided, in my view.

52   John Freind, "An Account of Books," in Sloane, ed., *Philosophical Transactions* (1710), 322.

53   For a recent overview of the spread of morphine use, see Black, "Doctors on Drugs."

54   On early modern state formation and government propaganda, see Burke, *Fabrication of Louis XIV*.

55 Not long before he died, Oliver Sacks wrote a beautiful piece on the complexities of drug addiction; see Sacks, "Altered States."

56 Medical discussions of addiction are relatively common in the eighteenth century, but the formal identification of addiction as a "disease" did not take place until the mid-nineteenth century. See Foxcroft, *The Making of Addiction*, 3–4 and ch. 6. Foxcroft argues that eighteenth- and early nineteenth-century physicians in Britain "did not seriously vilify the 'luxurious' use of opium" until the middle decades of the century. While it is true that opium use, especially by the upper classes, was tolerated by many pre-Victorian physicians, I believe a trend toward moralistic disapproval of opium usage in European medical writings is clear from at least the mid-eighteenth century onward.

57 Sonnedecker, *Emergence of the Concept of Opiate Addiction*.

58 De Quincey, "Confessions of an English Opium Eater," 295.

59 On the connections between metaphors of enslavement and the reality of the slave trade in zones of European colonization, see Derks, *History of the Opium Problem*.

60 Topsell, *Four-Footed Beasts*, 83.

61 On the late seventeenth-century European fascination with exotica and the Indies, see Schmidt, *Inventing Exoticism*.

62 Sala, an Italian Calvinist who resided in Germany for much of his professional life, was one of the leading popularizers of opium in seventeenth-century medical writings: the original version of his book on the topic, *Opiologia ou Traicté concernant le naturel, propriétés, vraye préparation et seûr usage de l'opium* (The Hague: de H. Jacobs, 1614), went into multiple printings in a half dozen languages.

63 Venette, *La generation de l'homme*, 229.

64 Ibid., 232.

65 Ibid., 233.

66 Ibid., 235.

67 Blount, *Natural History*, 118–19.

68 All quotes in this paragraph are from de Quincey, "Confessions of an English Opium Eater.," 3.

69 See, for instance, the widespread availability of morphine (and methamphetamine) in 1920s and 1930s Germany, or the widespread availability of legal, over-the-counter opiates in the late nineteenth-century United States (Ohler, *Blitzed*).

70 *The British Friend*, February 1, 1859, 42.

71 Norton, *Sacred Gifts*.

72 Chamberlayne, *Natural History of Coffee, Thee, Chocolate, Tobacco*, 22.

73 Ibid., 22–23.

74 Sahlins, "Royal Menageries of Louis XIV," 239. See also Sahlins's *1688: The Year of the Animal in France*.

75 Drayton, *Nature's Government*.

76 Anderson, *Creatures of Empire*; and Breen, "'The Elks Are Our Horses.'"

77 Chamberlayne, *Natural History of Coffee, Thee, Chocolate, Tobacco*, 22.

78 Because addiction was not used in relation to drugs until the nineteenth century,

early modern writers typically used the metaphor of enslavement to describe figures who today would be described as suffering from physical dependency. For instance, the reformed Formosan George Psalmanazar described himself as a "slave to youthful passions" during the time of his youthful imposture in London around 1704–5, clarifying that he was, specifically "a perfect slave" to opium (Psalmanazar, *Memoirs*, 49).

79 Cook, *Matters of Exchange*, 408.

80 Thomas Szasz, *Ceremonial Chemistry: The Ritual Persecution of Drugs, Addicts, and Pushers* (New York: Anchor Press, 1974).

81 For an excellent survey of the history of coca and cocaine, which this book has largely ignored because of the drug's late nineteenth-century rise to prominence, see Gootenberg, *Andean Cocaine*.

82 Quinones, *Dreamland*.

83 Quotes are from a 1998 promotional video for OxyContin (extended-release oxycodone) illegally distributed without FDA approval to approximately 15,000 physicians by Purdue Pharma. Purdue would later pay a penalty of almost $500 million, although this was dwarfed by the corporation's annual revenues of approximately $3 billion.

84 Van Zee, "Promotion and Marketing of OxyContin."

Conclusion

1 Other versions include two English-language prints that add a man and a woman holding a squirrel on a leash to the scene, an earlier German edition (c. 1600) also by Matthaus Greuter, and two early versions by Theodor de Bry, as well as another German-language version, which identifies the healer as Doctor Wurmbrandt (worm-burner). See Griffiths, *The Print in Stuart Britain*, cat. 91. The engraving also served as the model for a painted sign that survives in the Musée Rolin in Autun, France, which originally announced the wares of a seventeenth-century apothecary shop at 20 Grand Rue Chauchien, Autun (Vons, "Médecin guarissant phantassie").

2 Translation from Gilman, *Seeing the Insane*, 42.

3 Venette, *Tableau*, 281.

4 The best account of this period of change can be found in Courtwright, *Forces of Habit*, 1–9 and ch. 9.

5 Breen, "Drugs and Early Modernity."

6 Cooper and Stoler, "Tensions of Empire."

7 Milov, "Smoking as Statecraft."

8 New York Times Editorial Board, "China and the Toll of Smoking," *New York Times*, April 17, 2014, www.nytimes.com/2014/04/18/opinion/china-and-the-toll-of-smoking.html.

9 Ohler, *Blitzed*.

10 Cowan, *Social Life of Coffee*, 116.

11 As an example, see Jacques Derrida,"The Rhetoric of Drugs" (1990), reprinted in

Anna Alexander and Mark Roberts, eds., *High Culture: Reflections on Addiction and Modernity* (Albany: SUNY Press, 2002), ch. 1.

12 Müller and Schumann, "Drugs as Instruments."

13 White et al., "Lethal Malaria"; Kosanovic et al., "Rhodiola." On these difficulties, see Nappi, "Bolatu's Pharmacy."

14 Channing May, "Transnational Crime and the Developing World" (Washington, DC: Global Financial Integrity, March 2017), www.gfintegrity.org/report/transnational-crime-and-the-developing-world/.

15 International Federation of Pharmaceutical Manufacturers and Associations, "The Pharmaceutical Industry and Global Health: Facts and Figures 2017" (2017), www.ifpma.org/wp-content/uploads/2017/02/IFPMA-Facts-And-Figures-2017.pdf; CIA World Factbook, "Economy: World," 2017, www.cia.gov/library/publications/the-world-factbook/geos/xx.html.

16 Coppola et al., "3, 4-methylenedioxypyrovalerone (MDPV)."

17 Verweij, "Clandestine Manufacture of 3, 4-methylenedioxymethylamphetamine (MDMA)"; Schäffer et al., "Forensic Profiling of Sassafras Oils."

18 A 2013 report from the German newspaper *Der Spiegel* offered a generally positive assessment of the policy's social impact: Wiebke Hollersen, "'This Is Working': Portugal, 12 Years After Decriminalizing Drugs," *Spiegel Online*, March 27, 2013, www.spiegel.de/international/europe/evaluating-drug-decriminalization-in-portugal-12-years-later-a-891060.html.

Glossary

aldeia: a village

arroba: early modern Portuguese unit of measure equivalent to approximately 32 pounds

barbeiro: a barber or "barber surgeon"

bezoar: a mineral accretion found in the stomachs of some ungulates, particularly goats and camelids, which was prized for its medicinal properties in the early modern period

bezoartico: an "artificial" (i.e. human made) substitute for bezoar, popularized by the Portuguese apothecary João Curvo Semedo

*bhang (*or *bangue* or *bhanga):* a psychoactive preparation of cannabis popular in South Asia, typically involving a mixture of ground cannabis with milk or ghee

botica: the shop and workspace of an apothecary

boticário: an apothecary, one who converts "materia medica" into "simples"

cachaça: a high-proof alcoholic spirit distilled from the by-product of sugar refining

caixa: a box in which archival documents are stored, abbreviated here as "cx."

Capitão-mor: a military officer in the Portuguese Empire, typically commander of a fortress, municipality, captaincy, or city

Conselho Ultramarino: an administrative body of the Portuguese Empire; translated here as "Overseas Council"

cruzado: gold or silver coin typically worth 400 réis

degredado: a convicted criminal sentenced to labor in the Portuguese colonies

demoninhado: person possessed by a demon or spirit

feitiço: a magical charm, amulet, or spell created by a *feiticeiro*

Físico-mor: the chief physician of an administrative unit in the Portuguese Empire *gerebita:* a sugarcane-based liquor, the less-expensive cousin of *cachaça*

mestiço: of mixed race, analogous to the Spanish *mestizo*

miradouro: a look-out point or scenic overlook

pombeiro: a term used to describe mixed-race merchants and backlands traders in early modern Angola

presídio: a fortress, castle, or fortified position

real: a unit of currency used in the early modern Portuguese empire (plural: *réis*)

sertão: backlands or wilderness, often used to describe parts of Amazonia and Africa in seventeenth-century Portuguese

sertanejo: term originating in colonial Brazil used to describe the rural inhabitants of the *sertão*, comparable to the English term "frontiersman"

English

alkaloid: a class of naturally-occurring compounds; notable alkaloids include caffeine, cocaine, nicotine, theobromine, morphine, and psilocybin

compound: a prepared medicinal drug composed of multiple plant, animal, or mineral sources

electuary: a medicine mixed with sugar or other sweeteners to make it more palatable

empiric: early modern term for itinerant healers who promised miraculous cures

factor: a type of merchant in the early modern period, typically involved with the Indies trade

factory: a trading post, often associated with the various European East and West India companies

febrifuge: a fever-fighting drug

LD50: in toxicology, LD50 (or LD_{50}) is used as a shorthand to describe the "median lethal dose" required to kill half the members of a specific population.

materia medica: Latin term for the raw materials that apothecaries crafted into medicines; can also refer to a text about same

quack: a charlatan healer, from the Dutch term *quacksalver* ("hawker of salves")

simple: an unprocessed herbal, mineral, or animal medicine, often mixed by apothecaries into compound medicines

specific: in early modern European usage, a medicinal drug that treats a particular disease or ailment regardless of the humoral makeup of a patient

Bibliography

Archival Sources

Academia das Ciências de Lisboa
Archivum Romanum Societatis Iesu (ARSI), Rome
Arquivo Histórico Ultramarino (AHU), Lisbon
 Conselho Ultramarino: Angola, Bahia, Pará, and Maranhão
Arquivo Nacional da Torre do Tombo (ANTT), Lisbon
 Inquisitions of Lisbon and Coimbra
 Livro dos Feitos Findos (LFF)
 Manuscritos do Brasil (MSBR)
 Manuscritos da Livraria (MSLIV)
 Registo Geral das Mercês (RGM)
Biblioteca da Ajuda, Lisbon
Biblioteca Nacional de Portugal (BNP), Lisbon, Manuscritos Reservados
British Library (BL), London
 Sloane Manuscripts
 Additional Manuscripts
New York Academy of Medicine
Royal Society Archives (RSA), London
University of Pennsylvania Rare Book and Manuscript Library
Wellcome Library, London

Published Works

Abreu, José Rodrigues de. *Historiología Médica, fundada, e estabelecida nos princípios de George Ernesto Stahl.* Lisbon: Officina da Musica, 1733.
———. *Luz de Cirurgioens Embarcadissos.* Lisbon, 1711.
Acosta, Christoval de. *Tractado de las drogas y medicinas de las Indias orientales.* Burgos: Martin de Victoria, 1578.
Acosta, José de. *Historia natural y moral de las Indias.* Madrid: Ediciones de Cultura Hispánica y Agencia Española de Cooperación Internacional, 1998 [1590].
Acuña, Cristóbal de. *Nuevo descubrimiento del gran rio de las Amazonas.* Madrid: En la imprenta del Reyno, 1641.

Akyeampong, Emannuel Kwaku. *Drink, Power, and Cultural Change: A Social History of Alcohol in Ghana, c. 1800 to Recent Times.* Portsmouth: Heinemann, 1996.

Alden, Dauril. *The Making of an Enterprise: The Society of Jesus in Portugal, Its Empire, and Beyond, 1540–1750.* Redwood City, CA: Stanford University Press, 1996.

Alston, Charles. *Lectures on the Materia Medica: Containing the Natural History of Drugs, Their Virtues and Doses: Also Directions for the Study of the Materia Medica; and an Appendix on the Method of Prescribing.* London: Edward and Charles Dilly, in the Poultry, 1770.

Amaro, Ana Maria. "A famosa pedra cordial de Goa ou de Gaspar Antonio." *Revista da Cultura* 19, no. 22 (1988-89): 87–108.

Andrade, António Manuel Lopes. "Garcia de Orta and Amato Lusitano's Views on Materia Medica: A Comparative Perspective." In *Medicine, Trade and Empire: Garcia de Orta's Colloquies on the Simples and Drugs of India (1563) in Context,* edited by Palmira Fontes da Costa. London: Routledge, 2016.

Andrade Neto, Valter, et al. "Antimalarial Activity of Cinchona-like Plants Used to Treat Fever and Malaria in Brazil." *Journal of Ethnopharmacology* 87, nos. 2–3 (September, 2003): 253–56.

The Annual Register, or a View of the History, politics, and Literature for the Year 1801. London: Printed by T. Burton, 1802.

Antonil, André João. *Cultura e opulência do Brasil: Por suas drogas, e minas.* Lisbon: Deslandesiana, 1711.

Arrais, Duarte Madeira. *Arbor vitae, or a Physical Account of the Tree of Life in the Garden of Eden.* London: Thomas Flesher, 1683.

——. *Novae Philosophiae et Medicinae de Qualitatibus occultis.* Lisbon, 1650.

Arrow, Kenneth J. "Uncertainty and the Welfare Economics of Medical Care." *American Economic Review* 53, no. 5 (1963): 941–73.

Asúa, Miguel de. *Science in the Vanished Arcadia: Knowledge of Nature in the Jesuit Missions of Paraguay and Río de la Plata.* Leiden: Brill, 2014.

Atkins, John. *A Voyage to Guinea, Brasil and the West-Indies.* London: Caesar Ward, 1735.

Atkinson, Lesley-Gail, ed. *The Earliest Inhabitants: The Dynamics of the Jamaican Taíno.* Kingston, Jamaica: University of the West Indies Press, 2006.

Aulesa, Carles Vela. "Defining 'Apothecary' in the Medieval Crown of Aragon." In *Medieval Urban Identity: Health, Economy and Regulation,* edited by Flocel Sabaté, 127–42. Newcastle: Cambridge Scholars Publishing, 2015.

Ávila, Saint Teresa of. *The Life of Saint Teresa of Ávila by Herself.* Translated by J. M. Cohen. New York: Penguin, 2004.

Azevedo, Alonso de. *Repertorio de todas las pragmaticas y capitulos de Cortes, hechas por su magestad, desde el ano 1552 hasta 1564.* Salamanca: Andrea de Portonarius, 1566.

Bacon, Francis. *Sylva Sylvarum (New Atlantis) . . . Whereunto Is Newly Added the History Naturall and Experimentall of Life and Death.* London: T. Lee, 1677.

——. *Opera Omnia, Philosophica, Moralia, Historico-Politica.* Frankfurt: Joannis Baptistae Schonwetteri, 1665.

Baldwin, Martha. "The Snakestone Experiments: An Early Modern Medical Debate." *Isis* 86, no. 3 (1995): 394–418.

Barham, Henry. *Hortus Americanus: Containing an Account of the Trees, Shrubs, and Other Vegetable Productions of South-America and the West India Islands*. Kingston, Jamaica: Alexander Aikman, 1794.

Barrera-Osorio, Antonio. *Experiencing Nature: The Spanish American Empire and the Early Scientific Revolution*. Austin: University of Texas Press, 2010.

Barnett, Richard. *The Book of Gin: A Spirited World History from Alchemists' Stills and Colonial Outposts to Gin Palaces*. New York: Grove Press, 2012.

Bartlett, Robert. "Medieval and Modern Concepts of Race and Ethnicity." *Journal of Medieval and Early Modern Studies* 31, no. 1 (January 1, 2001): 39–56.

Bauer, Ralph, and José Antonio Mazzotti. *Creole Subjects in the Colonial Americas: Empires, Texts, Identities*. Chapel Hill: Omohundro Institute of Early American History and Culture and the University of North Carolina Press, 2012.

Bayly, C. A. *The Birth of the Modern World, 1780–1914*. London: Wiley, 2004.

Beckert, Sven, and Seth Rockman, eds. *Slavery's Capitalism: A New History of American Economic Development*. Philadelphia: University of Pennsylvania Press, 2016.

Beer, Edmund De. *The Correspondence of John Locke*. Oxford: Oxford University Press, 1976.

Belgers, M., M. Leenaars, J. R. Homberg, M. Ritskes-Hoitinga, A. F. A. Schellekens, and C. R. Hooijmans. "Ibogaine and Addiction in the Animal Model, a Systematic Review and Meta-Analysis." *Translational Psychiatry* 6, no. 5 (2016). https://doi.org/10.1038/tp.2016.71.

Benedict, Carol. *Golden Silk Smoke: A History of Tobacco in China, 1550–2010*. Berkeley: University of California Press, 2011.

Bennett, Judith M. *Ale, Beer, and Brewsters in England: Women's Work in a Changing World, 1300–1600*. Oxford: Oxford University Press, 1996.

Berlu, John Jacob. *The Treasury of Drugs Unlock'd, Or, A Full and True Description of All Sorts of Drugs, and Chymical Preparations, Sold by Drugists*. London: John Harris and Thomas Hawkins, 1690.

Berry, Chelsea. "Poisoned Relations: Medicine, Sorcery, and Poison Trials in the Greater Caribbean, 1680–1850." PhD diss., Georgetown University, 2019.

Bersselaar, D. Van den. "Who Belongs to the 'Star People'? Negotiating Beer and Gin Advertisements in West Africa, 1949–75." *Journal of African History* 52, no. 3 (2011): 385–408.

Bigelow, Allison Margaret. "Mining Empire, Planting Empire: The Colonial Scientific Literatures of the Americas." PhD diss., University of North Carolina at Chapel Hill, 2012.

Birch, Thomas. *The History of the Royal Society*. London, 1756.

Black, Sara E. "Doctors on Drugs: Medical Professionals and the Proliferation of Morphine Addiction in Nineteenth-Century France." *Social History of Medicine* 30, no. 1 (February 1, 2017): 114–36. https://doi.org/10.1093/shm/hkw065.

Blegny, Nicolas de. *La Découverte de l'admirable Remède Anglois pour la Guérison des Fièvres*. Paris: C. Blageart and L. d'Hourry, 1680.

————. *Zodiacus medico-gallicus sive Miscellaneorum medico physicorum gallicorum titulo recens in re medica exploratorum.* Geneva: Leonardi Chouët, 1679.

Bleichmar, Daniela. *Visible Empire: Botanical Expeditions and Visual Culture in the Hispanic Enlightenment.* Chicago: University of Chicago Press, 2012.

Bosman, Willem. *A New and Accurate Description of the Coast of Guinea, Divided into the Gold, the Slave, and the Ivory Coasts.* London: Sir Alfred Jones, 1705.

Boumediene, Samir. *La colonisation du savoir: Une histoire des plantes médicinales du "Nouveau Monde" (1492-1750).* Paris: Les éditions des mondes à faire, 2016.

Bourguignon, Erika. *Possession.* London: Chandler and Sharp, 1976.

Bowrey, Thomas. *Geographical Account of Countries 'round the Bay of Bengal, 1669-1679.* Edited by Richard Carnac Temple. London: Hakluyt Society, 1905.

Boxer, C. R. *The Golden Age of Brazil, 1695-1750: Growing Pains of a Colonial Society.* Berkeley: University of California Press, 1962.

Boxer, Charles Ralph. *The Dutch in Brazil, 1624-1654.* Oxford: Clarendon Press, 1957.

Boyle, Robert. *The Philosophical Works of the Honourable Robert Boyle Esq.,* vol. 2. London, 1725.

————. *Medicina Hydrostatica, or Hydrostatics Applied to the Materia Medica.* London: 1690.

Breen, Benjamin. "The Flip Side of the Pharmacopeia: Poisons in the Atlantic World." In *Drugs on the Page: Pharmacopoeias and Healing Knowledge in the Early Modern Atlantic World,* edited by Matthew Crawford and Joseph Gabriel. Pittsburgh: University of Pittsburgh Press, 2019.

————. "Semedo's Sixteen Secrets: Tracing Pharmaceutical Networks in the Portuguese Tropics. " In *Empires of Knowledge: Scientific Networks in the Early Modern World,* edited by Paula Findlen. London: Routledge, 2018.

————. "Opium or Cucumber? Debunking a Myth About Sumerian Drugs." *Res Obscura.* August 23, 2018.

————. "Drugs and Early Modernity." *History Compass* 15, no. 4 (2017).

————. "The Pharmaca of Jozeph Coelho: A Family of Converso Apothecaries in Seventeenth-Century Coimbra." *The Recipes Project,* November 20, 2014. https://recipes.hypotheses.org/4710.

————. "No Man Is an Island: Early Modern Globalization, Knowledge Networks, and George Psalmanazar's Formosa." *Journal of Early Modern History* 17, no. 17 (2013): 391–417. https://doi.org/10.1163/15700658-12342371.

————. "'The Elks Are Our Horses': Animals and Domestication in the New France Borderlands." *Journal of Early American History* 3 (December 2013): 188-205.

Brienen, Rebecca Parker. *Visions of Savage Paradise: Albert Eckhout, Court Painter in Colonial Dutch Brazil.* Amsterdam: Amsterdam University Press, 2006.

Brockey, Liam Matthew. *Journey to the East: The Jesuit Mission to China, 1579–1724.* Cambridge, MA: Harvard University Press, 2007.

Brook, Timothy. *Vermeer's Hat: The Seventeenth Century and the Dawn of the Global World.* New York: Bloomsbury, 2008.

Brunsman, Denver. *The Evil Necessity: British Naval Impressment in the Eighteenth-Century Atlantic World.* Charlottesville: University of Virginia Press, 2013.

Bunimovitz, Shlomo, and Zvi Lederman. "Opium or Oil? Late Bronze Age Cypriot Base Ring Juglets and International Trade Revisited." *Antiquity* 90, no. 354 (December 2016): 1552–61. https://doi.org/10.15184/aqy.2016.177.

Burke, Peter. *The Fabrication of Louis XIV*. New Haven, CT: Yale University Press, 1992.

Burnard, Trevor, and John Garrigus. *The Plantation Machine: Atlantic Capitalism in French Saint-Domingue and British Jamaica*. Philadelphia: University of Pennsylvania Press, 2016.

Burton, Robert. *The Anatomy of Melancholy vvhat it is*. Oxford: printed for Henry Cripps, 1621.

Cadornega, António de Oliveira de. *História geral das guerras angolanas*. Edited by José Matias Delgado. Lisbon: Agência-Geral do Ultramar, 1972 [1680].

Cagle, Hugh. *Assembling the Tropics: Science and Medicine in Portugal's Empire, 1450–1700*. Cambridge: Cambridge University Press, 2018.

———. "Cultures of Inquiry, Myths of Empire: Natural History in Colonial Goa." In *Medicine, Trade and Empire: Garcia de Orta's Colloquies on the Simples and Drugs of India (1563) in Context*, edited by Palmira Fontes da Costa. London: Routledge, 2016.

Caires, Alvaro Guimarães de. "Esbôço Histórico da Medicina dos Portugueses no Estrangeiro" in *Cursos e Conferências, Boletim da Biblioteca da Universidade de Coimbra*. Coimbra, 1935.

Calado, Manoel. *O Valeroso Lucideno e Triunfo da Liberdade*. Lisbon, 1648.

Calainho, Daniela Buono. "Jambacousses e Gangazambes: Feitiçeiros Negros em Portugal." *Afro-Ásia* 25–26 (2001): 141-76.

Camões, Luïs Vaz de. *Os Lusíadas*. Lisbon: Antonio Gôçalvez, 1572.

———. *The Lusiads*. Translated by Landeg White. Oxford: Oxford University Press, 2008.

Campos, Isaac. *Home Grown: Marijuana and the Origins of Mexico's War on Drugs*. Chapel Hill: University of North Carolina Press, 2012.

Candido, Mariana. *An African Slaving Port and the Atlantic World: Benguela and Its Hinterland*. Cambridge: Cambridge University Press, 2013.

Cañizares-Esguerra, Jorge. "On Ignored Global 'Scientific Revolutions.'" *Journal of Early Modern History* 21, no. 5 (2017): 420-32.

———. *Puritan Conquistadors: Iberianizing the Atlantic, 1550–1700*. Redwood City, CA: Stanford University Press, 2006.

———. *Nature, Empire, and Nation: Explorations of the History of Science in the Iberian World*. Redwood City, CA: Stanford University Press, 2006.

———. "New World, New Stars: Patriotic Astrology and the Invention of Indian and Creole Bodies in Colonial Spanish America, 1600-1650." *American Historical Review* 104, no. 1 (1999): 33–68. https://doi.org/10.2307/2650180.

Carney, Judith. *In the Shadow of Slavery: Africa's Botanical Legacy in the Atlantic World*. Berkeley: University of California Press, 2010.

Carod-Artal, F. J. "Hallucinogenic Drugs in Pre-Columbian Mesoamerican Cultures." *Neurologia* 30, no. 1 (February 2015): 42–49. https://doi.org/10.1016/j.nrl.2011.07.003.

Carpenter, Roger M. *The Renewed, the Destroyed, and the Remade: The Three Thought*

Worlds of the Huron and the Iroquois, 1609–1650. East Lansing: Michigan State University Press, 2004.

Carvalho, Rómulo de. *Portugal nas Philosophical Transactions no séculos XVII e XVIII*. Coimbra: Tipografia Atlântida, 1956.

Cavazzi, Giovanni Antonio. *Istorica descrizione de' tre' regni Congo, Matamba, et Angola*. Bologna: Giacomo Monti, 1687.

Cecyll, Ro., and Arthur Dimock. "The Conspiracy of Dr. Lopez." *English Historical Review* 9, no. 35 (1894): 440–72.

Chakrabarti, Pratik. *Materials and Medicine: Trade, Conquest and Therapeutics in the Eighteenth Century*. Manchester: Manchester University Press, 2015.

Chaplin, Joyce. *Subject Matter: Technology, the Body, and Science on the Anglo-American Frontier, 1500–1676*. Cambridge, MA: Harvard University Press, 2001.

Chamberlayne, John. *The Natural History of Coffee, Thee, Chocolate, Tobacco*. London: Christopher Wilkinson, 1682.

Chambouleyron, Rafael. "Cacao, Bark-Clove and Agriculture in the Portuguese Amazon Region in the Seventeenth and Early Eighteenth Century." *Luso-Brazilian Review* 51, no. 1 (May 25, 2014): 1–35. https://doi.org/10.1353/lbr.2014.0012.

———. "A Prática dos Sertões na Amazônia Colonial (Século XVII)." *Outros Tempos* 10, no. 15 (2013).

———. *Povoamento Ocupação e Agricultura na Amazonia Colonial*. Belém, Paráguay: Editora Açaí, 2010.

———. "Escravos Do Atlântico Equatorial: Tráfico Negreiro Para o Estado Do Maranhão e Pará (Século XVII e Início Do Século XVIII)." *Revista Brasileira de História* 26, no. 52 (December 2006): 79–114. https://doi.org/10.1590/S0102-01882006000200005.

Chapman, Allan. *England's Leonardo: Robert Hooke and the Seventeenth-Century Scientific Revolution*. London: CRC Press, 2004.

Chemist & Druggist, vol. 102. London: Benn Brothers, 1925.

Chevalier, Alexandre, and Dominique Bosquet. "Integrating Archaeological Data Toward a Better Understanding of Food Plants Choices and Territory Exploitation in the Northwestern European Early Neolithic: The Case of Remicourt 'En Bia Flo II.'" In *Social Perspectives on Ancient Lives from Paleoethnobotanical Data*, (2017) 15–54. https://doi.org/10.1007/978-3-319-52849-6_2.

Chuchiak John F., ed. *The Inquisition in New Spain, 1536–1820: A Documentary History*. Baltimore: Johns Hopkins University Press, 2012.

Clarkson, James J., Sandra Knapp, Vicente F. Garcia, Richard G. Olmstead, Andrew R. Leitch, and Mark W. Chase. "Phylogenetic Relationships in Nicotiana (Solanaceae) Inferred from Multiple Plastid DNA Regions." *Molecular Phylogenetics and Evolution* 33, no. 1 (October 1, 2004): 75–90. https://doi.org/10.1016/j.ympev.2004.05.002.

Coates, Timothy J. *Convicts and Orphans: Forced and State-Sponsored Colonizers in the Portuguese Empire, 1550–1755*. Redwood City, CA: Stanford University Press, 2001.

Cohen, Emma. *The Mind Possessed: The Cognition of Spirit Possession in an Afro-Brazilian Religious Tradition*. Oxford: Oxford University Press, 2007.

Cohen, Thomas M. *The Fire of Tongues: António Vieira and the Missionary Church in Brazil and Portugal*. Redwood City, CA: Stanford University Press, 1998.

Cohen, William B. "Malaria and French Imperialism." *Journal of African History* 24, no. 1 (1983): 23–36.

Collet, Andre. "Vieilles Enseignes de Paris." *Magasin Pittoresque*, Series II, Tome 16 (1899).

Columbus, Christopher. *Select Letters of Christopher Columbus: With Other Original Documents, Relating to His Four Voyages to the New World*. Edited by R. H. Major. London: Hakluyt Society, 1847.

Concepción, Luis de la. *Practica de Conjurar, en que se contienen exorcismos, y conjuros contra los malos espiritus*. Madrid, 1721.

Cook, Harold J. "Markets and Cultures: Medical Specifics and the Reconfiguration of the Body in Early Modern Europe." *Transactions of the Royal Historical Society* 21 (2011): 123–45.

———. *Matters of Exchange: Commerce, Medicine, and Science in the Dutch Golden Age*. New Haven, CT: Yale University Press, 2007.

———. *The Decline of the Old Medical Regime in Stuart London*. Ithaca, NY: Cornell University Press, 1986.

Cook, Harold J., and Timothy D. Walker. "Circulation of Medicine in the Early Modern Atlantic World." *Social History of Medicine* 26, no. 3 (August 1, 2013): 337–51. https://doi.org/10.1093/shm/hkt013.

Cooper, Alix. *Inventing the Indigenous: Local Knowledge and Natural History in Early Modern Europe*. Cambridge: Cambridge University Press, 2007.

Cooper, Frederick, and Ann L. Stoler. "Tensions of Empire: Colonial Control and Visions of Rule." *American Ethnologist* 16, no. 4 (1989): 609–21.

Copenhaver, Brian P. "A Tale of Two Fishes: Magical Objects in Natural History from Antiquity Through the Scientific Revolution." *Journal of the History of Ideas* 52, no. 3 (July–September 1991): 380–81.

Coppola, M., et al. "3, 4-methylenedioxypyrovalerone (MDPV): Chemistry, Pharmacology and Toxicology of a New Designer Drug of Abuse Marketed Online." *Toxicology Letters* 208, no. 1 (2012).

Correia, Gaspar. *Lendas da India: Collecção de monumentos ineditos para a historia das conquistas dos Portuguezes*. Lisbon, 1858.

Costa, Manuel Gonçalves da, ed. *Itinerário e outros escritos inéditos*. Lisbon: Livraria Civilização, 1971.

Costa, Palmira Fontes da. "Identity and the Construction of Memory in Representations of Garcia de Orta." In *Medicine, Trade and Empire: Garcia de Orta's Colloquies on the Simples and Drugs of India (1563) in Context*, edited by Palmira Fontes da Costa. Farnham: Ashgate, 2015.

Costa, Palmira Fontes da, and Henrique Leitão. "Portuguese Imperial Science, 1450–1800: An Historiographic Review." In *Science in the Spanish and Portuguese Em-*

pires, edited by Daniela Bleichmar et al. Redwood City: Stanford University Press, 2009.

Courtwright, David T. *The Age of Addiction How Bad Habits Became Big Business.* Cambridge, MA: Harvard University Press, 2019.

———. *Forces of Habit: Drugs and the Making of the Modern World.* Cambridge, MA: Harvard University Press, 2001.

Cowan, Brian. *The Social Life of Coffee: The Emergence of the British Coffeehouse.* New Haven, CT: Yale University Press, 2008.

Crawford, Matthew James. "A 'Reasoned Proposal' Against 'Vain Science': Creole Negotiations of an Atlantic Medicament in the Audiencia of Quito (1776–92)." *Atlantic Studies* 7, no. 4 (December 1, 2010): 397–419. https://doi.org/10.1080/147 88810.2010.516191.

———. *The Andean Wonder Drug: Cinchona Bark and Imperial Science in the Spanish Atlantic, 1630-1800.* Pittsburgh: University of Pittsburgh Press, 2016.

Croix, François Boissier de Sauvages de la. *Dissertation sur les médicaments qui affectent certaines parties du corps humain plutot que d'autres et quelle serait la cause de cet effet, qui a remporté le prix au jugement de l'Académie royale des belles lettres, sciences et arts de Bordeaux. (*Paris: Pierre Brun, 1752).

Croll, Oswald. *Basilica Chymica.* Frankfurt: Claudium Marnium, 1609.

Crosby, Alfred W. *The Columbian Exchange: Biological and Cultural Consequences of 1492.* Hartford, CT: Greenwood, 2003.

Curto, José C. *Enslaving Spirits: The Portuguese-Brazilian Alcohol Trade at Luanda and Its Hinterland, c. 1550-1830.* Leiden: Brill, 2003. https://brill.com/view/title/8290.

Cussen, Celia. *The Life and Afterlife of Fray Martin de Porres, Afroperuvian Saint.* Cambridge: Cambridge University Press, 2014.

Dampier, William. *A New Voyage Round the World: Describing Particularly, the Isthmus of America.* London: J. Knapton, 1705.

Dapper, Olfert. *Description de l'Afrique, contenant les noms, la situation & les confins de toutes ses parties, leurs rivieres, leurs villes & leurs habitations, leurs plantes & leurs animaux.* Amsterdam: Wolfang, 1686.

Daston, Lorraine. "The Empire of Observation, 1600-1800," in Daston and Lunbeck, *Histories of Scientific Observation.*

———. "Marvelous Facts and Miraculous Evidence in Early Modern Europe." *Critical Inquiry* 18, no. 1 (1991): 93–124.

Daston, Lorraine, and Elizabeth Lunbeck, eds. *Histories of Scientific Observation.* Chicago: University of Chicago Press, 2011.

Davy, Humphry. *Researches, Chemical and Philosophical, Chiefly Concerning Nitrous Oxide.* London, 1800.

Dean, Warren. *With Broadax and Firebrand: The Destruction of the Brazilian Atlantic Forest.* Berkeley: University of California Press, 1997.

Dear, Peter. *Discipline and Experience: The Mathematical Way in the Scientific Revolution.* Chicago: University of Chicago Press, 1995.

Delbourgo, James. *Collecting the World: The Life and Curiosity of Hans Sloane.* New York: Penguin, 2017.

Delbourgo, James, and Nicholas Dew, eds. *Science and Empire in the Atlantic world.* London: Routledge, 2008.

Denevan, William M. *Cultivated Landscapes of Native Amazonia and the Andes.* Oxford: Oxford University Press, 2003.

Derks, Hans. *History of the Opium Problem: The Assault on the East, ca. 1600-1950.* Leiden: Brill, 2012.

d'Esaguy, Augusto. "Agua de Inglaterra." *Bulletin of the Institute of the History of Medicine* 4 (1936): 404-8.

De Vos, Paula. "The 'Prince of Medicine': Yūhannā Ibn Māsawayh and the Foundations of the Western Pharmaceutical Tradition." *Isis* 104, no. 4 (2013): 667–712. https://doi.org/10.1086/674940.

———. "The Science of Spices: Empiricism and Economic Botany in the Early Spanish Empire." *Journal of World History* 17, no. 4 (2006): 399–427.

Diamond, Jared M. *Guns, Germs, and Steel: The Fates of Human Societies.* New York: W. W. Norton, 1997.

Donzelli, Guiseppe. *Teatro Farmaceutico, Dogmatico, Espagirico.* Venice: Gasparo Storti, 1696.

Dorner, Zachary. "'No One Here Knows Half so Much of This Matter as Yourself': The Deployment of Expertise in Silvester Gardiner's Surgical, Druggist, and Land Speculation Networks, 1734–83." *William and Mary Quarterly* 72, no. 2 (2015): 287–322. https://doi.org/10.5309/willmaryquar.72.2.0287.

Drayton, Richard. *Nature's Government: Science, Imperial Britain, and the "Improvement" of the World.* New Haven, CT: Yale University Press, 2000.

———. "Synchronic Palimpsests: Work, Power and the Transcultural History of Knowledge." In *Entangled Knowledge: Scientific Discourses and Cultural Difference,* edited by Klaus Hock and Gesa Mackenthun. Münster: Waxmann Verlag, 2012.

Duffy, Eamon. *The Stripping of the Altars: Traditional Religion in England, c. 1400-c. 1580.* New Haven, CT: Yale University Press, 2005.

Eamon, William. *Science and the Secrets of Nature: Books of Secrets in Medieval and Early Modern Culture.* Princeton, NJ: Princeton University Press, 1996.

Escohotado, Antonio. *Historia general de las drogas.* Madrid: Alianza Editorial, 1989.

Evans, Jennifer. *Aphrodisiacs, Fertility and Medicine in Early Modern England.* London: Boydell and Brewer, 2014.

Everett, Nicholas, and Martino Gabra. "The pharmacology of medieval sedatives: The 'Great Rest' of the Antidotarium nicolai." *Journal of Ethnopharmacology* 155, no. 1 (2014): 443–49.

Faria, Ana Maria Homem Leal de. "Duarte Ribeiro De Macedo: A Modern Diplomat (1618- 1680)." *e-Journal of Portuguese History* 4, no. 1 (Summer 2006).

Fernandes, Florestan. *Organização social dos Tupinambá.* São Paulo: Instituto Progresso Editorial, 1949.

Ferreira, Roquinaldo. *Cross-Cultural Exchange in the Atlantic World: Angola and Brazil During the Era of the Slave Trade.* New York: Cambridge University Press, 2012.

Floyd-Wilson, Mary. *Occult Knowledge, Science, and Gender on the Shakespearean Stage*. Cambridge: Cambridge University Press, 2013.

Fouquet, Marie. *Recueil de receptes choisies expérimentées & approuvées*. Paris: Pierre Grand'Aigne, 1675. http://archive.org/details/BIUSante_72042.

Foxcroft, Louise. *The Making of Addiction: The "Use and Abuse" of Opium in Nineteenth-Century Britain*. London: Routledge, 2016.

Franco, Antonio. *Imagem da virtude em o noviciado da Companhia de Jesus*. Coimbra: Real Collegio das Artes da Companhia de Jesus, 1719.

Freedman, Paul. *Out of the East: Spices and the Medieval Imagination*. New Haven, CT: Yale University Press, 2008.

Fromont. Cécile. *The Art of Conversion: Christian Visual Culture in the Kingdom of Kongo*. Chapel Hill: University of North Carolina Press, 2014.

Fryer, John. *A New Account of East-India and Persia, in Eight Letters*. London: R.R., 1698.

Fu, Lo-shu. *A Documentary Chronicle of Sino-Western relations*, vol. 1. Tucson: University of Arizona Press, 1966.

Furetière, Antoine. *Dictionaire Universel*. Paris, 1690.

Furtado, Júnia Ferreira. "Tropical empiricism: making medical knowledge in colonial Brazil." In *Science and Empire in the Atlantic World*, pp. 141–66. London: Routledge, 2008.

Gänger, Stefanie. "World Trade in Medicinal Plants from Spanish America, 1717–1815." *Medical History* 59, no. 1 (January 2015): 44–62. https://doi.org/10.1017/mdh.2014.70.

Gascoigne, John. "The Royal Society, Natural History and the Peoples of the New World(s), 1660-1800." *British Journal for the History of Science* 42, no. 4 (December 2009): 539–62.

Gaster, Moses. *History of the Ancient Synagogue of the Spanish and Portuguese Jews, the Cathedral Synagogue of the Jews of England, Situated in Bevis Marks*. London, 1901.

Gibbs, Frederick. "Poisonous Properties, Bodies, and Forms in the Fifteenth Century." *Preternature* 2, no.1 (2013): 19–46.

Gilman, Sander L. *Seeing the Insane*. Lincoln: University of Nebraska Press, 1982.

Godinho, Manoel. *Relação do novo caminho que fez por terra e mar, vindo da India*. Lisbon: Henrique Valente de Oliveira, 1665.

Goggin, John M. "Peyote and the Mexican Inquisition, 1620." *American Anthropologist* 44, no. 2 (1942): 324–26.

Gold, Joel J. "The Voyages of Jerónimo Lobo, Joachim Le Grand, and Samuel Johnson." *Prose Studies: History, Theory, Criticism* 5, no. 1 (1982): 20-42.

Goldman, Irving. *Cubeo Hehénewa Religious Thought: Metaphysics of a Northwestern Amazonian People*. Edited by Peter Wilson. New York: Columbia University Press, 2004.

Golinski, Jan. *The Experimental Self: Humphry Davy and the Making of a Man of Science*. Chicago: University of Chicago Press, 2016.

Gomes, Bernardino Antonio. *Ensaio sobre o cinchonino, e sobre sua influencia na virtude da quina, e d'outras cascas.* Lisbon, 1812.

———. "An Essay upon Cinchonin, and Its Influence upon the Virtue of Peruvian Bark, and Other Barks." *Edinburgh Medical and Surgical Journal* (1811): 420-31.

Gómez, Pablo F. *The Experiential Caribbean: Creating Knowledge and Healing in the Early Modern Atlantic.* Chapel Hill: University of North Carolina Press, 2017.

Goodman, Godfrey. *The Fall of Man, Or the Corruption of Nature, Proved by the Light of Our Naturall Reason.* London: Felix Kyngston, to be sold by Richard Lee, 1616.

Goodman, Jordan, Paul Lovejoy, and Andrew Sherratt, editors. *Consuming Habits: Drugs in History and Anthropology.* London: Routledge, 2014.

Gootenberg, Paul. *Andean Cocaine: The Making of a Global Drug.* Asheville: University of North Carolina Press, 2008.

———. "Secret Ingredients: The Politics of Coca in US–Peruvian Relations, 1915–65." *Journal of Latin American Studies* 36, no. 2 (May 2004): 233–65. https://doi.org/10.1017/S0022216X04007424.

Gordon, David. "The Political Economy of Khoikhoi Narcotic Consumption, 1487-1870." *South African Historical Journal* 35 (1996): 62-88.

Greenfield, Amy Butler. *A Perfect Red: Empire, Espionage, and the Quest for the Color of Desire.* New York: Harper Collins, 2009.

Grehan, James. "Smoking and 'Early Modern' Sociability: The Great Tobacco Debate in the Ottoman Middle East (Seventeenth to Eighteenth Centuries)." *American Historical Review* 111, no. 5 (December 1, 2006): 1352-77. https://doi.org/10.1086/ahr.111.5.1352.

Grew, Nathaniel. *Musaeum Regalis Societatis.* London, 1681.

Griffin, J. P. "Venetian Treacle and the Foundation of Medicines Regulation." *British Journal of Clinical Pharmacology* 58, no. 3 (September 2004): 317-25.

Griffith, Richard. *Observations Made upon the Brasillian root, Called Ipepocoanha, Imported from the Indies.* London, 1682.

Griffiths, Antony. *The Print in Stuart Britain.* London: Trustees of the British Museum, 1998.

Grisley, Gabriel. *Desengano para a medicina.* Lisbon: Henrique Valente de Oliveira, 1656.

———. *Viridiarum Lusitanum in quo arborum fruticum et herbarum differentiae onomasti insertae.* Lisbon: Antonio Craesbeek, 1661.

Grove, Richard H. *Green Imperialism: Colonial Expansion, Tropical Island Edens and the Origins of Environmentalism, 1600-1860.* Cambridge: Cambridge University Press, 1996.

Guest, Edwin. "On the Elements of Language." *Proceedings of the Philological Society,* vol. 4. London, 1850.

Guzmán, Gastón. "Nuevas observaciones taxonómicas y etnomicológicas en Psilocybe s.s. (Fungi, Basidiomycota, Agaricomycetidae, Agaricales, Strophariaceae) de México, África y España." *Acta Botánica Mexicana* no. 100 (July, 2012).

Hacke, William. *A Collection of Original Voyages.* London: James Knapton, 1699.

Hagen, Edward H., et al. "Ecology and Neurobiology of Toxin Avoidance and the Paradox of Drug Reward." *Neuroscience* 160, no. 1 (2009): 69–84.

Hall, Marie Boas. "Boyle's Method of Work: Promoting His Corpuscular Philosophy." *Notes and Records of the Royal Society of London* 41, no. 2 (June 1987): 111–43.

Alfred Rupert Hall and Marie Boas Hall, eds. *The Correspondence of Henry Oldenburg.* Madison, WI: University of Wisconsin Press, 1971.

Hamlin, Christopher. *More Than Hot: A Short History of Fever.* Baltimore: Johns Hopkins University Press, 2014.

Han, Beth, Wilson M. Compton, Carlos Blanco, Elizabeth Crane, Jinhee Lee, and Christopher M. Jones. "Prescription Opioid Use, Misuse, and Use Disorders in U.S. Adults: 2015 National Survey on Drug Use and Health." *Annals of Internal Medicine* 167, no. 5 (2017): 293–301.

Handler, Jerome. "Slave Medicine and Obeah in Barbados, circa 1650 to 1834." *New West Indian Guide / Nieuwe West-Indische Gids* 74 (2000): 50–79.

Handler, Jerome, and Neil Norman. "From West Africa to Barbados: A Rare Pipe from a Plantation Slave Cemetery." *African Diaspora Archeology Newsletter.* September 2007.

Harding, Rachel E. *A Refuge in Thunder: Candomblé and Alternative Spaces of Blackness.* Bloomington: Indiana University Press, 2003.

Hardwick, Julie. *Family Business: Litigation and the Political Economies of Daily Life in Early Modern France.* Oxford: Oxford University Press, 2009.

Harkness, Deborah E. "Managing an Experimental Household: The Dees of Mortlake and the Practice of Natural Philosophy." *Isis* 88, no. 2 (1997): 247–62.

Harris, John. *Lexicon Technium or, An Universal English Dictionary of Arts and Sciences.* London: Dan Brown, 1704.

Hart, Carl L., and Robert M. Krauss. "Human Drug Addiction Is More than Faulty Decision- Making." *Behavioral and Brain Sciences* 31, no. 4 (August 2008): 448–49.

Harvey, Gideon. *The Conclave of Physicians in Two Parts, Detecting Their Intrigues, Frauds, and Plots, Against Their Patients.* London, 1686.

Heckenberger, Michael J., James B. Petersen, and Eduardo Goés Neves. "Village Size and Permanence in Amazonia: Two Archaeological Examples from Brazil." *Latin American Antiquity* 10, no. 4 (December 1999): 353–76. https://doi. org/10.2307/971962.

Hedrick, Elizabeth. "Romancing the Salve: Sir Kenelm Digby and the Powder of Sympathy." *British Journal for the History of Science* 41, no. 149 (June 2008): 161–85.

Heintze, Beatrix. "The Extraordinary Journey of the Jaga Through the Centuries: Critical Approaches to Precolonial Angolan Historical Sources." *History in Africa* 34 (2007): 67–101. https://doi.org/10.1353/hia.2007.0005.

Hemming, John. "The Indians of Brazil." In *The Cambridge History of Latin America*, edited by Leslie Bethell. Cambridge: Cambridge University Press, 1985.

Henning, Basil Duke. "Montagu, Hon. Edward (c. 1636-65)." In *The History of Parliament: The House of Commons 1660-1690*, edited by B. D. Henning. London: Haynes, 1983.

Hernández, Francisco. *Quatro libros de la naturaleza, y virtudes de las plantas*. Mexico City: Diego Lopez Daualos, 1615.

———. *De Historia Plantarum Novae Hispaniae*, vol. 3. Madrid, 1790.

Heywood, Linda M. *Njinga of Angola: Africa's Warrior Queen*. Cambridge, MA: Harvard University Press, 2017.

———. "Portuguese into African: The Eighteenth-Century Central African Background to Atlantic Creole Cultures." In *Central Africans and Cultural Transformations in the American Diaspora*, edited by Linda Heywood. Cambridge: Cambridge University Press, 2001.

Heywood, Linda M., and John K. Thornton. *Central Africans, Atlantic Creoles, and the Foundation of the Americas, 1585-1660*. Cambridge: Cambridge University Press, 2007.

Hillig, Karl W., and Paul G. Mahlberg. "A Chemotaxonomic Analysis of Cannabinoid Variation in Cannabis (*Cannabaceae*)." *American Journal of Botany* 91, no. 6 (2004): 966–75. http://www.jstor.org/stable/4122711.

Hobhouse, Henry. *Seeds of Change: Five Plants That Transformed Mankind*. London: Counterpoint, 1985.

Hock, Klaus, and Gesa Mackenthun, eds. *Entangled Knowledge: Scientific Discourses and Cultural Difference*. Münster: Waxmann Verlag, 2012.

Hollersen, Wiebke. "'This Is Working': Portugal, 12 Years after Decriminalizing Drugs." *Spiegel Online* March 27, 2013, sec. International. www.spiegel.de/international/europe/evaluating-drug-decrimalization-in-portugal-12-years-later-a-891060.html.

Hong-Chunk, S. M. "An Aspect of East Asian Maritime Trade: The Exchange of Commodities Between Korea and Ryuku (1389-1638)." In Schottenhammer, *Trade and Transfer Across the East Asian "Mediterranean."*

Honigsbaum, Mark. *The Fever Trail: In Search of the Cure for Malaria*. London: Pan Macmillan, 2012.

Hooke, Robert. *Philosophical Experiments and Observations of the Late Eminent Dr. Robert Hooke*, edited by William Derham. London: W. and J. Innys, 1726.

Hooke, Robert, and H. W. Robinson, eds., *The Diary of Robert Hooke M.A., M.D., F.R.S. (1672- 1680)*. London: Taylor and Francis, 1935.

Hoorn, C., F. P. Wesselingh, H. ter Steege, M. A. Bermudez, A. Mora, J. Sevink, I. Sanmartín, et al. "Amazonia Through Time: Andean Uplift, Climate Change, Landscape Evolution, and Biodiversity." *Science* 330, no. 6006 (November 12, 2010): 927–31. https://doi.org/10.1126/science.1194585.

Hopkins, A. G. *Globalisation in World History*. New York: Random House, 2011.

Hutton, Charles, and Richard Pearson, eds. *The Philosophical Transactions of the Royal Society of London*. London: C. and R. Baldwin, 1809.

Ipsen, Pernille. *Daughters of the Trade: Atlantic Slavers and Interracial Marriage on the Gold Coast*. Philadelphia: University of Pennsylvania Press, 2015.

Jahangir. *The Jahangirnama: Memoirs of Jahangir, Emperor of India*. Translated by Wheeler Thackston. Washington, DC: Smithsonian Institution, 1999.

James I, King. *A Counterblaste to Tobacco.* London: R[obert] B[arker], 1604.

Janiga-Perkins, Constance G. *Reading, Writing, and Translation in the Relación Acerca de Las Antigüedades de Los Indios (c. 1498) by Fray Ramón Pané: A Study of a Pioneering Work in Ethnography.* Lewiston, NY: Edwin Mellen Press, 2007.

Jay, Mike. *Emperors of Dreams: Drugs in the Nineteenth Century.* London: Dedalus, 2000.

Jenner, M., and P. Wallis. *Medicine and the Market in England and Its Colonies, c. 1450-c. 1850.* London: Springer, 2007.

Johnson, Samuel. *A Dictionary of the English Language.* London, 1755.

Jones, Adam. *German Sources for West African History, 1599-1669.* London: Coronet, 1983.

Jones, John. *The Mysteries of Opium Reveal'd.* London: Richard Smith, 1701.

Juan-Tresserras, Jordi, and María Josefa Villalba, "Consumo de la adormidera (*Papaver somniferum L.*) en el Neolítico Peninsular: El enterramiento M28 del complejo minero de Can Tintorer." *SAGVNTVM* (1999): 397–404.

Keller, Vera. "The 'New World of Sciences': The Temporality of the Research Agenda and the Unending Ambitions of Science." *Isis* 103, no. 4 (December 2012): 727–34.

Kieckhefer, Richard. *Magic in the Middle Ages.* Cambridge: Cambridge University Press, 2014.

Kier, Gerold, Holger Kreft, Tien Ming Lee, Walter Jetz, Pierre L. Ibisch, Christoph Nowicki, Jens Mutke, and Wilhelm Barthlott. "A Global Assessment of Endemism and Species Richness Across Island and Mainland Regions." *Proceedings of the National Academy of Sciences of the United States of America* 106, no. 23 (June 9, 2009): 9322–27. https://doi.org/10.1073/pnas.0810306106.

Klayman, D. L. "Qinghaosu (Artemisinin): An Antimalarial Drug from China." *Science* 228, no. 4703 (May 31, 1985): 1049–55. https://doi.org/10.1126/science.3887571.

Klein, Herbert S. "The Internal Slave Trade in Nineteenth-Century Brazil: A Study of Slave Importations into Rio de Janeiro in 1852." *Hispanic American Historical Review* 51, no. 4 (1971): 567–85. https://doi.org/10.2307/2512051.

Klein, Joel A. "Corporeal Elements and Principles in the Learned German Chymical Tradition." *Ambix* 61, no. 4 (2014): 345–65.

Klockgether-Radke, A. P. "F. W. Sertürner and the Discovery of Morphine: 200 Years of Pain Therapy with Opioids." *Anasthesiologie, Intensivmedizin, Notfallmedizin, Schmerztherapie: AINS* 37, no. 5 (May 2002): 244–49. https://doi.org/10.1055/s-2002-30132.

Knox, Robert. *An Historical Relation of the Island Ceylon in the East-Indies.* London: Richard Chiswell, 1681.

Kosanovic, Djuro, Xia Tian, Oleg Pak, Ying-Ju Lai, Yi-Ling Hsieh, Michael Seimetz, Norbert Weissmann, Ralph Theo Schermuly, and Bhola Kumar Dahal. "Rhodiola: An Ordinary Plant or a Promising Future Therapy for pulmonary Hypertension?" *Pulmonary Circulation* 3, no. 3 (2013): 499–506.

Koschel, Klaus. "Opium Alkaloids in a Cypriote Base Ring I Vessel (bilbil) of the Middle Bronze Age from Egypt. *Ägypten und Levante/Egypt and the Levant* (1996): 159–66.

Kramer, John C. "Opium Rampant: Medical Use, Misuse and Abuse in Britain and the West in the Seventeenth and Eighteenth enturies." *British Journal of Addiction* 74, no. 4 (1979): 377–89.

Krikorian, Abraham D. "Were the Opium Poppy and Opium Known in the Ancient Near East?" *Journal of the History of Biology* 8, no. 1 (1975): 95–114.

Lacerda e Almeida, Francisco José de. *The Lands of Cazembe: Lacerda's Journey to Cazembe in 1798*. London: John Murray, 1873.

The Ladies' Dispensatory: Or, Every Woman Her Own Physician. London: J. Hodges, 1739.

Lahiri, Rashmi, R. K. Lal, Nupur Srivastava, and Karuna Shanker. "Genetic Variability and Diversity in Indian Germplasm of Opium Poppy (*Papaver Somniferum L.*)." *Journal of Applied Research on Medicinal and Aromatic Plants* 8 (March 1, 2018): 41–46. https://doi.org/10.1016/j.jarmap.2017.10.001.

Lahon, Didier. "Inquisição, Pacto Com o Demônio e 'Magia' Africana Em Lisboa No Século XVIII." *Topoi (Rio de Janeiro)* 5, no. 8 (June 2004): 9–70. https://doi.org/10.1590/2237-101X005008001.

Lamb, Kate. "Thousands Dead: The Philippine President, the Death Squad Allegations and a Brutal Drugs War." *Guardian*, April 2, 2017, sec. World News. www.theguardian.com/world/2017/apr/02/philippines-president-duterte-drugs-war-death-squads.

Lee, Henry. *The Vegetable Lamb of Tartary: A Curious Fable of the Cotton Plant. To Which Is Added a Sketch of the History of Cotton and the Cotton Trade*. London: S. Low, Marston, Searle, & Rivington, 1887.

Lémery, Nicolas. *Cours de Chymie Contenant la Manière de Faire les Operations Qui Sont en Usage dans le Medecine*. Paris: Nicolas Lémery, 1675.

———. *A Course of Chymistry: Containing an Easie Method of Preparing Those Chymical Medicines Which Are Used in Physick*. London: A. Bell, 1720.

Leong, Elaine. "'Herbals She Peruseth': Reading Medicine in Early Modern England." *Renaissance Studies* 28, no. 4 (September 2014): 556–78. https://doi.org/10.1111/rest.12079.

Leong, Elaine, and Sara Pennell. "Recipe Collections and the Currency of Medical Knowledge in the Early Modern 'Medical Marketplace.'" In *Medicine and the Market in England and Its Colonies, c. 1450–c. 1850*, edited by Mark Jennery and Patrick Wallis, 133–52. London: Palgrave Macmillan, 2007. https://doi.org/10.1057/9780230591462_7.

Lesch, John E. "Conceptual Change in an Empirical Science: The Discovery of the First Alkaloids." *Historical Studies in the Physical Sciences* 11, no. 2 (1981): 305–28.

Linschoten, John Huyghen van. *The Voyage of John Huyghen van Linschoten to the East Indies. From the Old English Translation of 1598 . . . Volume II*. Edited by P. A. Tiele. London: Hakluyt Society, 1885.

[Lobo, Jerónimo]. *A Short Relation of the River Nile . . . Translated out of a Portuguese manuscript, at the desire of the Royal Society, by Sir Peter Wych*. London: John Martin, 1669.

Lobo, Jerónimo. *Itinerário.* Translated by Donald M. Lockhart. London: Hakluyt Society, 1984.

Locke, John. *An Essay Concerning Human Understanding.* 3rd ed. London: John Churchil, 1695.

Loo, Mirjam van het, Ineke van Beusekom, and James P. Kahan. "Decriminalization of Drug Use in Portugal: The Development of a Policy." *Annals of the American Academy of Political and Social Science* 582 (2002): 49–63.

Losa, Francisco. *Vida del Siervo de Dios Gregorio Lopez . . . a que se añaden los Escritos del Apocalypsi, y Tesoro de Medicina.* Madrid: Juan de Aritzia, 1727.

Loureiro, Rui Manuel. "Enter the Milanese Lapidary: Precious Stones in Garcia de Orta's Coloquios Dos Simples, e Drogas He Cousas Mediçinais Da India." *Journal of History of Science and Technology* 8 (Fall 2013): 29–47.

Lovell, Julia. *The Opium War: Drugs, Dreams, and the Making of Modern China.* London: Picador, 2011.

Macedo, Duarte Ribeiro de. *Obras Ineditas de Duarte Ribeiro de Macedo.* Lisbon: Impressão Regia, 1817.

Mancall, Peter C. *Deadly Medicine: Indians and Alcohol in Early America.* Ithaca, NY: Cornell University Press, 1995.

———. "Tales Tobacco Told in Sixteenth-Century Europe." *Environmental History* 9, no. 4 (October 2004): 648. https://doi.org/10.2307/3986264.

Mann, Charles C. *1491: New Revelations of the Americas Before Columbus.* New York: Vintage, 2006.

Mapes, Russell W. "Past and present provenance of the Amazon River." PhD diss., The University of North Carolina at Chapel Hill, 2009.

Markey, Lia. "Stradano's Allegorical Invention of the Americas in Late Sixteenth-Century Florence." *Renaissance Quarterly* 65, no. 2 (2012): 385–442. https://doi.org/10.1086/667256.

Marques, Vera Regina Beltrão. "As 'Medicinas' indígenas ganham o mundo nas páginas das farmacopéias portuguesas do setecentos." *IX Encontro Regional De História*, 2004.

———. *Natureza em boiões: medicinas e boticários no Brasil setecentista.* Campinas, Brazil: Editora da Unicamp, 1999.

Marquese, Rafael de Bivar. *Feitores do corpo, missionários da mente: senhores, letrados e o controle dos escravos nas Américas, 1660–1860.* São Paulo: Companhia das Letras, 2004.

Massa, Nicolò. *Liber de morbo gallico.* Venice, 1532.

Matthee, Rudi. *The Pursuit of Pleasure: Drugs and Stimulants in Iranian History, 1500–1900.* Princeton, NJ: Princeton University Press, 2009.

May, Channing. "Global Financial Integrity: Transnational Crime and the Developing World." Washington, DC: Global Financial Integrity, March 2017. www.gfintegrity.org/report/transnational-crime-and-the-developing-world/.

Mccants, Anne E. C. "Exotic Goods, Popular Consumption, and the Standard of Living: Thinking About Globalization in the Early Modern World." *Journal of World History* 18, no. 4 (2014): 433–62.

McNamara, Patrick. *The Neuroscience of Religious Experience*. Cambridge: Cambridge University Press, 2009.

McNeill, J. R. *Mosquito Empires: Ecology and War in the Greater Caribbean, 1620-1914*. Cambridge: Cambridge University Press, 2010.

Mead, Richard. *A Mechanical Account of Poisons: In Several Essays*. London, 1702.

Menezes, Francisco Javier de. *Henriqueida: Poema heroico com advertencias preliminares*. Lisbon: na officina de Antonio Isidoro da Fonseca, 1741.

Merolla, Girolamo. *Breve e succinta relazione del viaggio nel regno di Congo nell' Africa meridionale, continente variati clima, arie, animali, fiumi, frutti, vestimenti con proprie figure, diversità di costumi, e di viveri per l'uso umano: Scritto, e ridotto al presente stile istorico, e narrativo dal Angelo Piccardo da Napoli*. Naples, 1726.

———. *Breve, e succinta relatione del viaggio nel regno di Congo nell'Africa meridionale*. Naples: Francesco Mollo, 1692.

Merret, Christopher. *A Short View of the Frauds, and Abuses Committed by Apothecaries: As Well in Relation to Patients, as Physicians, and of the Only Remedy Thereof by Physicians Making Their Own Medicines*. London: J. Allestry, printer to the Royal Society, 1669.

Merwe, Nikolaas J. van der, "Antiquity of the Smoking Habit in Africa." *Transactions of the Royal Society of South Africa* 60, no. 2 (2005): 147-50.

Miller, Joseph C. "Requiem for the 'Jaga' (Requiem Pour Les 'Jaga')." *Cahiers d'Études Africaines* 13, no. 49 (1973): 121–49.

Miller, Joseph Calder. *Way of Death: Merchant Capitalism and the Angolan Slave Trade, 1730–1830*. Madison: University of Wisconsin Press, 1997.

Milligan, Barry. *Pleasures and Pains: Opium and the Orient in Nineteenth-Century British Culture*. Charlottesville, VA: University of Virginia Press, 1995.

Milov, Sarah. "Smoking as Statecraft: Promoting American Tobacco Production and Global Cigarette Consumption, 1947–1970." *Journal of Policy History* 28, no. 4 (October 2016): 707–35. https://doi.org/10.1017/S0898030616000312.

Milton, John. *Paradise Lost*. London: W. Sharp, 1816.

Mintz, Sidney W. *Sweetness and Power: The Place of Sugar in Modern History*. Repr. ed. New York: Penguin, 1986.

Miranda, Evaristo Eduardo de. *Quando o Amazonas corria para o Pacífico: uma história desconhecida da Amazônia*. Petrópolis: Editora Vozes, 2007.

Miranda, João Cardoso de. *Relação cirurgica, e medica, na qual se trata, e declara especialmente hum novo methodo para curar a infecção escorbutica, ou mal de Loanda*. Lisbon: Na Officina de Manoel Soares, 1741.

Mithoefer, Michael C., et al. "Novel Psychopharmacological Therapies for Psychiatric Disorders: Psilocybin and MDMA." *Lancet Psychiatry* 3, no. 5 (2016): 481–88.

Moncrief, John. *The Poor Man's Physician, Or the Receipts of the Famous John Moncrief*. London: G. Stewart, 1716.

Monginot, François. *A New Mystery in Physick Discovered, by Curing of Fevers & Agues by Quinquina or Jesuites Powder*. London: Will. Crook, 1681.

———. *De la guérison des fièvres par le quinquina*. Paris, 1680.

Monroe, J. Cameron, and Seth Mallios, "A Seventeenth-Century Colonial Cottage

Industry: New Evidence and a Dating Formula for Colono Tobacco Pipes in the Chesapeake." *Historical Archaeology* 38, no. 2 (2004): 68–82.

Monteiro, Isabel. "A Escrita da História: Oriente, Occidente." *Revista Camões* 1 (1998).

Montoro, Dignacio de Altarribaram de, et al. *Ordinaciones de la imperial ciudad de Zaragoza: En veinte y tres dias del mes de deziembre del año 1669.* Zaragoza: Diego Dormer, 1675.

Moore, Thomas J., and Donald R. Mattison. "Adult Utilization of Psychiatric Drugs and Differences by Sex, Age, and Race." *JAMA Internal Medicine* 177, no. 2 (February 1, 2017): 274–75. https://doi.org/10.1001/jamainternmed.2016.7507.

Mora, Santiago. "Early Inhabitants of the Amazonian Tropical Rain Forest: A Study of Humans and Environmental Dynamics. PhD diss., University of Calgary, 2001.

Motolinia, Toribio de Benavente. *Historia de los Indios de Nueva España.* In *Collection de documentes para la historia da Mexico,* edited by Joaquin Garcia Icazbalceta. Mexico City: Libreria de J. M. Andrade, 1858.

Moura, Joseph Ferreyra de. *Syntagma chirurgico theorico-practico de Joam de Vigo . . .* Lisbon: Officina Real Deslandesiana, 1713.

Moxham, Noah, and Aileen Fyfe. "The Royal Society and the Prehistory of Peer Review, 1665–1965." *The Historical Journal* 61, no. 4 (2018): 863–89.

Moyle, John. *The Present Ill State of the Practice of Physick in This Nation Truly Represented; and Some Remedies Thereof . . . Proposed to the Two Houses of Parliament.* London, 1702.

Müller, Christian P., and Gunter Schumann. "Drugs as Instruments: A New Framework for Non- Addictive Psychoactive Drug Use." *Behavioral and Brain Sciences* 34 (2011): 293–310.

Nappi, Carla. "Bolatu's Pharmacy Theriac in Early Modern China." *Early Science and Medicine* 14, no. 6 (November 2009): 737–64. https://doi.org/10.1163/1383742 09X12542104914000.

Nelson, William Max. "Making Men: Enlightenment Ideas of Racial Engineering." *American Historical Review* 115, no. 5 (2010): 1364–94.

Neri, Janice. *The Insect and the Image: Visualizing Nature in Early Modern Europe, 1500–1700.* St. Paul: University of Minnesota Press, 2011.

Nesse, Randolph M., and Kent C. Berridge. "Psychoactive Drug Use in Evolutionary Perspective." *Science* 278, no. 5335 (October 3, 1997): 63–66. https://doi.org/10.1126/science.278.5335.63.

Nesvig, Martin. "Sandcastles of the Mind: Hallucinogens and Cultural Memory." In *Substance and Seduction: Ingested Commodities in Early Modern Mesoamerica,* edited by Stacey Schwartzkopf, Kathryn E. Sampeck. Austin: University of Texas Press, 2017.

——— "Peyote, Ever Virgin: A Case of Religious Hybridism in Mexico." In *A Linking of Heaven and Earth: Studies in Religious and Cultural History in Honor of Carlos M. N. Eire,* edited by Emily Michelson, Scott K. Taylor, and Mary Venables. London: Routledge, 2012.

Neto e Cova, Maria Teresa Trigo. "O Pensamento Politico de Duarte Ribeiro de

Macedo." *Do Tempo e da História*, vol. 3, Centro de Estudos Históricos, Faculdade de Letras da Universidade de Lisboa, 1970.

Neuwinger, Hans Dieter. *African Ethnobotany: Poisons and Drugs: Chemistry, Pharmacology, Toxicology*. Weinheim, Germany: CRC Press, 1996.

Newman, William R., and Lawrence M. Principe. *Alchemy Tried in the Fire: Starkey, Boyle, and the Fate of Helmontian Chymistry*. Chicago: University of Chicago Press, 2005.

Nichols, D. E., M. W. Johnson, and C. D. Nichols. "Psychedelics as Medicines: An Emerging New Paradigm." *Clinical Pharmacology and Therapeutics* 101, no. 2 (February 2017): 209–19. https://doi.org/10.1002/cpt.557.

Francesco Maria Nigrisoli, *Febris china chinae expugnata, seu illustrium aliquot virorum obuscula*. Ferrara: Bernardini Pomatelli, 1687.

Nóbrega, Manuel da, and Serafim Leite. *Cartas do Brasil e mais escritos (opera omnia)*. Coimbra, Portugal: University of Coimbra Biblioteca Geral, 1955.

Nogueira, André Luís Lima. *Entre cirurgiões, tambores e ervas: Calunduzeiros e curadores ilegais em acão nas Minas Gerais (século XVIII)*. Rio de Janeiro: Editora Garamond, 2018.

Norton, Marcy. *Sacred Gifts, Profane Pleasures: A History of Tobacco and Chocolate in the Atlantic World*. Ithaca, NY: Cornell University Press, 2008.

Odell, Sheperd. *The Lore of the Unicorn*. New York: Courier Corporation, 1930.

Ohler, Norman. *Blitzed: Drugs in the Third Reich*. New York: Houghton Mifflin Harcourt, 2017.

O'Malley, Gregory E. *Final Passages: The Intercolonial Slave Trade of British America, 1619-1807*. Chapel Hill: University of North Carolina Press, 2014.

Orta, Garcia da. *Coloquios dos simples e drogas da India*. Edited by Conde de Ficalho. Lisbon: Imprensa Nacional, 1891.

———. *Colóquios dos simples e drogas he cousas medicinais da India e assi dalgūas frutas achadas nella onde se tratam algūas cousas tocantes a mediçina practica e outras cousas boas*. Goa: Joannes de Endem, 1563.

Orozco, Juan Manuel de. *Directorio de beneficiadores*. Potosí[?], 1737.

Ovington, John. *A Voyage to Surat in the Year 1689*. London: Jacob Tonson, 1696.

Packer, Ian, and Lynda Pratt, eds. *The Collected Letters of Robert Southey, Part Two: 1798- 1803*. Romantic Circles Electronic Edition, 2011.

Palacios, Félix. *Palestra Farmacéeutica, chimica-galénica*. Madrid, 1706.

Parés, Luis Nicolau, and Roger Sansi, eds. *Sorcery in the Black Atlantic*. Chicago: University of Chicago Press, 2011.

Parfit, Derek. *Reasons and Persons*. Oxford: Oxford University Press, 1984.

Parrish, Sean David. "Marketing Nature: Apothecaries, Medicinal Retailing, and Scientific Culture in Early Modern Venice, 1565-1730." Duke University, 2015. https://dukespace.lib.duke.edu/dspace/handle/10161/11326.

Parrish, Susan Scott. *American Curiosity: Cultures of Natural History in the Colonial British Atlantic World*. Chapel Hill: University of North Carolina Press, 2012.

Parsons, Christopher M. "The Natural History of Colonial Science: Joseph-François

Lafitau's Discovery of Ginseng and Its Afterlives." *William and Mary Quarterly* 73, no. 1 (2016): 37–72.

Payne, Lynda. *With Words and Knives: Learning Dispassion in Early Modern England.* London: Ashgate, 2013.

Pelling, Margaret, and Frances White. *Medical Conflicts in Early Modern London: Patronage, Physicians, and Irregular Practitioners, 1550–1640.* Oxford: Clarendon Press, 2003.

Pereira, Jonathan. *The Elements of Materia Medica*, vol. 2. London: Longman, 1840.

Philips, John Edward. "African Smoking and Pipes." *Journal of African History* 24, no. 3 (1983): 303–19.

Philosophical Transactions, Giving Some Account of the Present Undertakings, Studies, and Labours of the Ingenious, in Many Considerable Parts of the World. London: C. Davis, Printer to the Royal Society of London, 1708.

Pietz, William. "The Problem of the Fetish, I." *RES: Anthropology and Aesthetics*, no. 9 (1985): 5–17.

———. "The Problem of the Fetish, II: The Origin of the Fetish." *RES: Anthropology and Aesthetics* 13 (1987): 23–45.

Pinker, Steven. *Enlightenment Now: The Case for Reason, Science, Humanism, and Progress.* New York: Viking, 2018.

Piso, Willem and Georg Marcgrave. *Historia Naturalis Brasiliae, Auspicio et Beneficio.* Amsterdam: Franciscus Hack, 1648.

Pitt, Robert. *The Craft and Frauds of Physick Expos'd, the Very Low Prices of the Best Medicins Discover'd.* London: Tim Childe, 1703.

Pollan, Michael. *The Botany of Desire: A Plant's-Eye View of the World.* New York: Random House, 2002.

Pomet, Pierre. *Histoire generale des drogues: Traitant des plantes, des animaux, & des mineraux . . . le tout tres utile au Public.* Paris: Chez Jean-Baptiste Loyson, 1694.

Portuondo, María M. *Secret Science: Spanish Cosmography and the New World.* Chicago: University of Chicago Press, 2009.

Prioreschi, Plinio. "Medieval Anesthesia–The Spongia Somnifera." *Medical Hypotheses* 61, no. 2 (2003): 213–19.

Pyrard, François. *The Voyage of François Pyrard of Laval to the East Indies, the Maldives, the Moluccas and Brazil.* Edited by Albert Gray. London: Hakluyt Society, 1890.

———. *Discours du voyage des François aux Indes Orientales, ensemble des divers accidens, adventures et dangers de l'auteur en plusieurs royaumes des Indes.* Paris, 1611.

Anonymous [W. M.], *The Queens Closet Opened: Incomparable secrets in physick, chirurgery, preserving, candying, and cookery.* London: N. Brook, 1656.

Quezada Ramírez, Noemí. "Prácticas terapéuticas y de magia amorosa en San Luis Potosí." *Estudios de Cultura Otopame* 3 (2002): 105–21.

Quincey, Thomas de. "Confessions of an English Opium Eater." *London Magazine* (September, 1821): 293–312.

Quinones, Sam. *Dreamland: The True Tale of America's Opiate Epidemic.* New York: Bloomsbury, 2015.

Ragland, Evan. "Chymistry and Taste in the Seventeenth Century: Franciscus Dele Boë Sylvius as a Chymical Physician Between Galenism and Cartesianism." *Ambix* 59, no. 1 (March 2012): 1-21.

Rankin, Alisha. *Panaceia's Daughters: Noblewomen as Healers in Early Modern Germany.* Chicago: University of Chicago Press, 2013.

Rau, Virgínia, María Fernanda Gomes da Silva, and Dukes of Cadaval. *Os manuscritos do arquivo da casa de Cadaval respeitantes ao Brasil.* Coimbra: Universidade de Coimbra, 1955.

["R. B."]. *The English Acquisitions in Guinea & East-India.* London, 1700.

Ribera, Francisco Suárez de. *Quinta essentia medica theorico-practica, in duos libros divisa, quorum prior theoricae fundamenta continens praeclarissimo doctori . . . Josepho Cervi . . . aucthore D. Francisco Suarez de Ribera . . .* ex typographia viduae Francisci del Hierro, 1732.

Riebeeck, Jan van. *Journal of Jan van Riebeeck. Volume II, 1656-1662.* Edited by H. B. Thom and translated by J. Smuts. Cape Town: A. A. Balkema, 1954.

Riley, Margaret. "The Club at the Temple Coffee House Revisited." *Archives of Natural History* 33, no. 1 (2006): 96.

Robbins, Louise E. *Elephant Slaves and Pampered Parrots: Exotic Animals in Eighteenth-Century Paris.* Baltimore: Johns Hopkins University Press, 2002.

Robert, Talbor. *The English Remedy, Or, Talbor's Wonderful Secret for Cureing Agues and Feavers: Sold by the Author Sir R. Talbor to the Most Christian King.* London, 1682.

Rocco, Fiammetta. *The Miraculous Fever-Tree: Malaria, Medicine and the Cure That Changed the World (Text Only).* New York: HarperCollins UK, 2012.

Rojo-Guerra, Manuel Ángel, Rafael Garrido-Pena, Íñigo García-Martínez-de-Lagrán, Jordi Juan-Treserras, and Juan Carlos Matamala. "Beer and Bell Beakers: Drinking Rituals in Copper Age Inner Iberia." *Proceedings of the Prehistoric Society* 72 (n.d.): 243–65.

Roma, Francisco Morato. *Luz da Medicina, pratica racional, e methodica, guia de infermeyros, directorio de principiantes.* Lisbon: na officina de Francisco de Oliveyra, 1753.

Romaniello, Matthew P. "Customs and Consumption: Russia's Global Tobacco Habits in the Seventeenth and Eighteenth Centuries." In *The Global Lives of Things: The Material Culture of Connections in the Early Modern World,* edited by Anne Gerritsen and Giorgio Riello. London: Routledge, 2015.

Rome, Jean-François de. *Relation brieve et fidelle du succez de la mission des Freres mineurs capucins du seraphique pere sainct François, au royaume de Congo.* Lyon: Pierre Muguet, 1649.

———. *Fondation de la Mission des Capucins au Royaume de Congo.* Paris: Pierre Muguet, 1648.

Roos, Anna Marie. "Perchance to Dream: Science and the Future. *The Appendix* 2, no. 3 (July 17, 2014).

Ruiz, Hipólito. *Quinologia, o tratado del árbol de la quina ó cascarilla.* Madrid: la Viuda é Hijo de Marin, 1792.

Russell-Wood, A. J. R. *The Portuguese Empire, 1415-1808: A World on the Move.* Baltimore: Johns Hopkins University Press, 1998.

Sacks, Oliver. "Altered States." *New Yorker,* August 20, 2012. www.newyorker.com/magazine/2012/08/27/altered-states-3.

Safier, Neil. "Fruitless Botany: Joseph de Jussieu's South American Odyssey." In *Science and Empire in the Atlantic World,* 217-38. London: Routledge, 2008.

——— "Global Knowledge on the Move: Itineraries, Amerindian Narratives, and Deep Histories of Science." *Isis* 101, no. 1 (2010): 133-45. https://doi.org/10.1086/652693.

———. "The Tenacious Travels of the Torrid Zone and the Global Dimensions of Geographical Knowledge in the Eighteenth Century." *Journal of Early Modern History* 18, no. 1-2 (February 11, 2014): 141-72, https://doi.org/10.1163/15700658-12342388.

Sahagún, Bernardino de, *Historia general de las cosas de Nueva Espanã.* Carlos Maria de Bustamante, ed. Mexico City: Alejandro Valdés, 1830.

Sahlins, Peter. *1668: The Year of the Animal in France.* New York: Zone Books, 2017.

———. "The Royal Menageries of Louis XIV and the Civilizing Process Revisited." *French Historical Studies* 35, no. 2 (2012): 237-67.

Salavert, Aurélie. "Agricultural Dispersals in Mediterranean and Temperate Europe." *Oxford Research Encyclopedias, Environmental Science,* August 2017. doi:10.1093/acrefore/9780199389414.013.307.

———. "Le pavot (*Papaver somniferum*) à la fin du 6e millénaire av. J.-C. en Europe occidentale." *Anthropobotanica* 1, no. 3 (November 26, 2010): 3-16.

Salmon, William. *Polygraphice; or, The Art of Drawing.* London: Richard Jones, 1672.

Sansi, Roger. "Sorcery and Fetishism in the Modern Atlantic." In *Sorcery in the Black Atlantic,* edited by Luis Nicolau Parés and Roger Sansi. Chicago: University of Chicago Press, 2011.

———. "Feitiço e Fetiche No Atlântico Moderno." *Revista Antropologia* 51, no. 1 (2008): 123-53.

Sarabia, Angélica Morales. "The Culture of Peyote: Between Divination and Disease in Early Modern New Spain." In John Slater, Maríaluz López-Terrada, José Pardo-Tomás, eds. *Medical Cultures of the Early Modern Spanish Empire.* London: Routledge, 2016.

Sauvages, François Boissier de Lacroix de. *Dissertation sur les medicamens, qui affectent certaines parties du corps humain plutot que d'autres.* Paris: Pierre Brun, 1751.

Santo António, Caetano de. *Pharmacopea Lusitana Reformada Methodo Pratico de preparar os Medicamentos na fórma Galenica, & Chimica.* Lisbon: Real Mosteyro de São Vicente de Fóra, 1711.

Santos, Vanicleia Silva. "As bolsas de mandinga no espaço atlântico: século XVIII." PhD diss., Universidade de São Paulo, 2008.

Sarianidi, V. "New Discoveries at Ancient Gonur." *Ancient Civilizations from Scythia to Siberia* 2, no. 3 (1996): 289-310.

Saunders, Nicholas, and Dorrick Gray. "Zemís, Trees, and Symbolic Landscapes: Three Taíno Carvings from Jamaica," in Atkinson, *The Earliest Inhabitants.*

Schäffer, M., T. Gröger, M. Pütz, and R. Zimmermann. "Forensic Profiling of Sassafras Oils Based on Comprehensive Two-Dimensional Gas Chromatography. *Forensic Science International* 229, no. 1 (2013): 108-15.

Schaffer, Simon. "Newton on the Beach: The Information Order of *Principia Mathematica.*" *History of Science* 47 (2009): 243-76.

Schiebinger, Londa. *Secret Cures of Slaves: People, Plants, and Medicine in the Eighteenth-Century Atlantic World.* Redwood City, CA: Stanford University Press, 2017.

Schiebinger, Londa L. *Plants and Empire: Colonial Bioprospecting in the Atlantic World.* Cambridge, MA: Harvard University Press, 2007.

Schiebinger, Londa, and Claudia Swan. *Colonial Botany: Science, Commerce, and Politics in the Early Modern World.* Philadelphia: University of Pennsylvania Press, 2016.

Schmidt, Benjamin. *Inventing Exoticism: Geography, Globalism, and Europe's Early Modern World.* Philadelphia: University of Pennsylvania Press, 2015.

Schmitz, Rudolf. "Friedrich Wilhelm Sertürner and the Discovery of Morphine." *Pharmacy in History* 27, no. 2 (1985): 61-74.

Schneider, John T. *Dictionary of African Borrowings in Brazilian Portuguese.* Hamburg: Helmut Buske Verlag, 1991.

Scholz-Böttcher, Barbara M., Arie Nissenbaum, and Jürgen Rullkötter. "An 18th Century Medication 'Mumia Vera Aegyptica'—Fake or Authentic?" *Organic Geochemistry* 65 (2013): 1-18. https://doi.org/10.1016/j.orggeochem.2013.09.011.

Schottenhammer, Angela. *Trade and Transfer Across the East Asian "Mediterranean."* Wiesbaden: Otto Harrassowitz Verlag, 2005.

Schultes, Richard Evans. *The Healing Forest: Medicinal and Toxic Plants of the Northwest Amazonia.* Portland, OR: Dioscorides Press, 1990.

Schwartz, Stuart B., ed. *Sugar Plantations in the Formation of Brazilian Society: Bahia, 1550-1835.* Cambridge: Cambridge University Press, 1985.

———. *Implicit Understandings: Observing, Reporting and Reflecting on the Encounters Between Europeans and Other Peoples in the Early Modern Era.* Cambridge: Cambridge University Press, 1994.

———. *Slaves, Peasants, and Rebels: Reconsidering Brazilian Slavery.* Champaign: University of Illinois Press, 1996.

———. *Tropical Babylons: Sugar and the Making of the Atlantic World, 1450-1680.* Chapel Hill: University of North Carolina Press, 2011.

Schwartzkopf, Stacey, and Kathryn E. Sampeck. *Substance and Seduction: Ingested Commodities in Early Modern Mesoamerica.* Austin: University of Texas Press, 2017.

Semedo, João Curvo. *Polyanthea medicinal: Noticias galenicas e chymicas repartidas en tres tratados.* Lisbon: na officina de Antonio Pedrozo Galram, 1727.

———. *Atalaya da vida contra as hostilidades da morte.* Lisbon: Office Ferreyrenciana, 1720.

———. *Observaçoens medicas doutrinaes de cem casos gravissimos.* Lisbon: Antonio Pedrozo Galram, 1707.

———. "Memorial de varios simplices que da India Oriental, da America, & de outras partes do mundo vem ao nosso reino." Lisbon: undated.

Sennert, Daniel. *Thirteen Books of Natural Philosophy*. London: Peter Cole and Edward Cole, 1661.

Sertürner, F. W. "Darstellung Der Reinen Mohnsaure (Opiumsaure) Nebst Einer Chemischen Untersuchung Des Opiums Mit Vorzuglicher Hinsicht Auf Einen Darin Neu Entdeckten Stoff Und Die Darin Gehorigen Bemerkungen." *Trommsdorffs Journal Der Pharmazie* 14, no. 1 (1805): 47–98.

Shapin, Steven. "The Invisible Technician." *American Scientist* 77, no. 6 (1989): 554–63.

Shirley, John. *The Accomplished Ladies Rich Closet of Rarities, Or, The Ingenious Gentlewoman and Servant Maids Delightfull Companion*. London: W. W., 1687.

Shurkin, Joel. "News Feature: Animals That Self-Medicate." *Proceedings of the National Academy of Sciences* 111, no. 49 (December 9, 2014): 17339–41. https://doi.org/10.1073/pnas.1419966111.

Siegel, Rudolph E., and F. N. L. Poynter. "Robert Talbor, Charles II, and Cinchona: A Contemporary Document." *Medical History* 6, no. 1 (January 1962): 82–85.

Siena, Kevin P. "The 'Foul Disease' and Privacy: The Effects of Venereal Disease and Patient Demand on the Medical Marketplace in Early Modern London." *Bulletin of the History of Medicine* 75, no. 2 (2001): 199–224.

Silva, José Ferreira da. *Observações sobre a propriedade da Quina do Brasil*. Lisbon, 1801.

Simões, Ana, Ana Carneiro, and Maria Paula Diogo. "The Scientific Revolution in Eighteenth- Century Portugal: The Role of the *Estrangeirados*." *Social Studies of Science* 30 (2000): 591–619.

Simpson, Eve Blantyre. "How Chloroform Was Discovered." *The Review of Reviews* (January 1894): 207–8.

Sloane, Hans, editor. *Philosophical Transactions Giving Some Account of the Present Undertakings, Studies, and Labours of the Ingenious*. London: H. Clements, 1710.

———. "On the Use of Ipecacuanha, for Looseness." *Philosophical Transactions* 238 (1698): 69.

Smail, Daniel Lord. *On Deep History and the Brain*. Berkeley, CA: University of California Press, 2008.

Smith, Anthony. *Explorers of the Amazon*. Chicago: University of Chicago Press, 1994.

Smith, G. C. Moore. *Gabriel Harvey's Marginalia*. Stratford-upon-Avon: Shakespeare Head Press, 1913.

Somavilla, Nádia S., Gustavo P. Cosenza, Christopher W. Fagg, and Maria G. L. Brandão. "Morpho-Anatomy and Chemical Profile of Native Species Used as Substitute of Quina (*Cinchona spp.*) in Brazilian Traditional Medicine. Part II: Remijia Ferruginea." *Revista Brasileira de Farmacognosia* 27, no. 2 (April 2017): 153–57. https://doi.org/10.1016/j.bjp.2016.09.005.

Sonnedecker, Glenn. *Emergence of the Concept of Opiate Addiction*. Madison, WI: American Institute of the the History of Pharmacy, 1962.

Sousa Dias, José Pedro. *A Água de Inglaterra: Paludismo e Terapêutica em Portugla no Século XVIII*. Lisbon: Caleidoscópio, 2012.

———. "Jacob de Castro Sarmento e a conversão à ciência moderna. In *Primeiro Encontro de História das Ciências Naturais e da Saúde*, edited by C. P. Correia. Lisbon: Shaker Verlag, 2005.

———. "A 'Água de Inglaterra' no Portugal das Luzes, contributo para o estudo do papel do Segredo na terapêutica no século XVIII. Doctoral thesis, Faculty of Pharmacy, University of Lisbon, 1986.

Souza, Bernardino José de. *O Pau-brasil na história nacional*, 2nd ed. São Paulo: Companhia Editora Nacional, 1978.

Souza, George Bryan, and Jeffrey Scott Turley. *The Boxer Codex: Transcription and Translation of an Illustrated Late Sixteenth-Century Spanish Manuscript Concerning the Geography, History and Ethnography of the Pacific, South-east Asia and East Asia*. Leiden: Brill, 2015.

Soyer, François. *The Persecution of the Jews and Muslims of Portugal: King Manuel I and the End of Religious Tolerance (1496-7)*. Leiden: Brill, 2007.

Specter, Michael. "Getting a Fix." *New Yorker*, October 10, 2011. www.newyorker.com/magazine/2011/10/17/getting-a-fix.

Stern, Philip J. *The Company-State: Corporate Sovereignty and the Early Modern Foundations of the British Empire in India*. Oxford: Oxford University Press, 2012.

Stewart, Alan. "The Early Modern Closet Discovered." *Representations* 50 (1995): 76–100. https://doi.org/10.2307/2928726.

Stolz, Yvonne, Joerg Baten, and Jaime Reis. "Portuguese Living Standards, 1720–1980, in European Comparison: Heights, Income, and Human Capital." *Economic History Review* 66, no. 2 (2012): 545–78. https://doi.org/10.1111/j.1468-0289.2012.00658.x.

Sweet, James H. *Domingos Álvares, African Healing, and the Intellectual History of the Atlantic World*. Chapel Hill: University of North Carolina Press, 2011.

———. "Mutual Misunderstandings: Gesture, Gender and Healing in the African Portuguese World." *Past & Present* 203, suppl. 4 (January 1, 2009): 128–43. https://doi.org/10.1093/pastj/gtp006.

———. "Slaves, Convicts, and Exiles: African Travellers in the Portuguese Atlantic World, 1720-1750." In *Bridging the Early Modern Atlantic World: People, Products, and Practices on the Move*, edited by Caroline Williams. London: Ashgate, 2009.

——— *Recreating Africa: Culture, Kinship, and Religion in the African-Portuguese World, 1441–1770*. Raleigh: University of North Carolina Press, 2003.

———. "The Hidden Histories of African Lisbon." In *The Black Urban Atlantic in the Age of the Slave Trade*, edited by Jorge Cañizares-Esguerra. Philadelphia: University of Pennsylvania Press, 2013.

Talbor, Robert. Πυρετολογία, *a Rational Account of the Cause and Cure of Agues*. London, 1672.

Taussig, Michael T. *Shamanism: A Study in Colonialism, and Terror and the Wild Man Healing*. Chicago: University of Chicago Press, 1987.

Tavárez, David. *The Invisible War: Indigenous Devotions, Discipline, and Dissent in Colonial Mexico*. Redwood City: Stanford University Press, 2011.

Tepaske, John Jay. "Regulation of Medical Practitioners in the Age of Francisco

Hernández." In *Searching for the Secrets of Nature: The Life and Works of Dr. Francisco Hernández*, edited by Simon Varey and Rafael Chabrán. Redwood City, CA: Stanford University Press, 2000.

Thornton, John. K. *Warfare in Atlantic Africa, 1500–1800*. London: Routledge, 2002.

———. *The Kongolese Saint Anthony: Dona Beatriz Kimpa Vita and the Antonian Movement*. Cambridge: Cambridge University Press, 1998.

———. *Africa and Africans in the Making of the Atlantic World, 1400–1800*. Cambridge: Cambridge University Press, 1992.

———. "New Light on Cavazzi's Seventeenth-Century Description of Kongo." *History in Africa* 6 (1979): 253–64.

Toit, Brian M. du. "Man and Cannabis in Africa: A Study of Diffusion." *African Economic History* 1 (1976): 17–35.

Tononi, Giulio, and Christof Koch. "Consciousness: Here, There and Everywhere?" *Philosophical Transactions of the Royal Society*. B 370, no. 1668 (May 19, 2015).

Topsell, Edward, Conrad Gessner, Thomas Moffett, and John Rowland. *The History of Four-Footed Beasts and Serpents*. London: Printed by E. Cotes, for G. Sawbridge [etc.], 1658. http://archive.org/details/historyoffourfoo00tops.

Torres, João Carlos Feo Cardoso de Castelo Branco e. *Memórias contendo a biographia do vice almirante Luiz da Motta Feo e Torres: A história dos governadores e capitaens generaes de Angola, desde 1575 até 1825*. Lisbon: Fantin, 1825.

Varey, Simon, and Rafael Chabrán, eds. *The Mexican Treasury: The Writings of Dr. Francisco Hernández*. Redwood City, CA: Stanford University Press, 2001.

Vasconcellos, Simão de. *Vida do P. Joam d'Almeida da Companhia de Iesu*. Lisbon: Oficina Craesbeeckiana, 1658.

Venette, Nicolas. *De la Generation de L'Homme, ou Tableau de l'Amour Conjugal*. Cologne: Claude Joly, 1696.

Verweij, Anthonie. "Clandestine Manufacture of 3, 4-methylenedioxymethylamphetamine (MDMA) by Low Pressure Reductive Amination: A Mass Spectrometric Study of Some Reaction Mixtures." *Forensic Science International* 45: 1 (1990): 91–96.

Vidal, Silvia, and Neil L. Whitehead. "Dark Shamans and the Shamanic State: Sorcery and Witchcraft as Political Process in Guyana and the Venezuelan Amazon." In Whitehead and Wright, *Darkness and Secrecy*.

Vieira, António. *Cartas a Duarte Ribeiro de Macedo*. Lisbon: E. Augusto, 1827.

———. *Cartas selectas*. Edited by José Ignacio Roquete. Lisbon: Livraria Portugueza de J. P. Aillaud, 1856.

Vigier, João. *Pharmacopea Ulyssiponense, galenica e chymica, que contem os principios, diffiniçoens e termos geraes de huma et outra pharmacia*. Lisbon: Na officina de P. da Sylva, 1716.

——— *Thesouro apollineo, galenico, chimico, chirurgico, pharmaceutico ou Compendio de remedios para ricos & pobres*. Lisbon: Na Officina Real Deslandesiana, 1714.

Vigo, Giovanni da, and Joseph Ferreyra de Moura. *Syntagma chirurgico theorico-practico*. Lisboa: Na officina Real Deslandesiana, 1713.

Villault, Nicolas. *Relation des costes d'Afriques appelées Guinée*. Paris: Denis Thierry, 1669.

———. *Relation of the Coasts of Africk Called Guinee*. London: John Starkey, 1670.

Voeks, Robert A. *Sacred Leaves of Candomblé: African Magic, Medicine, and Religion in Brazil*. Austin: University of Texas Press, 2010.

Vries, Jan De. *The Industrious Revolution: Consumer Behavior and the Household Economy, 1650 to the Present*. Cambridge: Cambridge University Press, 2008.

——— "The Limits of Globalization in the Early Modern World." *Economic History Review* 63, no. 3 (August 2010): 710–33. https://doi.org/10.1111/j.1468-0289.2009.00497.x.

Wadsworth, James E. "Charlatan in the Backlands: Inquisition and Imposture in Colonial Brazil." *Luso-Brazilian Review* 49, no. 1 (2012): 63–95.

Walker, Donald A. "Virginian Tobacco During the Reigns of the Early Stuarts: A Case Study of Mercantilist Theories, Policies, and Results." In Lars Magnusson, ed. *Mercantilist Economics*, 143–71. Recent Economic Thought Series. Dordrecht: Springer, 1993. https://doi.org/10.1007/978-94-011-1408-0_6.

Walker, Timothy D. "Acquisition and Circulation of Medical Knowledge within the Early Modern Portuguese Colonial Empire." In *Science in the Spanish and Portuguese Empires*, edited by Daniela Bleichmar et al. Stanford: Stanford University Press, 2009.

———. *Doctors, Folk Medicine and the Inquisition: The Repression of Magical Healing in Portugal During the Enlightenment*. Leiden: Brill, 2005.

———. "The Role and Practices of the Curandeiro and Saludador in Early Modern Portuguese Society." *História, Ciências, Saúde-Manguinhos* 11 (2004): 223–37. https://doi.org/10.1590/S0104-59702004000400011.

———. "Slaves, Free Blacks and the Inquisition in Early Modern Portugal: Race as a Factor in Magical Crimes Trials." *Bulletin of the Society for Spanish and Portuguese Historical Studies* 25, no. 2 (2000).

Wall, Wendy. *Recipes for Thought: Knowledge and Taste in the Early Modern English Kitchen*. Philadelphia: University of Pennsylvania Press, 2015.

Wallis, P. "Exotic Drugs and English Medicine: England's Drug Trade, c. 1550–c. 1800." *Social History of Medicine* 25, no. 1 (2011): 20–46.

Wallis, Patrick. "Consumption, Retailing, and Medicine in Early-Modern London." *Economic History Review* 61, no. 1 (2008): 26–53.

Wallis, Patrick, and Teerapa Pirohakul. "Medical Revolutions? The Growth of Medicine in England, 1660–1800." *Journal of Social History* 49, no. 3 (March 1, 2016): 510–31. https://doi.org/10.1093/jsh/shv091.

White, Nicholas J., Gareth D. H. Turner, Nicholas P. J. Day, and Arjen M. Dondorp. "Lethal Malaria: Marchiafava and Bignami Were Right." *Journal of Infectious Diseases* 208: 2 (2013): 192–98.

Whitehead, Neil L., and Robin Wright, eds. *In Darkness and Secrecy: The Anthropology of Assault Sorcery and Witchcraft in Amazonia*. Durham, NC: Duke University Press, 2004.

Whitehead, P. J. P. "The Biography of Georg Marcgraf (1610-1643/4) by His Brother Christian, Translated by James Petiver." *Journal of the Society for the Bibliography of Natural History* 9, no. 3 (November 1, 1979): 301-14. https://doi.org/10.3366/jsbnh.1979.9.3.301.

Willerslev, Rane. "Not Animal, Not Not-Animal: Hunting, Imitation and Empathetic Knowledge Among the Siberian Yukaghirs." *Journal of the Royal Anthropological Institute* 10, no. 3 (2004): 629-52.

Wilson, Catherine. "Visual Surface and Visual Symbol: The Microscope and the Occult in Early Modern Science." *Journal of the History of Ideas* 49, no. 1 (January 1988): 85-108.

Wink, Michael. "A Short History of Alkaloids." In *Alkaloids* 11-44 (Springer, 1998). https://doi.org/10.1007/978-1-4757-2905-4_2.

Woolf, Judith. "Seventeenth-Century Female Pharmacists." *Chemical Heritage Magazine* 27, no. 3 (Fall 2009).

Woolf, M. "Foreign Trade of London Jews in the Seventeenth Century." *Transactions of the Jewish Historical Society of England* 24 (1970-73): 38-58.

Vasconcellos, Simão de. *Vida do P. Joam d'Almeida da Companhia de Iesu, na provincia do Brazil.* Lisbon, 1658.

Villault, Nicolas. *A Relation of the Coasts of Africk Called Guinee.* Translated by John Starkey. London, 1670.

Vons, Jacqueline. "Le médecin guarissant phantassie, purgeant aussi par druges la folie." *Histoire des Sciences Médicales* 44, no. 2 (2010): 121-29.

Yangwen, Zheng. *The Social Life of Opium in China.* Cambridge: Cambridge University Press, 2005.

Zahedieh, Nuala. *The Capital and the Colonies: London and the Atlantic Economy 1660-1700.* Cambridge: Cambridge University Press, 2010.

Zapata, Lydia, Leonor Peña-Chocarro, Guillem Pérez-Jordá, and Hans-Peter Stika. "Early Neolithic Agriculture in the Iberian Peninsula." *Journal of World Prehistory* 18, no. 4 (2004): 283-325.

Zee, Art Van. "The Promotion and Marketing of OxyContin: Commercial Triumph, Public Health Tragedy." *American Journal of Public Health* 99, no. 2 (February 2009): 221-27. https://doi.org/10.2105/AJPH.2007.131714.

Zucchelli, Antonio. *Relazioni del viaggio, e missione di Congo nell' Etiopia inferiore occidentale.* Venice: Bartolameo Giavarina, 1712.

Županov, Ines G., and Ângela Barreto Xavier. "Quest for Permanence in the Tropics: Portuguese Bioprospecting in Asia (16th-18th Centuries)." *Journal of the Economic and Social History of the Orient* 57, no. 4 (September 26, 2014): 511-48. https://doi.org/10.1163/15685209-12341357.

Index

Acknowledgments

I t is with a sense of profound gratitude that I write to thank the people who have made this book possible.

Jorge Cañizares-Esguerra's tremendous work ethic, determination, and creativity remains an inspiration. I have also been lucky to benefit from the mentorship of Julie Hardwick and James Sidbury. Christopher Heaney and Cameron Strang read the complete manuscript and provided comments on nearly every page, and Felipe Cruz provided a wellspring of ideas, conversation, and friendship.

Numerous friends and colleagues have generously offered feedback on earlier drafts or provided help with research: Allison Bigelow, Matthew Crawford, Harold Cook, David Courtwright, Paula Findlen, Carl Erik Fisher, Pablo Gómez, Paul Gootenberg, Joel Klein, Elaine Leong, Barbara Mundy, Abena Dove Osseo-Asare, Christopher Parsons, Neil Safier, Pamela Smith, James Sweet, Timothy Walker, and Phil Withington. I also thank friends in Austin and beyond who have served as valued sounding boards over the years: Daniel Gackle, Hadi Hossainy, Brian Jones, Katherine Noble, and John Travis Lindner.

In 2015 and 2016, Columbia University's Society of Fellows in the Humanities was an ideal home for writing much of this manuscript. Thank you to my fellow fellows for providing such a supportive and friendly environment: Maggie Cao, Will Derringer, Christopher Florio, María González Pendás, Brian Goldstone, David Gutkin, Heidi Hausse, Arden Hegele, Murad Idris, Nori Jacoby, Whitney Laemmli, Max Mishler, Dan-el Padilla Peralta, Carmel Raz, Rebecca Woods, and Grant Wythoff. Christopher Brown was helpful at every stage of my time at Columbia. Above all, I want to thank Eileen Gillooly for her tireless work in making the Heyman Center what it is.

Researching and writing this book involved extensive travel, and I have accrued many debts in the process. In Philadelphia, I owe thanks to Mairin Odle, Claire Gherini, Matt Goldmark, Ashley Cohen, Sean Trainor, Mitch Fraas, and the staff and community of the McNeil Center, especially to the inimitable Daniel Richter. At the John Carter Brown Library, I thank Margot Nishimura, Ken Ward, and my fellow Fiering House residents Ben Reed, Celine Carayon, Julia Gaffield, and Sophie Brockmann. At the Huntington, I greatly enjoyed peaceful walks around the gardens in the company of Matt Sargent, Ran Segev, and Claudia Tobin. And in London, I owe a special debt to Patrick, Adam, Béné, Waddah, Asya, Juan, Seda, Cosette, and all the other residents of Bishops House for inviting me into their home and making me feel welcome.

In Lisbon, thanks are due to Daniela Mak, Stephanie Almeida, and Jason Keith Fernandes. The Luso-American Development Foundation and the Arquivo Nacional da Torre do Tombo provided financial support and an office space early on in my time in Lisbon that helped me get settled. Thanks as well to the staff of the Portuguese Fulbright Commission; to the librarians and archivists of the Biblioteca Nacional de Portugal, the Torre do Tombo, and the Arquivo Histórico Ultramarino; and to Liam Brockey for an extremely well-timed tutorial in paleography. It was also in Lisbon that I met Timothy Walker, whose intellectual generosity and friendship came at just the right time.

The archival research for this book was made possible through the generosity of the J. B. Harley Fellowship in the History of Cartography; the Luso-American Development Foundation; the American Institute of the History of Pharmacy at the University of Wisconsin–Madison; the Fulbright Commission; the Consortium for History of Science, Technology and Medicine; the New York Academy of Medicine; the John Carter Brown Library; the Huntington Library; the McNeil Center at the University of Pennsylvania; the Fellows of Lincoln College, University of Oxford; and the Mellon Foundation. Thanks also go to the staff of the Harry Ransom Center at the University of Texas at Austin, the Beinecke Library at Yale University, and the John Carter Brown Library at Brown University in Providence, as well as to audiences who provided valuable feedback at the University of Pennsylvania, the University of Texas at Austin, the John Carter Brown Library, Columbia University, the New York City Latin American History Workshop, the New York University Atlantic Workshop, the Omohundro Institute at Yale University, and the University of California, Santa Cruz. To these institutions and to their staff who work to make historical research possible in a difficult period for the humanities, I express my sincere gratitude.

At the University of Pennsylvania Press, Bob Lockhart has been incredibly supportive and helpful over the past two years. I also wish to thank series editor Peter Mancall and Penn's anonymous reviewers for their helpful and constructive comments on this manuscript.

UC Santa Cruz has been the ideal place to finish the work on this book. I am especially grateful to my neighbors in faculty housing for their warm welcome: Muriam Davis, Anna Friz, Amy Ginther, Alma Heckman, and Thomas Serres. Thanks also to my colleagues Alan Christy, Jennifer Derr, Kate Jones, Marc Matera, Matt O'Hara, Gregory O'Malley, and Elaine Sullivan. I also want to acknowledge the contributions of Adriane Ackerman, Andrew Bailey, Sophia Gold, Charley Lanyon, Dustin Neuman, and Samuel Rosen.

I want to end by thanking the Breen and Pakzad families. In Iran, I was shown a level of hospitality that truly moved me, especially from my mother-in-law Eshrat, my sister-in-law Roja, and her husband Ehsan. My mother Gloria, my father John, my sister Heather, and my brother Nathan have taught me an important lesson in love and determination. I dedicate this book to my parents and brother in recognition of the profound sacrifices they have made and continue to make.

Finally, I want to thank Roya Pakzad. Your enthusiasm for life, your idealism, and your unique perspective inspire me every day, and your love and support has meant more than you know. The past four years have been the happiest of my life. To many more.